gondolin press

CARMEN HERNÁNDEZ BARRERA

DIARIES
1979-1981

Foreword by
Cardinal Séan Patrick O'Malley

gondolin press

DIARIES 1979-1981 – *Carmen Hernández Barrera*

Original title: *Diari 1979-1981* (2017)
First published in Italian by Cantagalli
Translated by Pablo & Debora Martinez & Maria Gennarini Calderon
Edited by David & Michelle Rak & Peter Waymel

© gondolin press

1915 Aster Rd.
60178 Sycamore IL

www.gondolinpress.com
info@gondolinpress.com

2022 © Gondolin Institute LLC

ISBN 978-1-945658-32-7 *soft cover*
ISBN 978-1-945658-33-4 *hard cover*

All the literary and artistic rights are reserved. The rights for translation, electronic storage, copy and total or partial adaptation, by any equipment, (including microfilm and photostats) are reserved for all countries. The Editor remains at disposition for eventual holders of rights who have not been traced.

First U.S. edition: February 2023

NOTE FROM KIKO ARGÜELLO ON DIARIES

Dear Brothers,

Reading these diaries has been a moving experience, and a surprising one as well.

The Desert Fathers say, "Love Christ and thousands will follow you…" The love for Christ that appears in these diaries is impressive. Through intense suffering, it seems the Lord Jesus closed every door for Carmen so she would unite herself to Him, and Him alone. From this union came Carmen's extreme freedom: nothing interested her in this world, only love for Christ.

It is truly heroic that Carmen spent 50 years with me, always suffering in silence, without revealing it to anyone, alone with Him. One day she said, "Lord, on the eve of persecution, I no longer desire anything in this life. Poor and having nothing, I feel an intimate desire for your presence alone. Holiness, Lord, hidden desires for holiness, for sacrifice, to fill the day with you. Prayer. Lord, come fill goodness and all things with meaning. Strengthen Kiko's faith" (n. 77).

I now understand better so many fruits of the Way. God has given us a sister with a unique level of holiness and it could not have been otherwise, given the importance of the mission God has entrusted to us. Reading of her love for Christ, I feel small and poor and do not know how to thank God for the immense grace of having had Carmen as my companion in the mission.

50 years without a moment's rest: trips, scrutinies, visiting so many communities in Madrid, Zamora, Barcelona, Paris, Rome, Florence, Ivrea... Listening and listening to each brother speak about his life, his sufferings, and his history: enlightening it with the light of faith, of the glorious Cross of Our Lord Jesus.

I think you have the right to get to know Carmen's heart, her immense love for Jesus Christ. She constantly said, "My Jesus, I love you. Come, come, help me."

Carmen penned her diaries over the course of 30 years and we will transcribe them little by little for the spiritual good of the brothers of the Way and of the Church. Here, we have published the first three years (1979-1981), in which can be seen the enormous work of evangelization we have done.

Keep these writings with reverence. None of us deserves a sister like her.

Pray for me and for Carmen.

Kiko Argüello

FOREWORD

by Cardinal Séan Patrick O'Malley, GCIH

The most personal literary genre is the diary. In the English language, perhaps the most famous diarist who comes to mind is Samuel Pepys, whose writings have provided an insight into the lives of this man, his family and times; as well as moving descriptions of great events, like the London fire. In more recent times, Anne Frank's *Diary* has allowed the world to see the horrors of the Holocaust through the eyes of a young girl and her family.

Diaries are usually written for the benefit of the author and not for publication. This fact allows the one writing the diary to be completely open and honest in expressing their thoughts and feelings. Unamuno's *Diario Intimo* is a fine example of how a diary can be a window into a man's soul.

The diary that made the most impact on me was Pope John XXIII's *Journey of a Soul*, a personal, intimate diary which the then-young Angelo Roncalli began when he entered the seminary at 14 years of age and continued to write until his death. Many of the entries document spiritual reflections that came to him during retreats and periods of prayer. For a young seminarian like myself, I found the book very inspiring and that led me to keep a journal during my novitiate year; which I kept in Latin, trying to honor *Veterum Sapientia*, Pope John's apostolic Constitution, which promoted Latin in the seminaries. Needless to say, I have never shared those musings with anyone, and although I did not continue the practice, I came to have an appreciation of how valuable journaling can be. Alas, the ablative absolutes and the deponent verbs were the most interesting aspects of my humble attempts at a diary.

Carmen Hernandez's journal begins in January 1979. Although I had long abandoned my own diary by that time, the events of that month are as fresh in my memory, as if it were yesterday. Carmen embarks on her spiritual journaling at the same time that St. John Paul II makes his first missionary journey as the Roman pontiff. Pope John Paul traveled to Mexico for the Puebla conference in January 1979.

In the inscrutable designs of Providence, I was plucked like Habakkuk from my pastoral duties with the immigrants in Washington, D.C. to be the priest secretary for the president of the US Bishops conference, who did not speak Spanish and needed someone to translate for him. It turned out to be one of the most memorable events in my life.

John Paul arrived in Mexico and traveled by open car 80 miles to the city of Puebla, with the crowd extending the whole way. Many had slept on the highway to be there when the new pope would arrive. It occurred to me that it was like the early Christians placing the sick by the side of the road, so that Peter's shadow might touch them.

The shadow of the new pontiff certainly touched the lives of Kiko and Carmen and the members of the Neocatechumenal communities. The new pope brought us a realization of the need for a new evangelization, as well as the urgency of discovering and nurturing the charisms of the Spirit that were stirring the Church after the Second Vatican Council.

It is in that context that Carmen Hernandez picks up her pen and begins her diary with the plaintiff call to her hidden Lord, "Jesus, my Jesus, I cry out to you night and day. Come, come love of my youth and my hope." In the opening paragraphs, one can hear the poetry of St. John of the Cross, from *La Noche Oscura* and the *Cantico Espiritual*. Carmen's deep love for Christ is a constant theme in the diaries. As I read her words, I thought of the passage from the Gospel of the Transfiguration where, having experienced a theophany, the apostles saw *"neminem nisi Jesus."* Carmen's gaze was on "no one but Jesus."

Carmen was a spiritual daughter of the Second Vatican Council and she dreamed of becoming a missionary, of spending her life in service to others. However, as the *Diaries* clearly show, she was no actor rehearsing for a part but an active participant with God as she was forged into a disciple of Christ. After she met Kiko Argüello, the two went on to give birth to a charism in the Church known as the Neocatechumenal Way, which Pope John Paul II recognized as "an itinerary of Catholic formation valid for our society and for our time."

In the Acts of the Apostles, we see how the community is itself an instrument of evangelization. Ever since I first met Kiko and Carmen, I have always been impressed by the emphasis of the Way on the importance of the community for the renewal of the Church. Christian faith is essential for the Church today, yet it needs a community where it can grow and be nourished, just as a baby needs a mother's womb before being born. The Neocatechumenal Way is Christian initiation through the beauty of the liturgical signs and the saving grace of the sacraments celebrated in a community of brothers and sisters.

Carmen knew the difference between doctrine and faith, and she decried the risk of reducing faith to an exercise of the intellect, but also of priestly ministry degenerating into a bureaucratic function. The Way joins laity and priests in a way of conversion by discovering the graces of baptism that alone make us children of God. When Christian doctrine is taught without faith, Christianity becomes joyless discipleship of submission to a Law without the Spirit.

Carmen's life and writings underscore the identity and mission of the woman in the Church. If the evil of abortion has erased countless children that are missing today in our schools, churches and playgrounds, I am always amazed every time that I meet with the communities of the Way to see so many families with young children. The presence of so many children are an indelible sign of love for God and our best hope of a future for the Church. Now, this is even more telling as I hear the experience of some of these young mothers who say they used to be radical feminists who didn't want to get married, let alone have children. They are also quick to point out that "were it not for Carmen, my children would not have been born." Now, if only God can convince a woman to have children and these women confess that it was thanks to Carmen that they had children, Carmen is both a prophetess of our times or a spiritual mother to all these children!

One of the great insights that Carmen and Kiko have given us is the emphasis on Christian initiation and the courage not to confuse Christian faith with Catholic doctrine. For much too long we have presumed faith in people without concerning ourselves with the integrity of faith in people. Kiko and Carmen have helped us understand that faith needs to be proposed to people through the announcement of the Gospel, and should never be presumed. As a means of renewal in the Church, the Neocatechumenal Way touches both clergy and laity and calls both, not alone but in a community, to be light to the world and salt of the earth. Like a farmer who sets out to prune his vineyard, to correct it so that it may give more fruit, the

Way seeks to serve the Church through love and sacrifice – and no one better than Carmen embodies this concept. She was an indomitable force of nature whose constant fears and inadequacies did not prevent her from speaking openly to popes and bishops, to Kiko, to priests and to anyone who came within her radius in need of a plain and unfiltered word of truth. In a Church accustomed to assign power to men, Carmen personified a frightening authority to many powerful people, especially as she evinced a greater love for God and for the Church than for human affections and political sensibilities.

Much of Carmen's life, especially what she said publicly or officially, is already published and can be easily accessed. What the *Diaries* give the reader, however, both those who knew and did not know Carmen, is a glimpse into her soul as God alone knew her!

Apart from the historical value of these entries, in the ensuing pages, the reader will journey with Carmen through the early vicissitudes that gave birth to the Neocatechumenal Way as we know it today. We should not be surprised that this work of God was conceived through struggles and anxieties and amid Carmen's constant admission of her inadequacies and utter nothingness in front of God. If she felt out of place at times and grappled to comprehend what God was doing with her, prayer re-centered her and kept her always in the presence of God.

We often say that a person never tires of hearing another person say, "I love you!" By this standard, Carmen was a woman deeply in love with Christ, who each day before going to bed entrusted her soul to her beloved as her last will and testament. While the untrained reader in spiritual matters may find this repetition kind of childish, to anyone who knew Carmen and admired her humble yet fierce demeanor and the kind, yet prophetic force of her words, these pages are an epiphany of how God works, often fashioning his strongest warriors from among his weakest soldiers.

If daily conversion restores innocence and recreates a person anew, then every entry in these *Diaries* speaks of Carmen's conversion and of how she adjusted herself daily to the will of God, making herself vulnerable to the promptings of the Spirit, so that God could accomplish in her the purpose of his love.

PREFACE

MY GRATEFUL MEMORY OF CARMEN BEFORE GOD

This publication wishes to remember, with gratitude, the life and mission of Carmen Hernandez a year since her definitive call to God. Kiko and Carmen opened the Neocatechumenal Way in the Church. According to the competent ecclesial authority, it is a form of Christian initiation for our times. Rooted in the Second Vatican Council, it is spread throughout the world through numerous Christian communities and countless multitudes of catechumens. Carmen had planned for herself a missionary life in the Americas, but the providence of the Lord asked of her a different answer to her apostolic mission. She spent many years writing *Diaries* that were found only after her death. They tell of events, they remember people, but above all they manifest her personal relationship in dialogue with Jesus Christ. This book has offered a chance to collect a part of her vast writings, preserve the memory of her work, give her due recognition for her invaluable service, and prolong her impact.

Approximately 50 years ago, I met Kiko and Carmen when the Neocatechumenal Way first began in Rome and Avila. I followed the catechesis in the parish of the *Natività*, where I walked for the duration of my studies in Rome. I had at that time the conviction that something new, powerful and far-reaching, and in concord with the Council, was emerging. I was particularly impressed by the application of St. Paul's theology to current human existence. Kiko and Carmen, together with a priest, formed the team of initiators of the Way: *they are a word in which the Acts of the Apostles resounded*. Fr. Farnés had been Carmen's professor at the Pastoral Theology Institute of the Pontifical University of Salamanca in Madrid, and he advised the Neocatechumenal communities. Farnés recently died at the venerable age of 91 on March 24, 2017. It is out of a debt of gratitude that I also remember him here today. The development of the Neocatechumenal Way has been fostered by the liturgical formation,

Kiko's experience of personal conversion, witnessing the signs from God in the history of the Church and of humanity, and in the experience of a multitude of communities. In its unfolding have converged the original intuition of the initiators, the welcoming of the message by many listeners, the acceptance of the Way by those responsible for the pastoral action of the Church, the historical knowledge of the catechumenate restored by the Second Vatican Council, the liturgical reform, the constant faithful reading of the Sacred Scriptures that the itinerant catechist carries in his satchel, and the personal and communitarian experience of the work of the Holy Spirit. Whereas Kiko was the catechist who always spoke and Carmen almost always listened, at times praying, at other times with restlessness and sometimes intervening with a pertinent reflection, we must assume that the content of the catecheses, the development of the "steps" and of the "rites" of the catechumenal itinerary, as well as the organization of the evangelization through itinerant or local catechists and through families in mission, is due to the combined work of the initiating team. Each one contributed the gifts received by God.

In addition to their individual contributions, it is striking that both have remained faithful and united in fulfilling the mission that God entrusted to them. In the Church of our time they introduced a catechumenate for the already baptized, who in the majority of cases had not been initiated to faith. Little by little people who have not been baptized entered the catechumenate. Both Kiko and Carmen, notwithstanding their differences and occasional disputes, understood that they were beholden to an overwhelming mission of evangelization. Although the mission has been refining them, both are strong personalities and their distinct characters have always remained vibrant. God can unexpectedly touch the heart in spite of the limitations of the messengers of his mercy. The two were called to inseparably participate in the work for the Gospel (2 Tm 1: 8-12.) At every moment the realization of their shared mission necessitated their mutual agreement by repeatedly, humbly forgiving one another. Diaries have shown us how the attention that Carmen gave Kiko's catecheses would alternate between satisfaction, because he was inspired, petitioning God to grant him a sure word, and fury because from her perspective Kiko placed his "ego" at the center. They have surrendered their lives to the evangelization. They have not run away from the charge with which they were entrusted. Instead they have patiently fulfilled it. As St. Paul writes, they have suffered the death of Christ daily so that life might be manifest in their catechumens (2 Cor 7-12.) At Carmen's funeral, confident in the Lord who grants the crown of eternal life, we were also able to apply to her, further words of St. Paul, "I have fought the good fight, I have finished the race, I have kept the faith" (2 Tim 4:7). Kiko and Carmen are who they have become because of their mission. It has converted them and made of them witnesses of "the Gospel of the grace of God" (Acts 20:24.)

Carmen's *Diaries* show the exterior labor and the interior suffering, trials on the inside and adversities on the outside. The itinerant mission was a cross, on occasion a very heavy cross, for Carmen. The itinerancy brings with it uncertainties and privations. Not having a fixed placed to create a stable home, or in the words of Jesus, "no place to lay his head," (Lk 9:58) is a painful imperative. It was a visible mortification for her to live permanently on the road, without reading the books that she desired to read, and serenely reflecting on what she desired to contemplate. We can perceive throughout *Diaries* that the itinerant style was a difficult requirement for Carmen. She needed more stability in a concrete place to ensure her personal harmony. Every day she had to "pack up the house" going against her natural inclinations. To depend on the hospitality of others, to travel without pause, to be exposed to persecution and incomprehensible situations are all the ways her life was sacrificed. She lived an incredibly heavily loaded agenda with constant encounters with people who needed light and consolation, meetings, convivences, visits to communities, scrutinies, "steps" and "rites." Hers was an exhausting life. Carmen, because of her personality, would have preferred a tranquil life in a fixed place; Kiko and the requests they received subjected her to non-stop transience, which was a cross she carried uphill.

If the itinerancy was a heavy burden, *Diaries* shows that interiorly she endured the unimaginable. She repeatedly refers to sadness, anguish, the desire to flee, meaninglessness and even pain of the soul, of existence and of life itself. The interior suffering appears with many variations, doubts, frustrations, neuroses, dejections, and temptations on the meaning of a life spent in this manner of mission. I admit that I was particularly impressed by this facet of Carmen's life, unknown to most and so deep and continuous. At the same time, it has provoked in me feelings of deep gratitude for her perseverance in the trials and her patient surrender of her own life. Despite everything, she neither retreated from the mission nor rejected the apostolic cross.

She lived her interior suffering in affectionate communion with Jesus. She tells of her trials in a dialogue with Him. Her immense love of Jesus Christ must be inseparably united with her interior suffering, "My Jesus, I love you: do not abandon me. Come and help me." She suffered her pain in an intimate communion with the crucified Jesus, who is already glorious forever.

In the proper measure, this perspective reminds us of the crisis of faith suffered by St. Teresa of the Child Jesus and Teresa of Calcutta, that we only learned about after their own deaths. Through *Diaries* we have access to what Carmen maintained for the most part as secret. We can see on the one hand the cross of the mission and on the other, her love for Jesus Christ. These were the two faces of a woman in love with the Lord, and who was always faithful to the charge she received.

St. John of the Cross, eminent spiritual master, was an expert in painful trials and in the "rising of dawn." He called "night" the deep darkness that enveloped his soul and sensibilities. St. John of the Cross spoke of the "horrendous night." Carmen highlights a few words in *Diaries* in the entry of August 13, 1982, "For having passed through so many *torments, anxieties, doubts, misgivings and horrors* in this night and darkness... Not able to enjoy human or divine things; the affections of the soul: oppressed and constricted, *not able to move* towards them nor find *any support in anything;* the imagination: bound, not able to make any discourse of good; memory: finished, understanding: obscured, not able to focus on things, and from here even the will *dry and constricted*, and all the powers are *empty and useless*, and above all a thick and heavy cloud over the soul that keeps it in *anguish* and alien from God" (Dark Night of the Soul II, 1; 16,1.)

How can we not conclude that throughout years and years with Kiko, Carmen's suffering, carrying silently the cross of the mission, was also the secret of the fruitfulness of the Neocatechumenal Way? The words of Kiko and the prayer of Carmen have empowered the announcement of the Gospel and the call to conversion.

While praying for Carmen's eternal rest from her labors and for the light of the Risen One in her darkness, let us also thank the Lord for the gift of her person and of her life surrendered to the evangelization.

Valladolid, June 2017

Mons. D. Ricardo Blásquez Pérez
Cardinal-Archbishop of Valladolid
President of the Spanish Episcopal Conference

**DIARIES
1979-1981**

1979

1. When everything fades into the nothingness and the night into darkness, it eats the soul in the nothingness. Lord, where? How? Who are you? You are a mysterious, hidden God, and your absence makes joy impossible. This pain is devouring my life, killing every possibility and accusing every moment. Relentless, terrible, destructive accuser.[1]

Jesus, my Jesus, I cry to You at night and day. Come,[2] come, Love of my youth and my hope. Infuse me with energy, for I'm collapsing into the nothingness. Come, Jesus. I love you.[3] I hope only in You. Have mercy on my absolute impotence, my radical nothingness. Come, You, come. You alone are Truth. You exist.

(Castelldefels – Barcelona, January 13, 1979)

2. We've finished this convivence. I flee, Jesus, I flee from people to avoid showing the sadness that eats away at the depths of my being. Jesus, what's happening to me? Am I sick? My life is falling apart. I remember at 14 the drive you gave me to fight. Give me strength, energy. I neither want nor desire anything. To be alone. And this without You is absolute death.

I can breathe a little at night, Lord, and then understand how many thanks I should sing to you for so much wellbeing throughout my life. This oppressive agony is inexplicable, that eats up my soul, corroding it; inexplicable while it lasts. Lord, I love you for your great love. Gladden the life of your servant.[4] Bring me joy, my Jesus, have mercy on my suffering. Let your Face shine[5] on my heart...

Thank you, my Jesus, for your love. When I awake, come. Spend the night with me. Come, Jesus.

(Castelldefels – Barcelona, January 14, 1979)

---

[1] Cf. Rv 12:10.

[2] Carmen repeats this "come" continuously, almost always in capital letters, COME. Rv 22:17.20.

[3] Carmen repeats this "I love you" continuously, almost always in capital letters, I LOVE YOU. Jn 21:15-17; Ps 18:1; 86:2.

[4] Cf. Ps 86:4. As the reader will be able to verify, many of the biblical references echoing in Carmen's writings come from the daily liturgy (Psalter and Eucharist), which was her daily spiritual food (cf. for example, April 15, 1981). So much so that she would always say, especially to presbyters, that it is enough to follow the Liturgy of the Church with one's whole heart to be holy.

[5] Cf. Nm 6:25.

3. Free… But I'm not, Lord! I don't know how to tell you what I want. I'm consumed like the cigarettes I smoke, one after the other, uselessly.

Come, Jesus! Let me see things with simplicity, without so many burdensome problems, everything is problematic, dark grey. Come, light of my life! Come!

Joséfina's house[6] – two o'clock in the morning. Return to prayer. Fifteen minutes of quiet and my soul seems different. Is it possible? Jesus, I remember the days long ago and feel that I'm joyfully returning to that time, safe and with more humility. The serenity, goodness, peace, are incredible, Jesus, giver of peace, of love. Thank you, Jesus!

(Castelldefels – Barcelona, January 15, 1979)

4. Joséfina's house – Lord… Prayer and deep suffocation that doesn't let me live. To live? What for? Jesus! What incomprehensible pain, the pain of the nothingness! Save me, Lord, from the suffocation of powerlessness, have mercy!

It's night. The pharisee and the publican.[7] I doubt everything, Lord. You are a mysterious God, inexplicable, unreachable, "contradictory." I doubt what we say. You are the only one standing, Jesus, Lord, and crucified. Love is here. Why? I only know it can be experienced and is ineffable. Jesus, Lord. Your death is resurrection. Love, sweet Jesus, have mercy on me. Help me admit my sins, to say that I'm a sinner. I can admit that I am poor, but "I'm a sinner" doesn't come from my lips.

(Barcelona – January 16, 1979)

5. In bed, like an inner refuge. Escape, anguish, suffering… The catechesis tomorrow… total incapacity. My whole world with no preparation… terrible powerlessness. I don't want to go eat at the Salesians'.[8] I escape to bed; I don't even want to go out. Everything

---

[6] Josefina Jutglar, from the first community of the Parish of *Santas Juliana y Sempronia*, San Adrián de Besós, Barcelona.

[7] Cf. Lk 18:9-14.

[8] Parish of *María Auxiliadora*, Sarriá, Barcelona.

is like a roaring lion,[9] and I lie here abandoned and abandoning. What a mystery. What helplessness. What nothingness.

Lord, if you don't appear, I sink into the nothingness, in my neuroses, in my loneliness, in my death. Jesus, I have no words, not one idea in my head. How will I be able to say anything? I don't know how to speak. Come, Holy Spirit.

Jesus, what do you want? That I suffer? That I suffer? I already suffer, Lord, have mercy on me.

Night. After the catechesis, You, Lord. Good brushstrokes. I saw that contact is possible and better than long talks. I'm happy. Thank you, Lord. You help me continue. And it's Thursday…

(Barcelona, January 17, 1979)

6. Thursday. Catechesis. Kiko[10] is going to Madrid. And me? What fears, what helplessness, what neuroses. Lord, how mysterious You are. How miserable this man whom You have made to be so mysterious. I don't know how to speak. I'm terrified, persecuted, accused, torn apart, dead. Lord, come. Enlighten my incapacity, my darkness, my terrors. Come, Lord.

Night. After the catechesis. Thank you, Lord. I feel remade, renewed, healthy. Help me. It has helped me resurrect, to live. Thank you, Jesus. I'm happy. Open my lips. Help me go on. Do not leave me in the shadows and in the death of my sterility. Help me to love you. Come, Jesus.

(Barcelona, January 18, 1979)

7. Night. Deep, deep down, I'm happy. Peace. Jesus, I haven't felt this relaxed in a long time. I love You, Lord. Thank you, Jesus. When shall I see your face?[11] The only desire I have left is to contemplate You. My Jesus, suddenly my life lights up. Do not let me fall into the night. Help me. Open my lips. Enlighten my heart about the mission.

---

[9] Cf. 1 Pt 5:8.

[10] Kiko Argüello (Francisco José Gómez-Argüello Wirtz), the initiator, along with Carmen Hernández, of the Neocatechumenal Way. In 2002 the Holy See, through Statutes, named Kiko responsible of the International Team of the Neocatechumenal Way for life.

[11] Cf. Ps 42:2.

Increase and strengthen my faith. Come, Jesus. My God, mysterious, immense. Love. Love. Love. Give me joy.

(Barcelona, January 19, 1979)

8. In your light I see everything and the value of everything changes. The bed, like a pit of anguish, of death, is a jail cell that imprisons me, and I have no power to leave it. How is it possible to go from the joy of last night to this anguish upon waking? My life is falling on top of me. It all falls on me like a disgrace, an accusation of pessimism and repudiation.

Lord, arise, come resplendent in your Resurrection. Isn't it for man? Why are you silent? You withdraw from me, you leave me in the helplessness of the grave. I'm consumed with waiting. I hope in your Word. You, first, look into my eyes. I call upon you, Lord. Listen to my cry of fear and turmoil. Preserve my life. Give me the joy of the Easter Announcement. Life. Glory. Victory. God, one, mysterious, hidden, show yourself, come, savior.

Eucharist – children – prayer. Is it because of this? Jesus, I'm understanding improvisation and my neuroses of powerlessness. Come, open my mouth. Push me to risk, to improvise. What peace! What joy! Why do I embitter myself in my mind?

(Barcelona, January 20, 1979)

9. Come, Lord, when I awake. Heal my life. Heal me to my very depths... Ólvega[12] – Missions... I'm full of neuroses. Lord, take away my lifejacket, the books, the phrases. Throw me into improvisation, into the water.[13] Infuse me with energy, fortitude. Help me. You, with your presence, ask me, "Why are you afraid?" Peace.

Peaceful day, calm, with no pain.

I see my life and my mission as calm, spontaneous. Why do I always have to reluctantly force myself to speak? Do I secretly – though not that, either – want to be constantly creating ideas, after first having a plan of attack? Open my lips spontaneously, with faith,

---

[12] Carmen's birthplace, November 24, 1930.

[13] Here and elsewhere, Carmen, who has a degree in Chemistry, does not write "water" but H_2O.

with dialogue, not with novel ideas, but with the novelty of faith, present, daring, serene. Lord, thank you.

(Castelldefels – Barcelona, January 21, 1979)

10. It's always hard to wake up in the nothingness and to be in the nothingness of the day with only a single, agonizing source of support, being in between everything and nothingness or passively going along with it.

Lord Jesus, You know me. You know all things. What should I do, Lord? What should I do? I love you. Simplify me effortlessly. These unusual, neurotic pains, from my powerlessness… Lord, help me.

Matthew 14. The boat. "It is I."[14] Wonderful Jesus, the only one who remains in tribulation, in the night, in the sea. You lead me to look for You there, in the storm. You alone appear as a possibility, and you appear as a ghost. Let me hear your voice.[15] Call me, You Yourself, Jesus, console me, come tomorrow when I awake.

(Barcelona, January 22, 1979)

11. Me, in a day of indescribable, overwhelming sadness. Powerlessness in my bones. Nothingness, Lord. What's wrong with me? What do You want? I want to disappear into my bed, it's like a grave of loneliness. Am I sick? Is it a dark night? What's wrong with me, Lord, why don't I have any hope? Everything is sadness, sadness. I see the Church, the bishops, and even what we do as sterile, impossible nothingness, and the world stands alone and secure in its crimes. Come, Lord. Show me your face. You touch my soul and everything changes.

My only rest is later in the assembly. Puebla?[16] What powerlessness, Lord. Give my eyes faith to see you. Enlighten my life, Lord.

(Barcelona, January 23, 1979)

---

[14] Cf. Mt 14:27.

[15] Cf. Sg 8:13.

[16] Kiko and Carmen decided to meet with all the itinerant catechists of America in Puebla de los Ángeles (Mexico) during the meeting of the Third Latin American Episcopal Conference (CELAM), January 27-February 13, 1979.

12. What is it in my soul that pains me, Lord? To be here in a foreign place? We have nowhere to rest our heads.[17] Without the scandal of sleeping… And this? Why? Lord, everything seems absurd. My Jesus, I forget everything, the days of old, your mighty deeds. Come, Jesus, help my life. Come.

You give light and everything changes. How is it that suddenly my soul lights up, everything changes, suddenly I see everything with joy, with hope, differently? My Jesus, come when I awake!

(Barcelona, January 24, 1979)

13. Thursday – The Pope departs for Puebla.

Last day here. Another day, Lord. Mornings are darker than night itself. One day calls to another. Why? It seems like it's something incredible, wonderful, beautiful, dreams, hope, joy. I had never thought about it. It always seemed normal to me. These dark dawns and the generosity at nightfall leave me amazed by my helplessness and by how mysteriously you have formed man. Lord, come and save me!

After this gloomy day. Three o'clock in the morning. What free, deep peace; what joy! Jesus, how mysterious you are. Just a glimpse of your presence, to be with you in truth, changes everything from sadness to joy, from slavery to freedom. My Jesus, only redeemer, come fill my dawn. Come! Come when I awake, infuse me with energy.

(Barcelona, January 25, 1979)

14. Trip from Barcelona – Madrid. Night. My Jesus, peace, incredible. You are good. Thank you, Jesus. Do not take it away from me. Awaken me in peace. Inspire me, if you want. It's all the same to me. You are enough, Jesus, my Jesus. You have snatched me from the abyss, thank you, Jesus. Seeing the people gives me mercy for them. Console those who suffer, those who are afraid, those with anxieties. Jesus, how mysterious everything is. Thank you, Jesus. Come when I awake and satisfy me with your face.[18]

(Valle[19] – Madrid, January 26, 1979)

---

[17] Cf. Mt 8:20.

[18] Ps 17:15.

[19] Valle de los Caídos (San Lorenzo de El Escorial, Province of Madrid). Retreat house used for convivences.

15. It's raining but the day begins peacefully. Jesus, I'm surprised. Thank you. Suffering has made my heart merciful. Thank you, Jesus. Peace, joy. I'm surprised to see things calmly, looking forward to them, without ghosts, without fear, with power, with authority. Why, Lord? The heart of man is a mystery. And You? You, in You. Lord, thank you. Puebla. Help the Pope speak clearly.

(Valle – Madrid, January 27, 1979)

16. Elisa's house.[20] How uncontrollable the inner-being is: from joy to pain. Peaceful night.
Puebla. The outlook is good.
Everything looks uncertain, depending on You, Jesus. You, my Love.

(Madrid, January 28, 1979)

17. Day off. Amazing. A little bit of freedom. Lord, help me not to smoke two packs. How groggy it makes me… enormous headache… but a little encouraged. This morning to pray, work, do…
The Pope in Puebla. Magnificent. A positive outlook is appearing, Lord.
Thank you, Lord. Help us!

(Madrid, January 29, 1979)

18. *San José*[21] – Restlessness, Lord. Restless and dissatisfied to the bone. What loneliness! Poor Kiko, also alone, alone. Lord, where are you? The ghosts haunt me, accusing me, judging me, besieging me, like enemies. The fear, "What will they say?"… Lord, the truth makes one free,[22] freedom, your love, your presence, your word. Jesus, open up my perspective, my lips. Come, help me.

(Madrid, January 30, 1979)

---

[20] Carmen's sister, the eldest of nine siblings: Elisa (†), Félix (†), Telesforo (†), Pilar, Carmen (†), María Anunciación, Antonio (†), Elías, Milagros. Carmen died July 19, 2016, at Elisa's house on calle Samaria.
[21] *San José* Parish on Madrid's Gran Vía.
[22] Cf. Jn 8:32.

19. *S. Sebastián*[23] – Prayer.[24] I don't like Kiko… I return horrified and sad, and grumbling… How difficult men are, my Jesus! I feel besieged, as if by wasps.[25]

(Madrid, January 31, 1979)

20. Tragic awakening. What a night, Lord, what desolation, what sadness. In agony, Lord. How can this be? I thank you for life when you made me laugh, live. Jesus, everything seems like a dream, a vain illusion.

You console me a little when night comes. Why this powerlessness, this nothingness?

(Madrid, February 1, 1979)

21. Jesus, is it sickness? Is it the night? Is it my 'native' neuroses? What's wrong with me Lord? I'm sick. I pass the day in continual suffering.

Thank you, Jesus, that not even nightfall brings me serenity. Flight tomorrow. And Puebla on the 7th. Jesus, I understand nothing, I know nothing. Sorrows eat away at my heart. Only You remain, on the Cross, explaining everything. Come, Jesus.

(Madrid, February 2, 1979)

22. Listening to everyone consoles me. Eucharist. After enormous weariness, a moment of rest.

(Barcelona, February 3, 1979)

23. Once again all day today, morning and afternoon, listening. I don't know if we're crazy.

Still no sleep. Dead. Jesus, I can't go on.

(Barcelona, February 4, 1979)

---

[23] *San Sebastián* parish, Madrid.
[24] First Initiation to Prayer, step of the Neocatechumenal Way.
[25] Cf. Ps 118:12.

24. Slept poorly. Awoke disheartened. My mind, sick. Cardenal Jubany.[26] Airport.
Lord, you console my life for a little while. Thank you, Jesus.
(Barcelona, February 5, 1979)

25. We're going to Puebla. Why? So many doubts, uncertainties… Prayer in the night. Jesus, show yourself.
(Madrid, February 6, 1979)

26. The plane doesn't depart until night.
Airport. Three a.m. Departure for Puebla. My heart's in my boots. Too sad for words. Jesus!
(Madrid, February 7, 1979)

27. We awoke in Mexico after the cold of Montreal.[27] A world that seems better to me, more human, more real… And the love we feel for all the teams. Thank you, Jesus, for these Psalms. Teach me to pray. I would repeat each word to you from the depths of my heart. You free my life from the abyss. You make me live again. Your goodness reassures me. But you hid your face and I was put to confusion.[28]
(Puebla – Mexico, February 8, 1979)

28. Buried like poor little things… Lord, I believe in You even if I'm down, sad. You do all things well. Greatness in your creation. Mysterious in your works. Tragic is the life of man. The terrible problems in the Church. The only answer left is your Kingdom on the Cross. Jesus, my Love, mysterious, great, only one, give joy to my life. Come, Lord, come!
(Puebla de los Ángeles – Mexico, February 9, 1979)

---

[26] Cardinal Narciso Jubany Arnau (†), Archbishop of Barcelona, 1971-1990.

[27] Flight stopover.

[28] Cf. Ps 104:29.

Pope Francis greets Carmen Hernández during the meeting with 300 families from the Neocatechumenal Way that were sent out to all the world on February 1, 2014 in Paul VI Hall (photo from L'Osservatore Romano*)*

29. Eucharist with the Bishop of Honduras, Santos,[29] a truly holy and good man. Splendid Eucharist. Thank you, Jesus.

(Puebla – Mexico, February 10, 1979)

30. Visit to the holy city of Teotihuacán. Lord, mysterious God, great, immense.

(Puebla – Mexico, February 11, 1979)

Night: travel to CELAM by bus with "the 41."[30] We are a little consoled by Mons. Jorge Manrique's farewell.[31]

(Puebla – Mexico, February 11, 1979)

31. Finished the convivence with Lauds. Good, Lord. I return home happier. We leave for Madrid at 7. Stopover in Paris.

(Puebla – Mexico, February 12, 1979)

32. We arrived at night from the airport to the Easter announcement. The catechesis was very inspired. I leave very happy.

(Madrid, February 13, 1979)

33. Failed trip to Barcelona: ticket agents' strike. Jubany says it's all right.

Now, Jesus, it's night. I rested today. It is 3:30 a.m. and I can't sleep. The devil prowls around me[32] trying to make me sad. Come, Jesus, help me accept the present, the loneliness of this house. Help me read, work, pray. I love you, Jesus. I'm alone. Come.

(Madrid, February 14, 1979)

34. *Sta. Catalina*[33] – Gethsemane. You console me, Jesus, at nightfall, seeing you as a mystery in the proclamation of the Gospel.

---

[29] Mons. Héctor Enrique Santos Hernández, SDB (†), Archbishop of Tegucigalpa, 1962-1993.

[30] The number of itinerants at the convivence.

[31] Mons. Jorge Manrique Hurtado (†), Bishop of Oruro, 1956-1967 (where Carmen and several others had thought of going as missionary after her return from Israel in 1964) and Archbishop of La Paz, 1967-1987.

[32] Cf. 1 Pt 5:8.

[33] Parish of *Santa Catalina Labouré*, Madrid.

I'm envious, not doing it myself... but it's enough for me to accompany you, Lord, when you appear. Lord, let my heart rest in your will. My Jesus, I love you. Sanctify your name, your power. Allow me to enter into your rest. I love you. Good night.

(Madrid, February 15, 1979)

35. Lord, without a break. Why Lord? "Whom shall I fear?"[34] Jesus, I awake sad and afraid and in the nothingness. Everything, for what? Jesus, tell my soul You are the one behind all this. "It is I."[35] Say "It is I" to my life. Jesus, give me energy, hope, life. Come, Jesus.

Rite in *San Sebastián*. The vicar Agustín[36] consoles us. We're so poor, Lord, that even the little word of a poor Vicar feels like ecclesial paternity to us. Consolation. Dinner. Thank you, Jesus.

(Madrid, February 16, 1979)

36. After, Eucharist in *San Sebastián*. Children.

(Narváez[37] – Madrid, February 16, 1979)

37. At home in Narváez. All day in bed. Hemorrhage. I don't feel well. I'm not going to the Center,[38] to the meeting of the catechists of Madrid, of the "18."[39] I simply cannot go on today. My Jesus! How sad it is to be depressed, not to believe in life.

When night falls, I always feel a little better, see things differently. And the way this depressive darkness manages to take root and grow in my heart seems hopeless to me. Lord, should I have surgery? They believe this is the solution. I believe in You, Lord, enlighten my listless, distant, fearful faith. I understand nothing: the world, men,

---

[34] Cf. Ps 23:4.

[35] Cf. Mt 14:27.

[36] Mons. Agustín García Gasco (†), Episcopal Vicar of the third vicariate of Madrid. Later Cardinal Archbishop of Valencia from 1992 to 2009.

[37] Street of the apartment where Clemente Barrera Isla, Carmen's mother, lived, and where Carmen also lived in those years, when she was in Madrid.

[38] Neocatechumenal Center of Madrid, on calle Blasco de Garay 8.

[39] The way Carmen referred to the teams that coordinated the evangelization of the different sectors of the dioceses of Madrid and Rome.

the future. Eternity? You. The Resurrection. How dark everything is Lord! Isn't it for everyone? How can it be? If not, I don't understand it.

(Madrid, February 18, 1979)

38. By night, I can't sleep. I sleep and bleed all day. Continuous bleeding.

Lord, Love. You. I'm like Qoheleth: nothing matters, and all is vanity.[40]

Jesus, how mysterious life is, how mysterious man is. Jesus, is it possible? Come, Lord, have mercy on me, illumine your face, come. The night. Nothing interests me, I see nothing. Without you only nothingness exists. Without you, how is anything possible?

Jesus, when your love gladdened my face and everything shone with hope... Where are you? I believe in You at night. Jesus, I believe only in You. Come, come, Lord.

(Madrid, February 19, 1979)

39. Tests at La Paz.[41] No sleep. And all day on the move... my Jesus, I'm happy. Better in my house? The sun at dawn. It does me good to get out, in the street. What about the attic?[42] Is it a good idea? I'm thinking of trying it out, if they help me. Well, Jesus, should I have the surgery? When? Kiko is in Zamora. The letter to the Pope, long; I'm not fully convinced. I'm willing to spend money on the attic. Even though You are putting things in my hands, I resist.

Sleepless. Five a.m. and yearning to live. Thank you, Jesus. Make me sleep.

(Madrid, February 20, 1979)

40. Eight a.m. Still no sleep. Jesus, you are surprising. So many wonderful ideas. I see how to end the catechumenate and suddenly all is illuminated and has a future, little by little.

---

[40] Cf. Qo 1:2.
[41] "La Paz" General Hospital, Madrid.
[42] Near *San José* Parish on Madrid's Gran Vía, where Carmen considered going to live but never did.

1. Only the first community, the oldest one,[43] to see how it goes. Renewal at the Easter Vigil at *San Salvatore*.[44] Old garment and alb. Perfume. One by one: Do you believe? I believe. Dinner.

2. Invite Salimei[45] or Fr. Maximino.[46]

3. Honeymoon. Six days in Jerusalem, two in Tiberias, four in Jerusalem. Invite Salimei or Fr. Maximino.

4. Year of Neophyte. Song of Songs and sacraments of Baptism, Eucharist, and Confirmation. Should we invite Farnés?[47] And then we follow them.

It is best we try only with the first community, except for some we're not sure about: better they wait. Just to begin with. The first of *San Luigi*,[48] the first of *Natività*,[49] the first of *Santa Francesca*,[50] and the second of *Sacramentinos*[51] will come later.

Letter to the Pope, same: historically and without contention, asking for help.

Main idea: to create a nucleus in the parish that will serve to welcome.

---

[43] The first community of the parish of *Nostra Signora del Santissimo Sacramento e Santi Martiri Canadesi*, Rome.

[44] *San Salvatore in Campo* is a church in Rome that Cardinal Poletti granted for use by the Way. It served as the Neocatechumenal Center of the diocese for many years.

[45] Mons. Giulio Salimei (†), then Auxiliary Bishop of Rome, in charge of the Teams for Catechesis. Prematurely made emeritus due to illness, he served as the first rector of the "Redemptoris Mater" Diocesan Seminary of Rome (1988-1998).

[46] Mons. Maximino Romero de Lema (†), Secretary of the Congregation for the Clergy and Catechesis, 1976-1986. Once emeritus, he became spiritual director at the "Redemptoris Mater" Diocesan Seminary of Rome (1988-1998).

[47] Mosén Pedro Farnés Scheres (†), priest and liturgist of the Diocese of Barcelona.

[48] Parish of *San Luigi Gonzaga*, Parioli, Rome.

[49] Parish of *Natività del Nostro Signore Gesù Cristo*, Rome.

[50] Parish of *Santa Francesca Cabrini*, Rome.

[51] Parish of *Nostra Signora del Santissimo Sacramento e Santi Martiri Canadesi*, Rome.

Invite the 12 *Cefalos*.[52]

And also give strong scrutinies: change of life, not theology.

We're starting three nucleuses in Rome and three in Spain. And attending to the catechists and itinerants.[53]

We have to quickly organize houses, trips, etc.

Relying on Fr. Maximino, on Farnés, and on the Pope for support, keeping them well informed and asking for help.

Parache.[54] Vespers already. Truly, Lord, what can I say? Thank you for my life. Now it seems good. Do your will in me. Welcome me in your love and your grace, in your hands. I trust, falling asleep under anesthesia. Remember your love.

(Madrid, February 21, 1979)

41. La Paloma Clinic.[55] Lord, why is this mess with Fr. Jesús happening precisely today?[56] You are unpredictable and good. My Jesus, I love you with all my heart. Thank you for how much you have loved me and still love me. Help me to live and die according to your will. I love you, Lord, calm my heart in You.

(Madrid, February 22, 1979)

42. Finally in the operating room, Lord! I am happy. Thank you, my Jesus. I love you. You come to me. I love you. It is almost better for me to see you.[57] Thank you, Jesus. Help me! My life is in your hands.

Anesthesia. Afterwards, difficult afternoon, in pain. Lord, the patients, the surgeries, pain… my Jesus, man of sorrows, you who know every kind of suffering.[58] How hard it is, Lord. The body rebels

---

[52] Chosen during the world convivence for itinerant catechists in January 1978 at Arcireale to serve in an advisory capacity to the Initiators of the Neocatechumenal Way.

[53] Local catechists of Neocatechumenal communities that offer themselves to be sent to any part of the world to evangelize full-time.

[54] Dr. Enrique Parache Guillén, renowned Obstetrician/Gynecologist.

[55] In Madrid. Today it is called Virgen de la Paloma Hospital.

[56] Mons. Jesús Higueras Fernándes (†), pastor of *Virgen de la Paloma*, Madrid.

[57] Cf. Phil 1:23

[58] Cf. Is 53:3.

in its incredible helplessness. My bed… what pain, Lord. Where can I escape to?[59]

(Madrid, February 23, 1979)

43. La Paloma Clinic – Now it's another day. I almost feel well. The IV and bed keep me tied down here, tired, and helpless, but I'm doing very well. Jesus, all is now past. I'm terrified of another "appointment"… Visit the sick who are in pain. You, Servant, man of suffering,[60] the best consoler.[61]

(Madrid, February 24, 1979)

44. La Paloma Clinic. Good day.

Night, finally alone and doing well. My Jesus, thank you, you allow brief suffering but are bountiful in love. Will my sadness end now? I trust you, Lord. Help me to live with enthusiasm, with freedom, in your Love. Thank you, Jesus.

Vatican Radio: Częstochowa…

How will we end up? You know all things, Jesus, my Love. Good night.

(Madrid, February 25, 1979)

45. La Paloma Clinic – All alone. Lord, it seems my sadness is going to fade away. Let it be so! Lord, give me courage. I love you. Teach me to love people. Look at the state of the world, my Jesus.

Tranquil night, miraculous night.

(Madrid, February 26, 1979)

46. La Paloma Clinic – I wake up so-so. Parache says to wait until Friday.

Kiko returns from Paris.

Jesus, without a home, very lonely, everything far away. It is just You and me. I love you, Lord. Come, come, You. I believe in You alone.

(Madrid, February 27, 1979)

---

[59] Cf. Ps 139:7.
[60] Cf. Is 53:3.
[61] Cf. *Sequence of Pentecost.*

47. Ash Wednesday – La Paloma Clinic.

Last night? Thank you, Jesus, I feel like new. How can I not bless you?

Bless the Lord, my soul,
All that is within me, bless his holy name,
Bless the Lord, my soul,
Do not forget all the gifts of God,
Who forgives all your iniquity,
Who heals all your diseases,
Who redeems your life from the pit,
Who crowns you with love and tenderness,
Who fills your life with good things,
So that your youth is renewed like the eagle's.
The Lord does righteous deeds,
Brings justice to all the oppressed.
He made known his ways to Moses,
And his deeds to the children of Israel.[62]

My Jesus, I thank you with all my heart for this adventure. I love you, Jesus. "Adventure in its springtime flourish." "Even though I pass through a dark valley (anesthesia), I fear nothing, because You are with me."[63] Thank you, Lord.

(Madrid, February 28, 1979)

48. Departure. Freedom – It is like test driving life anew. Thank you, Lord. Your generosity is absolute in everything. Help me be like You, free me of my stinginess. Help me be like You, giver of life and joy and freedom, magnanimous. Lord, I love you. You are good and holy. Thank you, Jesus. Let the Glory of your *Shekinah* rest upon me.[64]

Election Day in Spain.

Scrutinies at night.

(Madrid, March 1, 1979)

---

[62] Ps 103:1-7.
[63] Cf. Ps 23:4.
[64] *Shekinah*: the presence (glory) of God amongst men.

49. Elections, elections, elections, newspapers, magazines, TV, interpretations…

I visit the Center in the afternoon.

(Madrid, March 2, 1979)

50. House, bed, rest. Mass at the *Sacramentinos*.[65] Preparing for a trip to the Vatican.

(Madrid, March 3, 1979)

51. Airport. Tried to leave for Rome. Strike at Alitalia. Home. Longest day of the year…

(Madrid, March 4, 1979)

52. Madrid-Rome. All day on my feet. Good, moving. Finally, night in Santa Marinella.[66]

(Santa Marinella, March 5, 1979)

53. I'm happy, Lord, optimistic. My outlook is clear. Ready for the fight. What more, Lord? Thank you for your love.

(Santa Marinella, March 6, 1979)

54. Since I've been happy, I don't know what to write… Working day. Creativity gives freedom. I read the old *Redditios*[67] and they give me joy. Remembering your wonders and your love for each person. It is four. Kiko returns from the *Redditio*. Good night, Jesus.

(Santa Marinella, March 7, 1979)

---

[65] Parish of *Santísimo Sacramento*, Madrid.

[66] Town on the Tyrrhenian Sea located some 60 km from Rome, in the house of Mimmo (†) and Angela (†) Gennarini, a couple from the first community of *San Luigi Gonzaga*, Rome. They put their house at the service of Kiko and Carmen so they could rest during the month of August.

[67] *Redditio Symboli* is a step of the Neocatechumenal Way. Carmen is speaking of the *Redditio Symboli* "directories" from past years. These volumes contain transcripts of recordings of the catecheses, convivences, steps, etc., of the Neocatechumenal Way.

55. I got up hopeless and making life impossible.
The long nights ... the time for rest is over...
Night. Rome.

(Rome, March 8, 1979)

56. Airport. Rome-Madrid, with a stopover in Barcelona. In a wheelchair.
Arrival. Parache.
Valle. The preaching consoles me: First Letter of St. John, new, fresh. Thank you, Jesus.

Redditio Scrutinies: three old ladies.
Cardinal Villot[68] has died.

(Valle – Madrid, March 10, 1979)

57. Lauds with the paralytic.[69] Freshness of the preaching. Incredible. I'm consoled seeing Kiko doing so well here. His stamina is incredible.
I love you, my Jesus. Eucharist. Willing to fight.

(Valle – Madrid, March 10, 1979)

58. Sunday. Older people. We've all gotten much older and yet the communion seems fresh and untiring. I love you, Lord.
Traffic jam on the way back. I want to act quickly on the attic. Shopping. Money. I love you, Lord. Give me energy when I awake and help me fight.
The Pope is at *San Basilio* – Tiburtina.

(Madrid, March 11, 1979)

59. Day off. Furniture, attic, Nebraska...[70] old times...
Standing before a mystery. Jesus, we are an incredible mystery: man is unfathomable, never comprehending the whole mystery. Lord, I believe in You. Have mercy on us. Help Kiko. Give him strength. Let your holiness descend upon us.

(Madrid, March 12, 1979)

---

[68] Cardinal Jean-Marie Villot (†), Secretary of State, 1969-1979.
[69] Cf. Acts 3.
[70] Cafeteria on Madrid's Gran Vía.

60. Kiko's new letter to the Pope. *Carina*.[71]

Climbed up to the attic with Antonio and Felix.[72] Kiko's and Jesus'[73] first night in the attic.

Jesus, I've had a sad, tense, heavy, stifling day. I'm tired, Jesus, I'm so tired.

First *Redditio* in Madrid. Jesus, gladden my life. Come, Jesus.

(Madrid, March 13, 1979)

61. I moan like a dove. Jesus, what a mystery depression is. Now I see how freely that hope, life, and light were given. Jesus, everything weighs on me, disappointment, everything. There were so many gifts… I don't see them. Money, the attic, Kiko, all weigh on me heavily. Everything is a shattering weight: itinerants, communities, bishops… Life itself. Everything is fear, worry, disappointment, death. <u>My Risen Jesus</u>, come in your manifestations of life to enlighten my land, fill the horizon with the future. Come, Jesus, to destroy death. I love you, my Jesus, I love you. Do not leave me in the hands of the night, of the enemy. I love you, my Jesus. In the day of distress, I seek the Lord. By night my hands are raised unceasingly.[74]

(Madrid, March 14, 1979)

62. Out of the depths I cry to you, Lord, distressed, restless, suffering greatly. Lord, Why? So many things, for what? I only need You, your presence, your countenance, your love. Show your power, Lord, excellent consoler. Come. Look at these depths that are unknown to me, the *kenosis*[75] where You have descended. Lord, have mercy on me. Give me strength. I can't do it. Peace, oh Jesus, peace.

(Madrid, March 15, 1979)

---

[71] Italian word, literally, 'cute, nice'.

[72] Antonio González (†) (presbyter – hereinafter, "pb"), and Félix Villegas (†) (pb), from the first community of *Virgen de la Paloma* parish, Madrid.

[73] Jesús Blásquez (pb) from the first community of *Nuestra Señora del Tránsito*, Madrid.

[74] Cf. Ps 77:3.

[75] Cf. Phil 2:6-8.

63. Tarancón[76] consoles us. Thank you, Lord. *Redditio* in *Canillas*.[77] This too is a consolation, but so cold. Thank you, Jesus.

(Madrid, March 16, 1979)

64. Meeting of "the 18." Eucharist with children. Thank you, Jesus. A surprise: Farnés visits Knox.[78] Easter? Lord, I'm not afraid, especially about Easter.

(Madrid, March 17, 1979)

65. Home. Large, dark, sad. Old age, my mother, Eulogia.[79] Everything passing away. Lord, what a mystery life is.

Kiko's going to *Valle* alone. Cantor's convivence. I'm not going. I'm listening to Vatican Radio: grassroots communities. It sounds the same, Lord, and yet it's not.

(Madrid, March 18, 1979)

66. *Redditio* at *La Paloma*.[80] What joy it gives me to listen. I go sad and return so happy when I contemplate you. Josemari Soler.[81] Thank you, Jesus, Love. Thank you. Jesus.

(Madrid, March 19, 1979)

67. *Redditio*. Marita, José, Rosario, Domingo.[82] What joy, Lord. You visibly guide and sustain your people, like a Good Shepherd. Thank you, my Jesus. We left the *Redditio* in the hands of the responsible.

(Madrid, March 20, 1979)

---

[76] Cardinal Vicente Enrique y Tarancón (†), Archbishop of Madrid, 1971-1981.

[77] Parish of *Nuestra Señora del Tránsito*, Madrid.

[78] Cardinal James Robert Knox (†), Prefect for the Congregation for Divine Worship, 1974-1981.

[79] Lifelong servant who worked in Carmen's mother's house.

[80] Parish of *Virgen de la Paloma y San Pedro el Real*, Madrid.

[81] José María Soler (†), from the community of the Neocatechumenal Center of Madrid.

[82] María Anoro, José y Rosario Agudo, Domingo Ramos (†), all belong to the community of the Neocatechumenal Center of Madrid.

68. Spring. After rushing around the whole day, the Paschal Preconium of the Easter announcement at the *Convención*.[83] I see a people walking toward Freedom, where the Passover is directing them. My Jesus, how happy I am. A small action and you fill the future and the depth of my *kenosis* with the sun.[84] Sweet Jesus, don't leave me. I love you. Thank you, Jesus.

(Madrid, March 22, 1979)

69. So happy, I didn't sleep all night. From Madrid to Rome. Arrival. A "Pharaoh" appears in the North who wants to oppose Easter. But he isn't taking from me the happiness of your power, of your presence.

Convivence of the Election with the first community of *Martiri*. Dominican nuns. We have reached the Election[85] with the first community. I see that you inspire Kiko. Help him. Thank you, Jesus.

Night. First Letter of St. John: Light = Love of Jesus Christ.

(Rome, March 23, 1979)

70. Convivence of the Election. Lauds. Philippians. New man. *Shema*[86] questionnaire. Eucharist. Thank you, Jesus. I'm happy, free. The Easter battle… Have mercy on me, Lord, You who love me.

(Rome, March 24, 1979)

71. My Jesus. When I feel good, I don't feel like writing here. Good night.

(Madrid, March 27, 1979)

72. Easter announcement at the *Antoniano*.[87] I feel impossibility, frustration, pain. Kiko… Jesus, how difficult everything is. Only your appearance, only your Holy Spirit coordinates, unites, loves, my Jesus.

(Rome, March 31, 1979)

---

[83] Convención Hotel, Madrid.

[84] Cf. Phil 2:6-8.

[85] Last step of the Neocatechumenal Way with the first community of the parish of *Nostra Signora del Santissimo Sacramento e Santi Martiri Canadesi*, Rome.

[86] Cf. Dt 6: 4-5. The *Shema* is a step of the Neocatechumenal Way between the First and Second Scrutinies.

[87] Pontifical University "Antonianum", Rome.

73. Cantors' Convivence at the *Antoniano*.

Thank you, Jesus, for the strength arising in me like a new youth: courage, <u>life</u>, my Jesus, thank you.

The enemies are rising up powerfully.

Easter gladdens me like a powerful <u>sanctuary lamp</u> in the middle of the night.

Lord, you are great. I love you. Thank you, Jesus.

74. Ideas for the 1979 Easter Vigil. Loins girded and the staff in our hands…

To depart on a journey with no return. What shall we take? You shall eat it in haste. It is the Lord's Passover. You shall anoint your doors with the blood of the lamb.[88]

Egypt is wounded, "the death" in my darkness, the body of the tyrant, "Sin", the accomplice of death. Israel baptized.

Easter = To suffer.

The <u>whole of creation is restored</u> revealing itself.

(April 3-4, 1979)

75. Easter Vigil in *S. Salvatore*.

So much anticipation, desire, eagerness, and then the squadron of children "put the brakes" on the Night for me. Contemplating in the depth of my soul… I love you, Lord. Come, Jesus.

(April 14, 1979)

76. I awake surrounded by problems, in anguish. Lord, teach me to cast off the ghosts. I love you, my Jesus.

(April 15, 1979)

77. Beatifications[89] – Lord, on the eve of persecution, desiring nothing more of this life. Poor and with nothing, I feel the intimate desire for your presence alone. <u>Holiness</u>, Lord, hidden desires for holiness, for sacrifice, to fill the day with your presence. Prayer. Lord,

---

[88] Cf. Ex 12:11.

[89] On this day St. John Paul II beatified Jacques-Désiré Laval (1803-1864) and Francisco Coll Guitart (1812-1875).

come fill the good and all things with meaning. Strengthen Kiko's faith.

(April 29, 1979)

78. Jesus, what a life this is, so forced in every way. Absolute uselessness. Dedicated to smoking… Lord, since I have nothing to do, I see that my only job is to be good and holy: in your presence, contemplating you and being good. That's what I'd like. Help me to continuously sacrifice myself, Jesus. I doubt everything and I fear everything. This life says nothing to me, oh Jesus. If only you would make yourself present again as in the past, and if only I believed, my Jesus, mysterious… Life and death are a great mystery. And You, My God, awesome mystery. You are difficult, Lord. How can it all be? I kneel before your mystery. Come, my Jesus, my love. Come, help me.

Night. Lord, I'm consoled by the brothers. My Jesus, help us continue.

(April 30, 1979)

79. On the day of distress I seek the Lord, I remember God and I moan.[90]

I keep silent, I don't speak, because it is You who will act.[91] I'm distraught and speechless.[92]

(May 2, 1979)

80. My Jesus, May 3, 1954. I was 23 years old. My Jesus, it was the day of "Victory."[93] I love you, my Jesus. How much you have loved

---

[90] Cf. Ps 77:2-3.

[91] Cf. Ps 39:9.

[92] Cf. Ps 77:4.

[93] This was the day she left her house in Madrid to go to Javier, to enter the *Misioneras de Cristo Jesús*. In Zamora on May 15, 1994, she recounted the event thus: "When I turned 23, and finished Chemistry, I escaped from my house and went to become a missionary. I remember that I escaped when my father was not in Madrid. He followed me but when he arrived in Madrid I was in already in Pamplona, and from there I reached the little town of Javier. I was no longer a minor and my father couldn't call the police. I finally reached Javier and joined a Missionary Institute… it had been formed just ten years before."

me. I don't regret it. I would leave again as I did on that day of my youth. Then I was happy, today I'm sad, and yet You are my only chance for happiness, for life. And I love you, my Jesus. Today you say, "Ask in my name."[94] I only want one thing: open my lips to the announcement of the Gospel, allow me to participate in your Word. Come, visit me, visit your land. I love you.

(May 3, 1979)

81. My Jesus, sadness is eating away at my heart all day long. All I know how to do is smoke, to escape with the smoke. What sadness. I see everything pessimistically: life, history, the future. Nothing exists. My God, so mysterious. Is it possible? Look on my affliction.[95] I'm not happy, but deep down I am. Jesus, you place a desert all around me and You are the only one there. I love You. Come, Jesus, speak to my heart, gladden me.

(May 4, 1979)

82. After a bleak day, the night. Easter, your presence mysteriously consoles me, changing everything. A crack opens and the light appears, the Love, the future, the power, the life. Yes, You are, you are life, the answer for man, the Resurrection. Lord, I love you. Do not leave me in the night, I wait for you; in the darkness, I believe in you. I love you. Come, Lord.

(May 5, 1979)

83. I fall asleep in peace and wake up sad and burdened. Lord, how can this be? Everything encircles me, disquieting, menacing, dangerous. Why? What do I care about anyone but You, Lord? Come, defend my life from darkness, from death, put your name on my lips. Jesus, I love you. Come. What to do today? Invigorate my limbs, get me moving, into life. Help me.

One-thirty in the morning. My heart breathes freely. My Jesus, thank you. Come when I awake. In peace, free.

(May 6, 1979)

---

[94] Cf. Jn 16:24.
[95] Cf. Sg 2:14.

84. "I am who I am."⁹⁶ God does not make theological declarations, but instead gives the answer his creatures need and that helps them, "I will be there as He who will be there; that is, you will not need to conjure Me up, because <u>I am there; I am with you</u>⁹⁷."

My Jesus, like a lace of humiliation, exasperation in the elevator… my Jesus, what pain.

(May 7, 1979)

85. Jesus, thank you for emptying me, for detaching my heart from all things. What remains is only You and living in your love, with the enemy at my side, being humbled, Lord. What pain, what worry, everything totters. Oh Jesus, cornerstone,⁹⁸ immovable life built on the Cross. Come, Jesus, shine your face on my life. Help me sustain my existence with You. My Jesus, lead me to prayer, to your holiness, my refuge, my life. Come, Most Holy Spirit, have mercy on my poverty.

(May 8, 1979)

86. Bouyer⁹⁹ makes me think more about how everything is relative. My Jesus, I hope only in the presence of your Consoling Spirit, Creator, Most Holy. Come, Holy Spirit, come, come, fill all my impossibility with your presence. My Jesus, come. Your presence makes life, intelligence bloom. Life, yes, Life. Everything as a surprise. Come, Holy Spirit, come.

(Santa Marinella, May 9, 1979)

87. I feel my heart revive as night falls. The sun, life, hope, my Jesus, mysterious God, excellent Consoler. People, the brothers, the Church, the others, cause me anguish. Itinerants, the future, they want to disappear amid the anguish. Now, in your presence, I'm willing to face reality, with the strength of your Holy Spirit. Come, Holy Spirit. Come, Holy Spirit, come, come.

(May 11, 1979)

---

⁹⁶ Ex 3:14.

⁹⁷ Carmen copies the text in English in her diary without referencing the quotation.

⁹⁸ Cf. Mt 21:42.

⁹⁹ Louis Bouyer (1913-2004), French theologian.

88. Eucharist in *San Salvatore*. Fifth Sunday of Easter. Sweet Consoling Spirit, I love you. Most Holy, Holy, Holy, breathtaking wind, impetuous, so good, you lead me to have love for each one, to sacrifice, to your holiness. Jesus, the only purpose of existence, the only happiness. Your Holiness. Take me, Jesus.

(Rome, May 12, 1979)

89. In the afternoon, second community of *Santa Francesca*. My Jesus, my Love, what uncertainty.

(Santa Marinella, May 13, 1979)

90. All my foundations are shaken, my Jesus, within me. Only You remain, only You, everlasting rock, only one. My Love, I sigh for your presence, your love, your sanctity. Come, my Love. You know all things. I'm waiting for you. I wait for you, Most Holy Spirit, good, consoler. I love you. Come to me. Transform me. Come, Jesus.

(May 14, 1979)

91. Jesus, I awake in Rome with pain in my heart, in my life, in my soul, restrained before everything, like a dying person.
Travel to Porto San Giorgio.[100] Spring. The center is rebuilt. Night: the brothers, Love… my Jesus, how is it that I see everything so, so black in the morning? The weight of the Vatican, the Church, the future and the present, all fall on my head; the responsibility terrifies me, darkness, death. How is this possible? Lord, I call upon you. Awaken me in You, open my lips. Help me in these days. Come, come, Lord.

(Porto San Giorgio, May 15, 1979)

92. The Spaniards are coming. My Jesus, I struggle sorrowfully with myself, constantly worrying. Amid all this, your Pentecost. My Jesus, You veil reality from me, I close my eyes and you comfort me. Your Word gives me life, but you don't open my mouth and I'm sad, not understanding myself or You. I feel like crying over my helplessness, my muteness. Jesus, have mercy on me, I hope in your

---

[100] "Servant of Yahweh" International Neocatechumenal Center, located in Porto San Giorgio (Fermo).

Most Holy Spirit, Wise, Eloquent. My Love, I abandon myself to You. Come.

(Porto San Giorgio, May 17, 1979)

93. Jesus, one invocation and you open life to me, this hidden life of mine, buried and sterile. Lord, thank you. I see the contrasts between life and death, but I'm dead in sterility. What sickness is this, Lord? Come.

(Porto San Giorgio, May 18, 1979)

94. This days feels closed, closed, closed. My Jesus, I'd like to escape. Where to? Frailty encompasses me, my Jesus. Why? Why? What's happening to me? I feel like the last one, the last, nothing in nothingness, and set in a display case of my shame and sadness. Jesus, if You would come... I know nothing, can say nothing, and am not interested in anything of this world or this life. I'm locked in a grave of death. I wait for you Jesus, and it is possible... I wait for You, weeping.

(Porto San Giorgio, May 18, 1979)

95. Eucharist and Africa. Day of pain. Two words, and badly said, and my heart opens up. My Jesus, sufferings, sufferings. Am I creating it all? Or is it Your work? Free me, Lord. Have mercy on me and on my people. Nothing consoles me. You do, Jesus; come.

(Porto San Giorgio, May 19, 1979)

96. 250 itinerants. Overwhelming.

(Porto San Giorgio, May 20, 1979)

97. 250 itinerants. Overwhelming. Joy too.

(Porto San Giorgio, May 21, 1979)

98. From Porto San Giorgio to the Vatican, to the Pope. With the Vatican, at nightfall, you remind me of your great Love, my Jesus, wonderful companion of my youth. How can I forget you in tribulation? You have loved me so much, so much, so much. Blessed are you. Jesus, my Love, only One, only One, wonderful. Come, You,

the anointed of the Holy Spirit, Sweetest one, come, come. I love you. Tomorrow in Jerusalem.

(May 22, 1979)

99. Sleepless night. Happy, taken by your presence. You remind me of all your wonderful presence, Jesus. I couldn't sleep. I love you for the great love with which you have loved me.

(May 23, 1979)

100. My heart takes flight. My tongue is loosed and my heart speaks. The bright light remains, wonderful, and I see everything comes from your hand, my Jesus. I see everything by the light of your face.

Israel. Tel Aviv. Tonight at the Ginosar.[101] "It seemed like a dream…"[102]

(Ginosar – Israel, May 24, 1979)

101. I didn't sleep well and wake up *"escorbútica,"*[103] and as if nobody were seeing the wonderful miracle it is to be here and in this hotel. My Jesus, you multiply things and I enter again into pain, unable to communicate, muteness. I would like to say so many wonderful things that I become mute, stupefied, ridiculous and useless. My Jesus, what must I do? Escape to be alone and love you. Come, Jesus.

(Ginosar – Israel, May 25, 1979)

102. Notre Dame of Jerusalem Center.[104]

This convivence stays open, it won't end here.[105] It's neither brainwashing nor tactical rearrangement.

---

[101] Hotel Nof Ginosar Kibbutz, Tiberias.

[102] Cf. Ps 126:1.

[103] In Italian the word *scorbutica* is used figuratively of a person who is sour, sullen, unfriendly, intractable, unsociable, sometimes for no particular reason.

[104] Written on a separate sheet bearing the Notre Dame of Jerusalem Center letterhead.

[105] This Itinerant Convivence which began in Porto San Giorgio – Holy Land, concluded, after the summer, in Chantilly (France) – two by two itinerancy throughout Europe for ten days – Porto San Giorgio.

The coming summer unfolds like a battlefield.

Not lack of sin. It's something else: an election that is verified by the battle in history. To demolish pride. Vigilance, prayer. To know how to be, "to live."

A *kairos*... The announcement of Jesus Christ. (To come out of the *status quo* and the daily grind, always returning to the freedom of the first announcement).

The opportunity for Europe.

The opportunity to enter into the full reality of others.

We have to re-make and complete teams, and this cannot be done long-distance, but instead in the freedom and public presence of everyone. And not now in the heat of the moment but later on, after a time of temptation and battle, keeping in mind that the "two-by-two itinerancy" is a week to "soak."

The *merkabá*[106] will depart from Porto San Giorgio toward the end of September. If you had plans, change them. You don't know if you'll return.

The whole summer will be up in the air: you don't know where you come from or where you're going.[107]

Chastity for those who are married.

(Jerusalem, June 1, 1979)

103. Cenacle. Pentecost – My Jesus, my soul is breaking from your love. You are wonderful and invincible, most sweet Consoler. I love you.

(Jerusalem, June 2, 1979)

104. Return from Tel Aviv to Rome after the Ascension, and Eucharist at the Intercontinental.[108]

At the Ascension. Eucharist. My Jesus, your promises fully realized. You are magnificent in your wonderful mysteries. I love you,

---

[106] "Chariot"-throne of the glory of God, of the Son of Man, that goes out in all four directions: Ez 1:4-28. In the Neocatechumenal Way the term *merkaba* refers to the itinerant evangelization and more specifically the assigning of the new mission destinations at the end of the convivences.

[107] Cf. Jn 3:8.

[108] Seven Arches Hotel, Jerusalem.

my Jesus. I love you. I love you. To sing eternally of your faithful love... I love you. Make the Word arise in me.[109] I love you.

(Rome, June 5-6, 1979)

105. Hotel Cristallo – Initiation to Prayer: second community of *Sta. Francesca*, first of *San Juan de Dios*, first of *Nuestra Señora de Lourdes*.

My Jesus, I'm deflated like a balloon. I was hoping for inspiration from you, from the many graces that you uncovered for me in the Valley of the Well,[110] and then everything I said was heavy and... Well, better that way. I wait for your coming. Take away my shame. I love you. Whatever You want. I love you.

(Arcinazzo,[111] June 8, 1979)

106. Mountain road. What joy.

Jesus, I wait here for your love, your grace, to finally have Rest, disconnect from everything. I entrust to You each worry, each itinerant. I desire you with all my heart, my Jesus. In the mountain, finally, I am alone with you. I love you. I wait for you. I want you. I fervidly desire you. Come, defend me.

(Venice, July 20, 1979)

107. My heart leaps to the rhythm of the brook. A stream of delights[112] You are for me, love of my life. You bring me back to my youth. How much You have loved me. Thank you, Jesus.

(Cortina,[113] July 21, 1979)

108. You bring me back to Ólvega, St. John of the Cross. Jesus, most faithful, most good, I love you. Thank you, Lord. How can I repay you?[114] Console my heart, freely, Jesus.

(Cortina, July 22, 1979)

---

[109] Cf. *Veni Creator Spiritus (sermone ditans guttura)*.
[110] Jesus and the Samaritan at Jacob's Well (cf. Jn 4).
[111] Altipiani di Arcinazzo, Province of Rome.
[112] Cf. Ps 36:8.
[113] Cortina d'Ampezzo, in the Dolomite Alps.
[114] Cf. Ps 116:12.

109. The mountains, the solitary valleys, delicious dreams of surrender, of helplessness. My Jesus, your angels. Yes, Jesus, you are wonderful. I love you, I love you. You manifest your presence to those whom You elect. Most faithful love of mine, always present. Jesus, I love you. Support those You try in tribulation. What consolation. I love you.
(Cortina, July 23, 1979)

110. The mountain, the cloud, the stream… my Jesus, my heart breaks at the tenderness of your presence. The same gestures from long ago… I desire to enter into your holiness, loving you. My heart beats fast, effortlessly, and I love you. Thank you, my Jesus, my love, my love. Thank you, Jesus.

(July 24, 1979)

111. My Jesus your wonderful signs… You know I'm waiting for your Word. Come, Jesus. Tell me whether You are there in all of this with the teams. Speak to me, calm me. I am happy. My Jesus, thank you.

(Santa Marinella, August 1, 1979)

112. Lord, fill my life with blessings. Your generosity, your love console me and move me. Jesus, I remember the sufferings reverently. I love you. Thank you, Jesus. The sea, the water. I'm in great shape, free. Thank you, Jesus. In the morning your sweet love awakens me. I love you.

(Santa Marinella, August 3, 1979)

113. Jesus, how can I give you thanks? You fill me with fortitude, with love, with consolation, with energy. I love you, my Jesus. You surround me with good things. Lord, you are great, immeasurable, the only one, wonderful. What joy, Jesus. You lift me up, give me life, my Jesus, my Rock, my Love. I love you.

(Santa Marinella, August 8, 1979)

114. Storm. Lord, you are great in all your works. Blessed are you, Lord. I love you.

(Santa Marinella, August 9, 1979)

115. Time flies and I don't care because you love me and I feel life eternally renewing. You, Eternal one, invincible. Lord, I love you.
(Santa Marinella, August 10, 1979)

116. To love each other, the sun, the night and the Eucharist – embattled – and you. Bread, Wine. I love you. I love you. You taste of eternal life, You, Lord, the Eternal One. I love you.
(Santa Marinella, August 11, 1979)

117. Lord, I have sinned. Offending you weighs on me, most merciful, holy one. Do not withdraw your Spirit of Love, of life, of fortitude. I love you. Jesus, teach me, help me to confess my sins, not to scandalize, to love you. Help me live in the Freedom of your Love. I love you, Jesus. I have sinned a lot. I confess your infinite mercy. I love you. Thank you, Lord. You bless me with good things and I am blind and stupid.
(Santa Marinella, August 12, 1979)

118. 1. *Oh living flame of love,*
how tenderly you wound
my soul in its deepest center!
Since you no longer elude,
end it now, if you wish;
rend the fabric of this sweet encounter![115]

My Jesus.
(Santa Marinella, August 13, 1979)

119. 2. *Oh gentle captivity!*
Oh gifted wound!
Oh soft hand! Oh delicate touch,
that feels like eternal life,
and pays all debts!
In death you have transformed it into life.[116]
(Santa Marinella, August 14, 1979)

---

[115] ST JOHN OF THE CROSS, *Living Flame of Love*.
[116] Ibid.

120. 3. *Oh lamps of fire*
in whose splendors
the deep caverns of the sense,
once dark and blind,
with strange beauty,
give color and light together with their Beloved![117]

Assumed one, Sweet Virgin Mary. I remember you in Barcelona and I abandon myself, past and future, within which I… Sweet Virgin Mary.

(Santa Marinella, August 15-16, 1979)

121. 4. *How meek and loving*
I remember you in my bosom,
where you alone secretly dwell,
and with your delectable breath
of good and glory filled
how delicately you seduce me![118]

(Santa Marinella, August 17, 1979)

122. A stormy sea today. How great you are, Lord, and unpredictable. Thank you, Lord, for your love. I no longer expected it, and then sweetly you make me fall in love. I can almost say I love you. I love You for you, since you have let me know you so well. Thank you, Jesus, beautiful as Lebanon, slender as a cedar.[119]

(Santa Marinella, August 18, 1979)

123. The sea is still stormy, and You console me without measure. You anoint me with new oil and renew my life as in my youth. Jesus, and the Pope? Can it be true? What? Lord, you keep me in suspense.[120]

(Santa Marinella, August 19, 1979)

---

[117] Ibid.
[118] Ibid.
[119] Sg 5:15.
[120] The possibility arises of a private audience with St. John Paul II.

124. *How well I know that fountain's rushing flow, although by night!*[121]

I cannot say whether it's night for me, Jesus, but how well I understand. That eternal fountain is hidden. Most sweet consoler, wonderful Jesus. I love you, my Jesus. Your consolations and your graces, toward this poor, unworthy wretch move me. You are great, Lord, splendid, generous, infinite. I love you.

(Santa Marinella, August 20, 1979)

125. Music: the despair felt in the throat upon encountering a loved one who no longer recognizes you. My God, your Word!

You console me with St. John of the Cross. You teach me and gently lead me to solitude, to prayer, and fill my will with love and fortitude. Blessed are you, Lord, in all your works. I remember other times. It's my womb, right? Right? I was already free in Jerusalem, and how dark, how ill-tempered. It is You, and only You, and I love you. Thank you, Jesus.

(Santa Marinella, August 21, 1979)

126. Elías' Saint Day.[122]

Lord, you console me so undeservedly that I'm moved. But what can I say to you? Life is already an undeserved gift. My Jesus, I recall the tribulations, the darkness, the sufferings and having lived them fills me with joy. Truly, You have heard my cries. You have made me cry out to you, call you. And You are indescribable, present, so loving, infinite and eternal. Sweet One, you encircle me wonderfully, you anoint me with new oil,[123] with strength, and You are my Only One. Thank you, thank you, Lord.

(Santa Marinella, August 22, 1979)

---

[121] ST. JOHN OF THE CROSS, *Canticle of the Soul*.
[122] Elías Hernández Barrera, Carmen's brother.
[123] Cf. Ps 92:10.

127. I don't know how to tell you what I want…

Jesus, your voice like the many waters.[124] To sing of your love… You are, Lord, and the Only One. My heart exults in your name. Jesus, Jesus, Lord, Christ. Come, Lord Jesus.

(Santa Marinella, August 25, 1979)

128. Lord, the Pope is at la Marmolada, in the mountains. You, here, are consoling me intimately. You are strengthening me like a newfound youth and loving me so undeservedly that you make me cry; delicately, you move me. Thank you, Jesus. Take away my animosity. Send me, free, Lord.

(Santa Marinella, August 26, 1979)

129. It's been so long since I last saw you, Jesus. Your presence luminously enlightens my history. It is filled with your presence. My Jesus, I'm deeply moved at feeling you again, feeling your sweet strength, your wonderful action, sure, tender, strong. I feel like I'm dreaming. Like a deer, you fled after wounding me[125] and I have been waiting for you, with my heart always open for You. Your return, Lord, your voice, your sweet being here, the quiet, and the ox's strength[126] with which you lift me up. You are wonderful and I love you. Thank you, Jesus.

(Santa Marinella, August 27, 1979)

130. My Jesus! 28. St. Augustine.

"You have seduced me and I let myself be seduced; you overpowered me and prevailed",[127] Lord, Lord Jesus. From August 28, 1962[128] to the 28th of August, 1979: 17 years. Thank you, Jesus, for all the times you have consoled me. Thank you, Lord, for how wonderfully you have acted in these 17 years of joys and sufferings. Today you renew my life with energy. Blessed may You be, Eternal, invincible, Holy.

---

[124] Cf. Ps 93:4.

[125] ST. JOHN OF THE CROSS, *Spiritual Canticle*.

[126] Cf. Ps 92:10.

[127] Cf. Jr 20:7.

[128] The date Carmen was "invited to leave" the Instituto de las *Misioneras de Cristo Jesús* in Barcelona.

We are going to see the Pope, and why not? You direct everything and are wisest. Let your will be done.[129]

(Santa Marinella, August 28, 1979)

131. Ideas – Penitential.[130] A Word for those who are in doubt or temptation about changing their situation: the devil distracts you to prevent you from entering into conversion today.

Climb Mount Moriah with your Isaac,[131] those of you who aren't yet 30 or 40 years old: I exhort you to be generous. Do not cheat the Lord of the last years of your first youth, if He, in reality, has already claimed them. I say 'first' because we are all there in the second, more mature one.

You anoint me with new oil.[132] Renew my strength, as in my youth.

(Santa Marinella, August 29, 1979)

132. Ideas. One thing is sure: the Word of God. "Let each one remain in the state he was first called."[133] And let no 'cretin' here say there isn't a clear call from the Lord weighing on your life because you will expose yourself to a Voice of Thunder that will leave you deaf…

Do not be cheap, haggling with the Lord over the last rays of youth and beauty. I say this for the 'pretty faces' constantly bargaining with God over their lives.

The Lord has called many of us here in our first youth, and has matured us, with blows and without, up to this moment of *Kairos*.

(Santa Marinella, August 30, 1979)

133. Ideas – women – changing teams.

I don't feel called to found a "female branch." I'm sure and free in the Lord, because He has proven it to me with clear events, like the Mission that God in his mercy has entrusted me with, as well as the

---

[129] Cf. Mt 6:10.

[130] Celebration of the Sacrament of Reconciliation, following the Rite for Reconciliation of Various Penitents with Individual Confession and Absolution.

[131] Cf. Gn 22:2.

[132] Cf. Ps 92:10.

[133] Cf. 1 Cor 7:20-24.

collaboration with Kiko, I don't know how long it will last; not eternally, obviously, even if it might be forever. Here lies my present and my future. And the one collaborating with me is Jesus Christ. And this exceptional collaboration is part of the whole tradition of the Church.

What I'm not so sure about, and is not in the tradition of the Church, is institutionalizing this. I'm not the model of a team to be perpetually reproduced.

Thus, I want to call the celibate and married women, at their own risk, to see if this collaboration is possible. Everything is biblical, but not standardized. This demands high morals as well as freedom from affections and sexuality.

To be able to collaborate with everyone everywhere: with the men of the team and with the catechumens, in each nation. We all have the same source, the *kerygma*. Do not come with sentimental excuses, or illusions: no one is indispensable.

I invite you to climb onto the evangelization with Jesus Christ, the four-wheeled *merkaba* in every direction.

Forget the past and when you have fallen. Use them neither for masochism nor timidity, but instead as a memorial of the faithfulness of God. And set your eyes on Jesus Christ and not on your hearts.

Movement, changes are not tactics but instead a wonderful help the Lord is giving you to detach your heart, strengthen it and give you a mission, a wonderful adventure. (Just like with the little plants that are transplanted from the winter nursery).

The same goes for the married couples. Do not be afraid of having many children, or few. The one who called you knows everything and knows why.

Virginity – The myth of having experiences so as to know… There is everything: the Virgin, Magdalen and the married woman (Joanna, the wife of Chuza).[134] All of them necessary. Do not follow "my standard."

Raise young women from your families, from your communities, to virginity and to the mission.

(Santa Marinella, August 31, 1979)

---

[134] Cf. Lk 8:2-3.

134. The wonderful vacation here is coming to an end. May your consoling spirit always continue. Let's go. Come, Lord, help us, inspire us. Come, come, come. Thank you, Jesus.

(Santa Marinella, September 3, 1979)

135. Great are you, Lord. Blessed are you.

Mario[135] and Fr. Francesco[136] with the Pope.

My Jesus, and tomorrow… Holy Spirit, you who enter and exit without a door, precede, enlighten, console, prepare the Pope, help him understand deeply.

My Jesus, I love you.

(Santa Marinella, September 4, 1979)

136. Ideas – Penitential – Intercession of Moses for the people: slaves for 400 years, in an idolatrous environment, and you want to change immediately? No changing of state. Remain in the state in which God has called you.

Do not be afraid of the children God gives you. We need two wonderful things: 1) life, children, which the world wants to reduce, cancel out, out of fear of life and love; 2) virginity, eschatology, the Messiah ("at the resurrection they neither marry nor are given in marriage").[137] Two wonderful things, and both necessary, neither is better or worse than the other.

That incomprehension of the absolute that is always life, which leaps to Eternal Life.[138]

---

[135] Mario Pezzi (pb) today belongs to the first community of the parish of *Sacra Famiglia*, Rome. This community began in the parish of San Giovanni di Dio and then continued for a time in the parish of *Nostra Signora di Coromoto*. Mario began collaborating intermittently with Kiko and Carmen in 1971 and permanently in 1982.

[136] Fr. Francesco Vergine (pb) (†), from the first community of *Santi Pietro e Paolo* in Gottolengo (Brescia). Pastor emeritus of that parish, he was the director of the "Redemptoris Mater" Diocesan Seminary of Rome until his death.

[137] Cf. Mt 22:30.

[138] Cf. Jn 4:14.

Repent of your sins of affection and when you have fallen in sexuality, and begin anew a wonderful, healthy collaboration. Take advantage of today's *kairos*.

Doubts? Know that today this is the way; yesterday, convents; tomorrow… whatever God wants. He always makes everything new, he knows deeply the problems of man. He is Love.[139]

(Chantilly[140] *– Paris – September 6 – 7, 1979)*

137. Making teams today. What a mess!
The morning exegesis, wonderful.

(Chantilly – Paris – September 8, 1979)

138. Eucharist. 100 teams depart today, like the "72."[141]

(Chantilly – Paris – September 9, 1979)

139. "She gave the holy ones the wages of their labors, she guided them along a <u>marvelous road</u>, herself their shelter by day and their starlight through the night."[142] How great you are, Lord, magnificent in all your works. Wonderful are your ways. I love you. Thank you, Lord.

(Santa Marinella, September 13, 1979)

140. Exaltation of the Cross – Courage, strength. Mysterious Jesus, wonderful, close. I love you.

(September 14, 1979)

141. Travel to Porto San Giorgio. Happy, encouraged.
Change. A lonely arrival. It looks like a desolate, cold wasteland. I find myself without the right clothes.[143]

(Porto San Giorgio, September 15, 1979)

---

[139] Cf. 1 Jn 4:8.16.
[140] Chateau de Montvillargenne, School of the Sisters of the Sacred Heart. Today it is a hotel.
[141] Cf. Lk 10:1.
[142] Wis 10:17.
[143] Cf. Mt 22:12.

142. Eucharist waiting for the itinerants.

(Porto San Giorgio, September 16, 1979)

143. Waiting for the itinerants. Jesus, I'm scared.

(Porto San Giorgio, September 17, 1979)

144. Boat. Fishing. Town.
Lord, it already feels like winter. Loneliness, sadness, worry, fear. Jesus, You are close, consoling, possible, accessible, God-with-me. Great are you, Lord, boundless, infinite. Thank you, Jesus. I love you, wonderful, holy. I'm worried about each itinerant. Why? Lord, aren't they free? Don't you exist? Gladden me, Lord, with holiness in You. Your gifts… counsel… Come, Holy Spirit. Come.

(Porto San Giorgio, September 18, 1979)

145. The *merkaba* sets out from Porto San Giorgio. New teams. Three o'clock in the morning.
How great you are, Lord, wonderful in your works, invincible![144] The enemy, sower of slander, is uncovered. Lord, convivence of the Good Shepherd, of the interior fight of the two brothers, the prodigal son and the older brother[145] who doesn't accept that the other confesses and receives freely, freely. And above all, Lord, convivence of the Glorious Cross.

(September 30, 1979)

146. How can I bless you, Lord? You are magnificent, wonderful. Thank you. Full of strength, grace, joy, consolation. Thank you, Jesus. May your name be blessed.

(October 1, 1979)

147. You are great, Lord. All your works are magnificent, sweet one, gentle, powerfully consoling, always present in all the convivences, wonderful and beyond words. My Jesus, two months of mission in your continuous action. Thank you, Jesus, I love you. How charming you are, my love, thank you. The Italian itinerants

---

[144] Cf. Ps 92:5-9; Jdt 16:13.
[145] Cf. Lk 15:11-32.

convivence finished today in Ostia, Rome. The last two months have been continuous itinerants convivences.

(Ostia – Rome, November 6, 1979)

148. Jesus calls so many vocations… at the beginning it scared me. Now you console me, Jesus, God, only God. I prostrate myself on the ground before your greatness. Faithful, faithful, great, Only One, Lord.

(November 7, 1979)

149. Life… Jesus, teach me to live, live, live. Jesus, my life, put your name on my lips.

(Santa Marinella, December 25, 1979)

150. Jesus, free me, Your love… Jesus, light, my life, come. Free me, Jesus.

My God, wonderful Creator, holy, you know me. Thank you, Jesus. Have mercy on me. Let your goodness, your mercy, freedom pass over me. Come, tear me away, take me to freedom with you, free me from the paths of people, of worries, of itinerants, Lord, put my life in your hands. Let me desire You alone. Free me from tobacco. Come, help me, give me courage, strength of will, heart. Jesus, Jesus put your name on my lips, your faithfulness, your love. Jesus, You love me. Show yourself, visit me, love me. Jesus, I love you.

(December 30, 1979)

1980[146]

---

[146] All the texts from this year are written on the loose pages of a diary from 1980 and another from 1978, which Carmen arranges, giving them continuity. At the beginning of the diary, Carmen writes: "Night, tribulations, ghosts, worries, suffering, sadness. Liberation as well. Chronic crisis. Year of sorrows, sufferings. Your absence, Lord."

151. Jesus! Jesus, my Jesus. Take my soul out of the darkness of the night. In the nothingness, in the not being, life doesn't exist, there is only darkness, death and sadness, sadness, sadness and depression.

Today is Kiko's birthday. He's sick. And I sit on my hands, stupid, lazy, hopeless, stationary, without anything to look forward to, or hope or options. Absolute indifference. I wait for you, Jesus, I wait for you to appear, your face, your presence, your prayer, your generosity and love. Jesus, the sufferings… you know it all.[147] I love you.

(January 9, 1980)

152. What serenity, Lord. I lie down in peace. Come, Lord, enlighten my awakening, give me hope for life. Let your presence enlighten my past because the accuser persecutes me, accusing me. Lord, I only believe in You. Have mercy on me. How difficult men, history, life are. Truly, Lord, you are God to hold everything steady. Lord, you are eternal. Can it be that You love me? Truly you are great, infinite, my Jesus. You try me in the crucible.[148] You see me staggering. Have mercy on me. Give me the depths of your mercy. Teach me to contemplate it for hours. I love you, Jesus, Jesus, my Jesus. I love you. Come tomorrow when I awake. Come, Jesus.

(January 10, 1979)

153. All day I'm sad, sad, sad, my head down, sad, with nothing to look forward to, no energy, nor strength, in the nothingness. Absolute indifference about everything and in everything. What could I desire? Only your presence, Lord, that You Are. Tell my heart, "I am," "I am,"[149] and you will give me life. Sweet Jesus, always my love, the accuser persecutes me, as do doubts, sadness, death. You are, Lord. How is this world possible for you, with all its people, each one of us? It all seems impossible to me. You are, Lord. You, Yahweh. Speak to me, let your voice resound in my ears. When I awake, Jesus, come, come, come.

(January 11, 1980)

---

[147] Cf. Jn 21:17.
[148] Cf. Ps 17:3.
[149] Cf. Ex 3:14; Mt 14:27.

154. Waking up hurts, life, the bed. A deep wail calls to you, searches for you. The accuser persecutes me, killing in me all hope, every future, and embittering the past. Jesus, Jesus, Jesus, consoler, defender, forgiver, generous, I want you, I search for you, I love you. Pull me out of this darkness. Come, Jesus. Come, Holy Spirit.

It is night now. After the Eucharist, serenity. My Jesus, how much I'm learning from loneliness, suffering, terrible ghosts. Truth is the Other, Love. Jesus, Lord, come illuminate my waking. You, You are the Other and You love me. Thank you, Lord. Who can accuse me?[150]

(January 12, 1980)

155. An anguished awakening: the itinerants, the teams, the women's collaboration… everything is impossible to maintain. My Jesus, if you are here, show yourself. Come, my Jesus, send your Holy Spirit, soothe me.

(January 13, 1980)

156. Itinerants convivence. Italy. Ergife Hotel – Rome. New, big.

I keep passing from suffering to a deeper contemplative serenity, deeper…

I don't know. Yes, you have freed me Lord from all the Neocatechumenal mess, from "electronically" governing the teams and the evangelization. You, Lord, are unpredictable, irresistible, terrifying and immeasurable. Thank you, Lord, that you allow me to be serving you. You are. Blessed are you.

(January 14, 1980)

157. Convivence Ergife Hotel – As if freed, I'm silent and serene, here. I see your action, your power, your mystery, and I admire you. Lord, you are great, infinite, grand, eternal. Yes, You, the Eternal. I love you. Thank you, Jesus. The uncontrollable evangelization, its inspiration, your action. Blessed are you.

(Rome, January 15, 1980)

158. Moving to the Midas Hotel – Everything is simplified. You make me see a people in which You echo so that your Word resounds

---

[150] Cf. Rom 8:33.

in the Universe. And it's your action that does it, makes it a reality, that acts. And everything is possible, especially what is not. This way you confound what is.[151]

And the libraries, the intelligence, the power, the institution... Our intelligence can preach the law... as well as permissiveness. Only your presence announces the Gospel, Being, Life, Love. And only You can make of us a sounding board of your Word.

(Rome, January 16, 1980)

159. Trip to Madrid – My heart hurts again when I awake, when I travel, when I arrive in Spain, at Elisa's house, and I suffer. Lord, I cry out to You incessantly from the pit of suffering. Listen to me, hear me, have mercy on me.

(January 17, 1980)

160. Sleepless night in Narváez.

Spain-Portugal itinerants convivence. House of the Sacred Hearts, El Escorial.

Serene, happy, free, suddenly free, in Peace. Jesus, Peace is possible because You exist. How incredible, Lord. Thank you, my dear, don't leave me, don't constrain me, have mercy on me. Terrible pain, unspeakable, when You are as if you were not. Terrible, Jesus, your absence. When you don't appear I am nothing but a scream in the night and the pain consumes me. Breathing is sweet in the presence of your wonderful being. To let go... Thank you, thank you, Jesus. Do not disappear. My Jesus, don't leave me.

(January 18, 1980)

161. We finished the day at Elisa's house. So many sufferings, Jesus. Eucharist. Return to peace.

(January 19, 1980)

162. Jesus, not-being haunts me and throws me into the nothingness, with no purpose, with no interest in anything. Jesus, if You would come... Yes, You exist, my Jesus.

(January 20, 1980)

---

[151] Cf. 1 Cor 1:27-28.

Carmen with Pope St. John Paul II

163. Jesus, catechists meeting at the Wellington Hotel (Madrid) and I am sad, sad, all day, in a sadness that submerges me in the nothingness, in absolute helplessness, in not-being. What do you want Lord? I can't be here "indifferent to everything" while your Name is being announced... Throw me out, Lord. Where? To do what, Lord? I'm not interested in anything. Moving... cleaning...

Lord. I smoke "like an addict" in this absence, growing old in the nothingness. Have mercy on me.

Jesus, thank you for all the days you visited me with joy. Come, Lord.

Paris tomorrow. I don't care about anything.

(January 21, 1980)

164. Cardinal Marty[152] – My Jesus, what could pull my heart out of this sadness? Only your name, Lord, only You. Your absence kills me, in the nothingness, in the sadness. Jesus, what is wrong with me? Am I sick? What is this not living not to live? My Jesus give me the will to live, to be. Everything seems like nothing of nothing for nothing to me. Jesus, life of life, victor, come, come, come.

Community of St. Honoré.[153] Pain.

(Paris, January 22, 1980)

165. Sadness, uselessness. I know nothing of nothing in nothing. With nothing to look forward to, with no word, and not enthusiastic about anything. My Jesus, where am I going? Who am I? To disappear... where? How?

The first community. The announcement. Kiko...

Lord, I go from the nothingness to the everything of your possibility, of your Being. You exist, Lord, come.

(Paris, January 23, 1980)

166. Morning meeting with the priests of *S. Honoré*. What sleepiness, what pain... Jesus, mission accomplished.

Absolute indifference felt in absolutely everything. Paris, boutiques, oysters, everything leaves me absolutely indifferent. The

---

[152] Cardinal Gabriel Auguste Francois Marty (†), Archbishop of Paris, 1968-1981.

[153] Parish of *Saint Honoré d'Eylau*, Paris.

movies... everything speaks of death to me. I look at the people, old age as the mysterious mystery. My Jesus, my companion, my Love of my youth, come, speak to me, love me, inspire me. Prepare my meeting with the Lord. My God, mysterious, holy, incredible: where are you?

(Paris, January 24, 1980)

167. Paris – Madrid - Valle – Time passes, dying painfully in the nothingness. What is wrong with me? This not-being that eats me up. I have death inside me. I'm already dead. What's killing me? Not having a word of inspiration to announce You? Or is it my fault? What can I do, Lord? Your will is that I accompany your Word. Ghosts surround me, filling me with accusations and sadness that gnaw at my soul. You say, "Do not abandon yourself to sorrow, do not torment yourself with brooding. Chase sorrow far away from you..."[154] How Lord? Free me, free me, Jesus.

Crowded night in the Valle. Jesus, serenity. Thank you, Lord. Freedom, indifference, peace. My sweet Jesus, grant me words of Love, of Light to reveal your Name. Help me, inspire me or let me be present in the silence. Let it be your work.

(Valle – Madrid, January 25, 1980)

168. Lauds. First time I almost fall asleep while Kiko speaks announcing the *kerygma*. Full room. Heat. I want to run away from all this, Lord. Where to?

Eucharist. Assembly. From indifference to peace, to the encounter with the assembly, with the mission. Lord, I feel the desire to receive you daily, to return to my youth. Give me the desire to work, Lord, to be. I love you. My Jesus, help me. Stay with me, come.

(Valle – Madrid, January 26, 1980)

169. End of the *Traditio*.[155] Crowded Valle: two communities from Barcelona,[156] one from Zamora,[157] one from Seville,[158] one from

---

[154] Cf. Sir 30:21.23.

[155] *Traditio Symboli*, a step of the Neocatechumenal Way.

[156] Today they are the first community from the parish of *Santas Juliana y Sempronia*, San Adrián de Besós.

[157] First community from the parish of *San Frontis*.

[158] First community from the parish of *Sagrada Familia*.

Baracaldo,[159] four from Madrid (first *Sta. Catalina*, first and second *S. Sebastián*, third *San José*), etc.

I come to Narváez happy. Tomorrow is free. Help me to work, to live, to be, my Jesus. Tell me, "I am."[160] Tell me that you are, that you were, that you will be. Jesus, life of my past, of today, of tomorrow. Come.

(Valle – Madrid, January 27, 1980)

170. It's already six in the morning and I can't sleep. From sadness to insomnia. Because of ideas? Because of joy. My intuitions bouncing around. Jesus, you have surprised me with satiety. This is what you do to me for my being stingy. Lord, teach me to live. I begin to see everything through the prism of your action, of your fantastic action, and I see you great, unique, baffling and wonderful. The gospel on the lips of a people without culture, without intellectual misrepresentations. Your presence keeps me awake. You are here and the joy confounds me. My Jesus, help me sleep…

Jesus, the CEI,[161] Cardinals and Bishops, Pope, it looks like everything is coming together. Lord, my eyes are fixed only on You. Help me.

(January 28, 1980)

171. Return from the second of *San Sebastián*. Money, the CEI, Lord, I don't care about anything. And my neuroses about not speaking surface as absolute powerlessness. Muteness, muteness, stupid ignorance. My Jesus, Knowledgeable, present. Are You here? Who are you? More than your throne, more than your face, more, more. You, my God. I want to see you, to be with you. Your Love. Help me. Pull me out of sadness, disenchantment, indifference. Jesus, your love of old, You.

(January 29, 1980)

172. My Jesus, these depressing awakenings, full of anguish… The sorrows of evangelizing in helpless silence. In one minute to voice an

---

[159] First community from the parish of *Nuestra Señora del Carmen*.
[160] Cf. Ex 3:14; Mt 14:27.
[161] The Italian Bishops' Conference.

"idea" that then becomes Kiko's word, and then is impossible to repeat. My Jesus, I can only escape in the contemplation of your being. You.

And the only contribution I can make is the smoke from my smoking... have mercy on me.

Return from *Sta. Catalina.* Two-thirty in the morning. Lord, how great you are in your works. Awesome, Lord: and I? Mute, mute inside. Jesus, have mercy on me. Worried... about what? Everything seems like the nothingness, not being, not living, and all of a sudden everything can change. How mysterious man is. Jesus, You know him. You are. Say to me, "I am."[162] Welcome me, have mercy on me.

(January 30, 1980)

173. Return from the third of *S. Sebastián.* It is already three o'clock in the morning. Breath of freedom, of your possibility, of the beauty of the desert, and I see a chasm of mystery within the life of man, the *kenosis*,[163] the suffering, the loneliness, the nothingness. My Jesus, liberator from sin, from death, blessed are you. What am I, Lord? Why do I remain mute, incapable of publicly calling myself a sinner? Mute, Lord. In the suffering you teach me to see each one. Jesus, don't leave me in this loneliness, in the nothingness. Come.

(January 31, 1980)

174. From Madrid to Barcelona – After spending the day suffering in sadness, inexplicably, you visit me with serenity, peace, my Jesus. To see life full of life... It's incredible. Everything changes. The past is enlightened. You open the future and living is living. You are Life.[164] Awaken me in You, my Jesus.

(February 3, 1980)

175. Second community. Wake up feeling sick and sad, sad, and alone, and they point it out to me. Wanting to escape, I don't even know to where or to do what.

(Barcelona, February 4, 1980)

---

[162] Cf. Ex 3:14; Mt 14:27.
[163] Cf. Phil 2:6-8.
[164] Cf. Jn 14:6.

176. Rite with Jubany. Good, good, and I'm left unfulfilled, lost, far away... nothing interests me interiorly. Deep down, I see this people and la Tragura:[165] your Word, la Princesa,[166] Santa María del Mar, leaving with the promise, Museo Marès,[167] Modrego,[168] and your great faithfulness.

I worshiped here with a people. Lord, I can't even put it into words because it's incredible. You know it all and I love you.

(Barcelona, February 5, 1980)

177. Farnés. Airport. Madrid. Rite at *S. Sebastián*. Return to Narváez.

I'm more satisfied today. My feelings, the satisfaction, and the loneliness, are inexplicable. I love you, Lord, give me courage, light, life. Your presence opens my future, the valley, my mouth. I love you, Lord. Have mercy on me. I love you. Help me wake up courageous, abandoned, have mercy on me.

(Madrid, February 6, 1980)

178. Narváez. I sleep all morning. Two in the afternoon and I can't get going.

Night. Already 3 a.m. Finished the *Traditio* in Madrid, finally, and in the Valle tomorrow, *Redditio*. My Jesus, life passes, the day passes in a moment, and it seems like I'm doing nothing but smoking cigarettes. I reach for them in anguish. At night, calm serenity. Jesus, if I saw your face when I woke up, if you would infuse energy, freedom, strength into me, Lord, I would live. And I'm dying, bleeding out life profusely. Jesus, Lord, raise me up.

(Madrid, February 7, 1980)

---

[165] On August 28, 1962, when Carmen left the *Misioneras de Cristo Jesús*, she lived in Barcelona for a time with some companions. They stayed with the poor in the projects of Casa Antúnez ("Eduardo Aunós" projects) located in calle Tragura, number 21.

[166] Calle de la Princesa, the street on which one of the houses of the *Misioneras de Cristo Jesús* was located.

[167] Museo Frederic Marès located near the cathedral of Barcelona, where Carmen found consolation contemplating the Romanic crucifixes.

[168] Mons. Gregorio Modrego Casaus (†), Archbishop of Barcelona, 1964-1972.

179. *Redditio* – My Jesus, in the Valle in tears. I can't go on. Uncovered, ridiculous and afterward, so much suffering. Lord, speak to me. Is it my fault? Is this your will for me? Is it an invasion from Kiko? Lord, I can't take any more, have mercy on me: I languish, dying of ridicule, in the nothingness. Jesus, I don't know what to say, I don't know how to speak. Mute and ridiculous. And I cannot endure the chair. I want to escape and I am dying. What can I do? I always wait for a miracle from you, like at Pentecost, and you don't appear. Lord, I no longer care about anything except to see you, to see you, to see you, to see you. Come Jesus, open my heart, unbind it. I love you. Thank you, Jesus, you give me peace amid ridicule.

(Valle – Madrid, February 8, 1980)

180. Profound *kerygma*, with power, and I almost fell asleep. Jesus, son of David, have mercy on me, don't leave me in death.

Jesus, serenity in the afternoon. You allowed me to speak calmly in the Eucharist. Thank you, Lord. Peace. It's possible to see everything in another way and live. My Jesus, don't leave me, because it's already Sunday. Help me tomorrow when I awake. Come, Lord, liberator. Free! Thank you, Jesus.

(Valle – Madrid, February 9, 1980)

181. Until 10 p.m. I am completely exhausted from listening and listening to so many people. Jesus, you are here, and everything is a miracle.

The Pope at Spinaceto.[169] Everything went so well, and my heart won't budge an inch. Jesus, only your presence says anything to me. Come.

(Valle – Madrid, February 10, 1980)

182. The Lake of Entrepeñas[170] – wrested from my bed by the blinding sun. And I can't see either; I'm still sleeping. This life of man

---

[169] Parish of *S. Giovanni Evangelista* in Spinaceto, Rome, where the Pope had one of his first meetings with the Neocatechumenal communities.

[170] Summer home of José Luis and Polis Bellido who began the Way in the first community of the Parish of *San Matías*, Hortaleza, Madrid, and who today walk in the first community of the parish of *Nuestra Señora del*

seems useless to me. How can man have such zest for life? Everything seems like enormously unbelievable nonsense. How can this be? With this inner eye through which I see life, alone and indifferent, to me everything seems like nothingness. I marvel at their enthusiasm for fishing. I'm sitting and waiting only to see you, to see You, my Jesus. Come.

Night. In bed. Jesus, it's sweet to breathe in your faithfulness at night. Jesus, allow me to sing your love in the morning. Your loving comforts me amid this disillusionment that oppresses, causing me sadness and inertia all day long. At night freedom, freedom. I see all things again, my life is upside down: during the day I'm in the night and at night there is light. How mysterious!

(Lago de Entrepeñas – Alocén, February 11, 1980)

183. Entrepeñas. I see skydivers, the world's doings, and it seems pointless. In this moment of nothing, of not being, that kills me at my core. What is it for? My Jesus, I sit, paralyzed in life contemplating existence, surprised at the world's lust for life all the while surrounded by death like Sheol.

S. Roque[171] – I leave *S. Roque* happy, seeing the possibility to announce the gospel to the poor. "The poor are evangelized."[172]

Redditio in the parish. Inspiration? We shall see. My Jesus, at night I see things in the light. Awaken me in your love. Have mercy on me, help me.

(Madrid, February 12, 1980)

184. Narváez – This waking up, fighting in the tomb of fear, pain, darkness, and the nothingness is terrible. My Jesus, I cry to You in this painful loneliness, and you don't hear me. Give me life: I'm drowning in dread, nausea, headache. Am I sick? You are trying me. My Jesus, you make me see man in the mystery of human *kenosis*,[173] in pain and fear. Have mercy on me. Raise me from this grave that is imprisoning me, killing me, eating me.

Tránsito, Madrid. The home is located in Alocén (Guadalajara) near the Entrepeñas reservoir.

[171] Parish of *San Roque*, Carabanchel, Madrid.
[172] Lk 7:22.
[173] Phil 2:6-8.

Night. Center. Three old communities and *La Paloma*.[174] Pastoral of mediation.[175]

Terrified, Lord, of so much, so much, so much…

I feel I'm someone who does absolutely nothing, an uninterested bystander. I left sad and fatigued. Nothing fits into plans and calculations. Lord, You are here. Good night. Oh, tomorrow! I offer you the sufferings of waking up. Do not leave me, have mercy on me.

(Madrid, February 13, 1980)

185. First and second of *S. José*.

Night. Already 3 a.m. My Jesus, I came back neither hot nor cold, feeling wholly indifferent. I admire the courage you give Kiko. If what happens to me were to happen to him, it would be catastrophic. I feel apathetic, I take a pass on everything; just stupidly smoking and smoking like an addict. Oh Lord, if you came, if you broke open the heavens and appeared, everything would change into life, into light, into day.

Travel tomorrow. Help me. Cheer me up.

(Madrid, February 14, 1980)

186. Madrid. Plane. Rome – It's cloudy and sad. Maura's house.[176]

Convivence (second *S. Luigi* and fourth *Martiri*), and you light up my life. With your light, My Jesus, surprisingly, everything changes, joy, happiness, peace, freedom. Life, Light, Eternal Life. Thank you, Lord. The Word, Life… There is no darkness in You.[177] You are light without any darkness, and I love you. My Jesus, you know the reason for all things. I don't understand myself. If You would give me life tomorrow when I awake… come, come, come.

(Rome, February 15, 1980)

---

[174] Community of the Neocatechumenal Center, first community of San José, first community of San Sebastián, first of La Paloma.

[175] After the *Redditio*, members of the community participate in the different pastoral services of the parish as integral part of their Christian formation and according to each one's vocation.

[176] Maura Aita (†), from the first community of the parish of *Santa Francesca Cabrini*, Rome.

[177] Cf. 1 Jn 1:5.

187. Hotel. *Redditio* Convivence with second *S. Luigi* and fourth *Martiri*.

I am happy, Lord. Why, my Jesus? Because of You, liberator, holy one, wonderful, light, life, resurrection of the dead, just and crucified one. I love you, Jesus, because of your great love, wonderful, destiny of man, of life. Bread, wine, freedom. I love you. Come, help me walk.

(Rome, February 16, 1980)

188. End of convivence.

My Jesus, we're alone. Help me to live with you. Help me, let me look forward to walking with you in freedom.

(Rome, February 17, 1980)

189. Center. Second *S. Luigi*.

Sadness has been my inseparable companion all day. Sad, indifferent. Lord, don't you feel pity for me? I consider life lost and I grab hold of your mercy because I know neither how to live nor how to be. What am I worried about? Truly nothing. I'm absolutely indifferent to everything. Am I sick? Lord, set me in motion, have mercy on me.

(Rome, February 18, 1980)

190. *San Salvatore*. North sector. Catechists meeting.

Kerygma – flesh – justice. My Jesus, you are great: catechists, a whole people evangelizing. I see a future yet my deep sadness doesn't budge. The only thing that fills me is your personal presence and your face, your love. Your work is yours. You are Eternal, almighty. You could do it all much more easily and resoundingly. You don't need us. I do, Lord, I need You, You, You, You, your love, your life, your joy, your eternity, You, Your being, your presence. My Jesus, the days you make me go through, wandering in darkness and helplessness.

Consolation from the Fathers in the Our Father, Tertullian, Cyprian, Origen, Cyril.

Jesus, my Jesus, the bread, the desert, the Scriptures... Sweet consolation of Scripture[178] amidst the darkness of doubt. Raise me up!

(Rome, February 19, 1980)

191. Ashes. Wasted day. Loneliness, interior pain, waiting... and nothing. My Jesus, if tomorrow your Sun were to shine on my life and I were to rise again from the mound of this grave, from this bed... my Jesus, to live, to live waking up to joy, to prayer, to work. Everything is possible for You,[179] save me. Jesus, awaken me in faith. I love you. I trust in You, liberator from sin and death. Show yourself.

(Rome, February 20, 1980)

192. Maura's house – Prayer. My Jesus, this interior point, restless, dark and painful... My Jesus, liberator, break this chain of worry and terror, set me on my feet, give me life, make me walk, attracted to You. Come, my Jesus, tenderness, compassion.

Fourth of *Martiri*. Better than I expected. So much worry... My Jesus, why do I complicate my existence with so many worries and with mountains of endless mysteries? You are. You make my life easier and I complicate it, my Jesus. How easy it is to see how easy everything is... and tomorrow, why should I see it as all dark, sad, counting on it to be terrible? Jesus, you who makes everything clear, you, who are good. I love you.

(Rome, February 21, 1980)

193. Ergife Hotel. Our Father.[180] First *Florence*, first, second and third *Martiri*, first *S. Luigi*, first *Natività*, first *Sta. Francesca*. *Abba*, my Father![181] Finally, this mumbling groans from the depth of my nothingness, trying to recognize you, seek you, feel you. My Sweet Jesus, who descends to the depth of suffering, of not being, and makes this cry emerge that clamors for the Homeland, destiny, the origin, identity, being. Holy Father, I love you. Through Jesus Christ,

---

[178] Cf. Rom 15:4.
[179] Cf. Mt 19:26.
[180] A step of the Neocatechumenal Way (2nd Initiation to Prayer).
[181] Cf. Mk 14:32; Rom 8:15.

our Lord, you fill each word with dense, infinite, eternal meaning. You, the Father of light, of the ingrafting,[182] of love, graft us on, enter into each one of us. In You is the destiny of the nations, of man. My Jesus, I love you.

(Rome, February 22, 1980)

194. Ergife Convivence – my Jesus, this interior temptation, painful, accusing, terrible... lead me not into temptation. When dusk becomes night, I can't believe I'm like this, bedridden, sad about everything and nothing. I flee from encountering others. I close myself in the gloom of this nothingness. My Jesus, what absurd sadness. I think everything's like this. That would be terrible. And I feel compassion for people who are suffering, and I laugh at the vain joys that last as long as a flash of lightning. Lord, only your mercy can speak words of eternity, gratuitously.

(Rome, February 23, 1980)

195. Ergife. End of the convivence.
This idleness is an unbearable horror. First time that I don't see you. I leave sad. Kiko admires me, but I find him unbearable... I admire this people's faith. My Jesus, tomorrow at six, cheer me up, wake me up, I also want to receive communion.

(Rome, February 24, 1980)

196. Lauds at six in the morning.[183] Happy. Everything is a mystery. Kiko like a saint. I slept two hours and now I'm happy. I want to wake up early tomorrow, too. Today's early rising has taken away my sadness. It's already midnight. I am happy. I remember the happy years of the novitiate, of the consolations, of the struggles, of your presence. Help me when I wake.

(Rome, February 25, 1980)

---

[182] Cf. Rom 11:17-23.

[183] After the step of the Our Father, during Lent and Advent and before going to work, the Neocatechumenal communities celebrate the Office of Readings and Lauds in the parish as a community with a time of contemplative prayer.

197. Lauds at six. Everything seems impossible to me and this stress in the people overwhelms me. Why? They're happy and it seems crazy to me.

My Jesus, I worry all day long with plans, impossible foresight and preparations, trying to control everything, thinking everything depends on me. Kiko creatively improvises as if nothing were necessary and everything was possible.

My Jesus, mysterious, magnificent on the Cross, I love you. Amid the darkness and sorrow, You are my only love. In the midst of my incredulity, I only have faith in You and I love you. Have mercy on me. Come visit me because I am afraid, terrified, so sad, detached from everything, wanting to hide and disappear, speechless, speechless, absolutely speechless and very sad.

Great are your works, Lord of the heavens. So many flocks of birds… You are great and wonderful, unpredictable, infinite. Lord, I prostrate myself before You. Love me. Draw this *Abba*[184] from my lips, great One, holy One.

(Rome, February 26, 1980)

198. My Jesus, merciful, good, I am adrift in the nothingness. To go, to come, to stay, and what is it all for? Nothing from nothing is nothing, if You don't make yourself present.

My Jesus, sustain Kiko. The last thing I need is to infect him with my sadness, with the nothingness and everything mysteriously falls to pieces… How horrible if your holy presence doesn't resound, Lord, my Jesus. Let's not return to the tragic, the mysterious, the terrible. "*Abba*", "*Abba*,"[185] my Father, Father, allow me to call to you, to wait for you, to see you. Come, Lord, to accompany you was enough for me and then you leave. No, my Jesus, come, come, come.

(Madrid, February 27, 1980)

199. First *Redditio* in *La Paloma*. Finally the deaf-mute.[186] You open my lips.[187] Thank you Jesus. You have freed me after the hellish pains

---

[184] Cf. Mk 14:32; Rom 8:15.
[185] Cf. ibid.
[186] Cf. Mk 9:14-29.
[187] Cf. Ps 51:15.

of this night, after the demonic attacks, accusers, deniers, destroyers and murderers. What terror, Lord, to eliminate your history of actions, of miracles, of life. Thank you, Jesus, for opening my perspectives and the end of the way of prayer. What an incredible birth. Now you give me peace, serenity, life and I no longer feel like writing, I only want to sing to you, to bless you, to love you, my Jesus. At your side, with you, You lead me to holiness. Thank you, thank you, my Jesus.

(Madrid, February 28, 1980)

200. First *Redditio* in *S. Sebastián* – Day full of prospects, sun, home, a little prayer and sleep. I couldn't sleep last night because of the excitement. My Jesus, I see the future more clearly, but I recoil from speaking, thinking that I might undo yesterday. The accuser pushes me, throws me into the abyss.

Jesus, liberator, free. Serenity. Consoler, in You I trust, come. The *Redditio* moves, the confession of faith. The mystery of man. My Jesus, I love you.

(Madrid, February 29, 1980)

201. Mass in Aravaca.

Center. Eucharist. Stars, Abraham and the Transfiguration.[188] Lord, so faithful, so clear… How can I be so blind? Your faithfulness is so clear, so evident, and the night blinds me. Lord, that day in Javier,[189] at dawn, you showed me the stars. Today, the descendants, the flocks of birds. So many times I've witnessed the glory of your wonderful transfiguration. And this bleak night makes life look foggy, sad, mysterious to man. You, Lord… I don't understand anything and I am afraid. I trust in You, Lord, help me.

(Madrid, March 1, 1980)

202. *Redditio* during Mass. From *S. Sebastián*, the second. From *La Paloma*, the first. I am terrified. Alocén. Prayer at nightfall, but the cloud of gloom overtakes me even though your Transfiguration

---

[188] Cf. Gn 15; Mk 1:8.

[189] Villa located in the Province of Navarra that is the mother house of the *Misioneras de Cristo Jesús*.

always accompanies me to the depths. Return to Madrid. Narváez. Alone. Coming back with Bellido[190] helped me. I love you, Lord. Tomorrow?

(Madrid, March 2, 1980)

203. Monday free. Red Sea. I see it with a true language: these deadly waters, enemies, my following you, my Jesus, an experience, this true story. I trust in You, Lord, even though you see me sad. Is this my home? I see everything demolished, walking toward death. I ask myself – to live, what for? Why live? I'm full of sadness, loneliness, misery. Nothing tells me nothing in the nothingness.

My Jesus, Kiko is back from Alocén; I make him miserable with my sadness.

In bed. A little better. Tomorrow Tarancón, and I don't care at all about that either.

(Madrid, March 3, 1980)

204. Tarancón, *calle Bailen*[191] and Cueto.[192] Far from everything. All seems soulless, far. Day of suffering, as always. I stroll while preparing the Palm Sunday procession: from the seminary to La Paloma. I am distant, with no spirit for anything.

Afternoon. Center. Catechists meeting. You bring life to life with your unexpected and inexpressible presence. My Jesus, You exist, and the world and life move, and everything changes. Sun, light, life, joy, future, present and past, full of your love, of your presence, of freedom. Thank you, Jesus, for your presence. Do not leave me. Traveling tomorrow.

(Madrid, March 4, 1980)

205. Madrid – Barcelona – Rome – First of *Martiri*. I desire to return to renunciation, to sacrifice, to youth. To move, to accept the battle, the fight, your constant presence, detachment, love, my Jesus. To get up, to get up, to get up. Let me sleep tonight. Tomorrow with

---

[190] José Luis Bellido.
[191] Location of the Madrid chancery.
[192] Mons. Antonio García del Cueto (†), Vicar General.

you at six-thirty. Infuse me with energy, to return to youth, to mortification, to the secret of your company. Jesus, if You came, what joy. Pull me out of the grave.

(Rome, March 5, 1980)

206. Lauds at *Martiri*.

Afternoon. My Jesus, how mysteriously you have created man. Problems, bishops, darkness. Are you here? Where are we going? My Jesus, my only destiny, fortune, being. Why and for what? Shine your face upon us.[193] Are You in the midst of everything? If not, I die. What? Why? Don't stay silent. Help me.

(Rome, March 6, 1980)

207. Lauds at a quarter past seven. I arrive late.

Meeting with Brandolini.[194] My Jesus, you allow me to speak of Easter.

Having to wake up early gets me on my feet, not smoking is fabulous. Help me, my Jesus, Holy one, faithful, Lord.

Afternoon. First of *S. Luigi*, first *Natività*. Jesus. My Jesus? You are the liberator. Help me. When I'm better, I no longer know what to write. Help me prostrate myself alone in prayer. I love you.

(Rome, March 7, 1980)

208. Lauds at a quarter past seven at *Martiri*. Meeting with "lost sheep"...[195] They almost anti-catechize me... my Jesus, my soul stings, my life, the day. What to do? Kiko gets in my way here, but at the same time, what else?

Eucharist. The Word... my Jesus, finally with your Word, you open a future to this Way that worries me, my Jesus.

(Rome, March 8, 1980)

---

[193] Cf. Ps 4:6.

[194] Mons. Luca Brandolini, CM, at the time Vicar for Liturgy of the Diocese of Rome. Later, he was auxiliary bishop of Rome, 1987-1993.

[195] Members of the Way that need special attention because of a crisis or grave difficulty.

209. My Jesus, the accusations are distressing me to the point of nausea. What a turbulent awakening! Everything is rattled and terrifying. My Jesus, you are here, come, help me against this accuser[196] who's killing me. Free me, help me. Get away from me, Satan.[197] Discovery: the strength of your Word. Terrifying awakenings. Serene nights, abandoned. Thank you, Jesus.

(Rome, March 9, 1980)

210. Lauds at *Martiri*.

Afternoon, *Sta. Francesca*, prayer. My Jesus, it seems you're presenting a marvelous future. Renew in them the love of youth. I love you.

Letter to the Pope on Easter.

Lord, I feel relieved this night. Day of battle. Help me tomorrow, enlighten my struggle. My Jesus, your sweet presence… how I miss it. Living just for You and with You, what memories of love. My Jesus, I love you.

(Rome, March 10, 1980)

211. Lauds at *Martiri*.

Vatican. Fr. Maximino. Presbyter of *S. Tito*.[198] I return happy having seen the community, each one. Lord, they seemed resurrected since Arcinazzo.

(Rome, March 11, 1980)

212. I didn't get up. My heart is consumed, scarred by *S. Tito* and Riva,[199] and the black, painful misunderstanding. Now that I write it down with a clear head, all this suffering for nothing seems hopeless. It seems like darkness, night, fog in broad daylight, and now I feel free. My Jesus, is it feelings, temptations, is it sickness? What is this,

---

[196] Rv 12:20.

[197] Mt 4:10.

[198] Fr. Domenico Piusco, CSI (†), pastor of *San Tito*, which later became *San Leonardo Murialdo*, Rome.

[199] Mons. Clemente Riva, IC (†), Auxiliary Bishop of Rome, 1975-1998. He was responsible for the Southern Sector of the diocese where the parish of *San Tito* was located.

Lord, this dying? You, You are here, your sweet company. Teach me how to search for you when I awake.

(Rome, March 12, 1980)

213. Suffering because I did not get up for morning prayer in the parish. Regret. Terrible night.

Finally out of the grave.

Night. Meeting with "the 18" and pastors. I'm consoled that Easter is so close. You open my lips to Easter. Tomorrow Poletti.[200] Defend Easter. Thank you, Jesus. And the Pope?

(Rome, March 13, 1980)

214. Chancery.[201] Poletti. Luca Brandolini. How mysterious, Lord, and what weariness.

Third of *Martiri*. Prayer. Jesus, your former graces come like an echo to become reality in a people. Possible? For You everything is possible.[202]

(Rome, March 14, 1980)

215. St. Peter's. *Angelus*. The cantors of the communities are present.

Thank you, Lord, for the Pope, "a gradual and intense itinerary of evangelization, catechesis, and participation in liturgical life, that in a way reminds us of the ancient catechumenate. 'Go and teach all the nations, baptizing them in the name of the Father, of the Son and of the Holy Spirit' (Mt 28:19)."[203]

(Rome, March 16, 1980)

216. With *S. Tito*. Tired. From what? Sleep. My Jesus, what futile powerlessness. We don't know anything.

The words of the Pope in the *L'Osservatore Romano* with pictures. Good. It gave me great joy. Terrible humiliation.

---

[200] Cardinal Ugo Poletti (†), Vicar General of the Diocese of Rome, 1973-1991.

[201] Chancery of the Diocese of Rome.

[202] Cf. Mk 10:27.

[203] Words of the Pope.

I'm consoled, Jesus, because you lead the communities to prayer. My Jesus, all day was cloudy and now, at night, the horizon opens for me. Infuse me with energy when I awake. Help me.

(Rome, March 17, 1980)

217. Lauds. A good day. Vespers at *Martiri*.

Prayer. You bring me back to the old times. If only, Lord, you would make me fall in love with you as you did then; I wish I could feel the fire in my heart and your continuous, unique, wonderful company. My Jesus, your presence and the eternity of that holy ascension remain as an eternal memorial amid this destructive, dangerous, terrible darkness that eats away at my soul and my life. Lord, have mercy on me. Raise me up.

(Rome, March 18, 1980)

218. *S. José* – Lauds.

My Jesus, all that longing to have some time, and now that I'm surrounded by it in abundance, absolute emptiness. Why?

Day at night. And You console me in the evening. St. Joseph… Mystery. <u>Sweet Virgin Mary</u> I am consoled by your life, your mystery, everyone's suspicion. Most sweet one, blessed are You. I love you. Thank you for this comforting insight into your nature that consoles me, encourages me, comforts me and makes me love you… Intercede for me.

(Rome, March 19, 1980)

219. To sleep… I hope, "like a bullfighter", the meeting with the pastors and responsibles to speak of Easter… my Jesus, suffering. And later, serenity.

Nothing matters to me at all. You hold the world and the Church in your hands. My Jesus, also this silent, secret battle, for the celebration of the Easter Vigil… You direct life and these sufferings of mine. You know all things. You know I love you.[204] I hope in you, in your action. You are the defender. Let your Consoling Advocate[205]

---

[204] Cf. Jn 21:17.
[205] Cf. Jn 14:16.

resound in the depth of my sufferings. I love you, Lord, help me. I am consoled by the figure of the Virgin.

(Rome, March 20, 1980)

220. Travel to *Firenze* – My heart is stirred. Lord, raise me up, set me walking toward eternal life. You are the only one who awakens in me the desire to live. Make me live, Lord, by raising me up, by acting. Take me out of the idiotic passivity of cigarettes.

My Jesus, is it an illness or is it all from my soul? My Jesus, only the eternal is indispensable. Lord, You are the Eternal One. Pull me in, drag me, come, Lord.

(Florence, March 21, 1980)

221. Meeting with the second, meeting with the third, and Eucharist with all of them. Welcoming of the new community. Dinner. The presbyter was a bit discouraged.[206]

My Jesus… I want to hide with you, far away and alone. I don't feel comfortable with anybody and I want to disappear. Only You are eternal, only You are Love, You alone. The image of Mary accompanies me, stunned in your mystery, alone, hidden, silent. I want to be alone with you and with absolutely no one else. It all seems so long. It's as if I can't stand anything anymore and nothing moves me.

(Florence, March 22, 1980)

222. From *Firenze* to Rome – with Fr. Dino.[207] I return happy from *Firenze*. With Fr. Dino… history, Lord. Who wouldn't recognize you in your works? Formidable crisis. Lord, your manifestation changes my death to life. My sorrow is that you might not exist. The earth covers your paths with sand, with death. With no meaning, Lord. Wake me.

(Rome, March 23, 1980)

---

[206] Fr. Piero Paciscopi (†), pastor of the parish of *San Bartolomeo in Tuto*, Scandicci (Florence).

[207] Fr. Dino Torreggiani (pb) (†), founder of *los Servos de la Iglesia*. In 1968 he met Kiko in Ávila, and later he accompanied Kiko and Carmen to the parishes of Rome and Florence.

223. Thank you, Lord, for the echoes of your consoling encouragement that come to me from deep within you. Sill, since morning, my Jesus, these struggles, this battle is what you're training me for in the night. Prayer, the sweet occasions of your loving, continual company, to be with you… your presence alone fills each moment, each instant, and everything becomes eternal, and life is amazing.

My Jesus, "Light", light of life, I love you.

S. Tito. My Jesus, I seem to get discouraged at night, instead of the day. I believe in You, Lord. I love you. Have mercy on me. Love me. Everything is possible for you.[208] I love you. Help me.

(Rome, March 24, 1980)

224. Annunciation – Sweet Virgin Mary. Prayer at the *Sacramentinos* pulls me out, to the point that I return consoled. Tonight, you remake the past into an immense sea of your powerful, magnificent manifestations. The burning love with which you led my youth… you make me feel like everything is possible in the future: freedom, uprooting, poverty. My Jesus, Most sweet one, I love you. I remember that day on the mountain in Javier where you submersed me in the "let it be done" of your sweet Mother.[209] My Jesus, everything is possible for you.[210] Don't mind me. Continue your works. Take me out of the night. Help me fight. Raise me up!

(Rome, March 25, 1980)

225. You raise me up. Joy of freedom. My Jesus, wonderful, incredible, I love you. Thank you, my Jesus, thank you. Thank you, Holy, Holy One. I love you. Do not let me sink in the night. Keep me standing, my Jesus. "Freedom." Breathing. My Jesus, have mercy on the man who suffers. You, Savior, Risen One, make your momentous manifestation in the night of man. My Jesus, the desert, the dryness, the terror… Sweet Jesus, your manifestation is illuminating. Thank you, Jesus.

---

[208] Cf. Mt 19:26.
[209] Cf. Lk 1:38.
[210] Cf. Mt 19:26.

Day of consolation, of life. My sweet Jesus, thank you. Peace.

At *Natività* in the morning and at night. You are invincible, my Jesus. Get me up tomorrow. Have mercy on me. I'm going to Madrid. Light me up inside.

(Rome, March 26, 1980)

226. Rome – Madrid – Once again struggling not to sink into sadness. Flight. Román[211] from *S. Anselmo.*[212]

My Jesus. Easter announcement in the Eurobuilding. The accusations eat away at my soul. My Jesus, don't abandon me, gladden my life, my existence. Open my mouth. I love you.

Areneros.[213] Prayer. My Jesus, "Easter." You have put life in our hands, your Passover. My Jesus, incredible, great, immense. Your faithfulness when I was 15 years old, the first time I entered these walls. Truly, you have surpassed your promises. How can I be sad? Raise me up.

(Madrid, March 27, 1980)

227. I get up, my heart eaten away. My Jesus, sadness expands like a cloud that wants to cover me, eating away at my soul.

My Jesus, a people. *Redditio* at *S. Sebastián*. The teams worry me. Lord, if you lead all these things, if you are in all of this, what is it that distresses me? You lead the Church, your People, and Kiko. Why so much suffering and anguish? Why the muteness? My Jesus, you gave me a day of freedom, of light, and I keep searching for you who are enveloped in light and life. *Areneros*. Tomorrow, I want to pray too. Move me. Awaken me!

(Madrid, March 28, 1980)

228. Failure. I was unable to preach you, my Jesus, and it's like my heart is wounded. Is this century possible without faith…? Kiko is sick. Tomorrow is the Palms. Agitated, suffering. Badly. Lord…

(Madrid, March 29, 1980)

---

[211] Román Encabo.
[212] Pontifical Atheneum San Anselmo, Rome.
[213] Chapel of the *Colegio de la Inmaculada y San Pedro Claver*, also known as *Colegio de Areneros*, Madrid.

229. Palm Sunday.

From the Seminary to *La Paloma*. Ascent to Jerusalem. My heart feels it in the suffering, the loneliness… My Jesus.

(Madrid, March 30, 1980)

230. Last day here, thank God. I'd like to never return, my Jesus. The family, the neuroses, the TV, Kiko's house, they are all meaningless to me, distant, dead, old, finished. My Jesus, I feel like it's a wasted day. To give… what? Love, my Jesus. To smoke, to smoke, to smoke, smoke into the nothingness, to make smoke.

My Jesus, "prayer"… nostalgia. The one thing necessary.[214] My love, to escape to search for you in solitude. This whole mess is crushing me. Listening to the catechists, my Jesus, and I keep quiet. The sign that you sustain Kiko with a living word, helps me see that this truly is a serious charism. You, Yourself, are the only Lord. My good Jesus, most sweet one, I'm no help at all. I'm like an idiot, smoking amid the nothingness. My Jesus, everyone seems to be in the nothingness, the vacuum, the nothingness. My Jesus.

(Madrid, March 31, 1980)

231. Madrid – Barcelona – Rome.

My Jesus, to escape from Spain. Arrival in Rome. Night. Crypt.[215]

It's already one in the morning. I want to get up tomorrow, my Jesus.

"Hide me in the secret of your presence."[216] To pray, to live, Jesus, to live. You are Life, Resurrection, Love. My sweet Jesus, I love you. Hide me in the secret of your presence. You know the heartaches of my life. You have seen my misery, my affliction, my Jesus. Who am I that You should visit me? But you are Holy, infinite, most sweet. And you are crucified for love of me. I love you, my Jesus. Wake me up. Hide me in the secret of your Presence, Sweet Jesus. This mystery of accompanying your voice… and I'm in the silence of this tomb. Lord,

---

[214] Cf. Lk 10:42.
[215] Of the parish of *Nostra Signora del Santissimo Sacramento e Santi Martiri Canadesi*, Rome.
[216] Cf. Ps 31:20; 27:5-7.

open my heart to your Passover. All the catechists are contributing and I'm mute, my Jesus. Easter is coming.

(Rome, April 1, 1980)

232. Doctor. Looking at the room for the Vigil on Via Aurelia.

All day, since Lauds this morning, from one place to another other and worried. Why? Then Kiko sets sail kerygmatically in meeting after meeting, and I, like an idiot, suffering from the schedule. *S. Salvatore.* Penitential. Presentation of the communities. Welcoming the new ones… my Jesus, some are in crisis… Help them, my Jesus.

(Rome, April 2, 1980)

233. Holy Thursday – *Martiri* – *"In coena Domini"*… my Jesus, to be alone, let us escape, finally, alone. My Jesus, in Viviana's[217] house: participation, community, Love.

My Jesus, living and being hurts me. Where? How? My Jesus, nothing says anything to me. Why?

(Rome, April 3, 1980)

234. Good Friday. *Martiri.* Wake up. Suffering. Ah, my Jesus, at night I cry out and there's no comfort for me.[218] Like a mute man, I open not my mouth.[219] And the grave is my home. Terrible, Jesus, this anguish. And the darkness surrounds me. I do not see, hear, or live. My Jesus, companion in death. Sweet, strong, invincible.

Fighting the attack on the liturgy gives me purpose in this battle. I love you, my Jesus, help me. Are the people at the service of the liturgy, of the solemnity of worship, or is the liturgy for the people, to nourish faith?

Passivity. Years to create communion, love, and we have to hand over the catechumenate as fodder for the clergy. What is important? Is the communion (love) that the sacraments want to foster and realize, solemnity… or participation?

(Rome, April 4, 1980)

---

[217] Viviana Zarattini from the first community of the parish of *Nostra Signora del Santissimo Sacramento e Santi Martiri Canadesi*, Rome.
[218] Cf. Ps 22:2.
[219] Cf. Is 53:7.

235. Dinner at Franco Voltaggio's[220] house: Kiko, Stefano,[221] Romano,[222] Mario, Toto,[223] etc.

My Jesus, it all should make me extremely happy, and I'm like this, only half happy. My Jesus, to be, to live, to be. My Jesus, only You can give me life. The trips, the brothers, the meals, the money, to me, nothing at all speaks to me. Ah, my Jesus, if only You would appear. My Jesus…

(Rome, April 7, 1980)

236. Trip to Rome – Palermo – Monreale. Cathedral: all the catechesis, Lord, and Jacob with the Angel[224] and the *Traditio*…

My Jesus, how powerful the Church is in history. And now? Lord, if you are present, all goes well. But I care for nothing, except to see you, my Jesus. Do not get angry with me. It's all the same to me and I see nothing. Apathy eats up my soul and I don't know how to live. If You come, your voice, Lord, changes everything in everything.

My Jesus, a voyage of adventure and nothing speaks to me anymore, nor does it move me. Forgive me, Lord. Night on the seashore, path of the famous Aeolian Islands.

(April 8, 1980)

237. Milazzo – Ship – Salina Island – Volcano, Lipari, etc. – Too much, too much. My Jesus, what are we doing here? Why here? Lord I'm almost afraid… these dreams… and this resting in Easter, after so much fasting… my Jesus, how? My Jesus, have pity, have mercy on me. Sometimes I believe that the source of this sadness is also this human side. My Jesus, have mercy on me.

(April 9, 1980)

---

[220] Franco Voltaggio (†) from the first community of the parish of *Nostra Signora del Santissimo Sacramento e Santi Martiri Canadesi*.

[221] Stefano Gennarini from the first community of the parish of *San Luigi Gonzaga*, Rome.

[222] Fr. Romano Fucini (†) from the first community of the parish of *Santa Francesca Cabrini*, Rome.

[223] Antonio Piccolo from the first community of the parish of *San Leonardo Murialdo*, Rome.

[224] Cf. Gen 32:25-33.

238. Lipari – My Jesus, I don't fit in anywhere or with anybody. I'm in a lost part of the planet and even here I cannot escape. With the Voltaggio family in their home.[225] The sea is cold, cold like the house of my heart: lonely, sad, distressed, distressed and *"escorbútico."*

My Jesus, my only warm refuge is my coat.

If you were to wrap me up like this, my Jesus, Life, Resurrection, Easter… Where are you? Why life? Who are we? My Jesus, what is everything for? Life has no taste to me, and everything is an apathy of death. I seek Your Face.[226] Come, Lord.

(Rinella – Salina Island, April 10, 1980)

239. And it's night. Deadly ghosts. Terrible night. Soaring ghosts consume me in helplessness, in my blame, in pain. My Jesus, as if I were to blame for everything. I cry out to You at night… with no answer.

To wake up – why? My Jesus, I'm consumed in sadness and nothingness. Jesus, I'm dying waiting for you. Life!

(Rinella, April 11, 1980)

240. *I, John, your brother and partner in <u>hardships</u>… and in perseverance in Jesus. I was on the <u>island</u> of Patmos… It was the Lord's Day and I was in ecstasy, and I heard a loud voice behind me… like a Son of man, dressed in a long robe and tied at the waist with a belt of gold. His head and his hair were white with the whiteness of wool, like snow; his eyes like a burning flame… his voice like <u>the sound of the ocean</u>. When I saw him, I fell at his feet as though dead. He laid his right hand on me and said, 'Do not be afraid. It is I, the First and the Last, I am <u>the Living One</u>; I was dead but now I live forever and ever, and I hold the keys of death and of Hades.'*[227]

I will fight against the ghosts of darkness. I will not dialogue with them, I will not let them rope me in. Away with you, Satan.[228] The

---

[225] The family of Franco (†) and Margherita Voltaggio, of the first community of the parish of *Nostra Signora del Santissimo Sacramento e Santi Martiri Canadesi*.

[226] Cf. Ps 27:8.

[227] Rv 1:9-18.

[228] Cf. Mt 4:10.

risen Lord... Gladden me Lord, fight at my side, invigorate and enliven my bones. Come, Lord. The Pope is in Turin.

(Rinella, April 12-13, 1980)

241. Thank you, Lord, for raising me up from the pit. The ghosts, the night, the sadness, the apprehensions, and the fear disappear. My Jesus. "Peace", freedom, love. Everything is incredibly changed, without anything being outwardly different. Everything is a mystery in my heart, my Jesus, where only You reach. Thank you, Lord, for encouraging me to pray. So much to do... pray, make a plan for tomorrow. Get me up.

Grotto. "You are my God."[229] *"Hide me in the secret of your presence, far from plotting enemies... hide me under the cover of your tent far from their plotting... Be for me a rock of refuge, a mighty fortress that saves me."*[230] "Savior", be my Savior. You have seen my misery, you have known my anguish. My Jesus, you train me for war. Lord, strong, powerful, don't remain distant lest I fall in the night. Fight! Sweet Jesus, invoke your powerful, saving name.

I return to the grotto. Nightfall. The sea moves. "Fight." My Jesus, I fix my eyes on You.[231] My soul is almost leaping now, joyously. If only I could bury the ghosts here. Take me, with my eyes fixed on You, fighting, with neither future nor past, with eyes fixed on the present. You are the present. Your robes are myrrh and aloe,[232] Sweet Jesus, liberator.

(Rinella – Salina Island, April 14, 1980)

242. Rinella – Lipari – Volcano – Milazzo – Catania (Pippo)[233] and Rome.

Jesus, a swim. You keep raising my head to freedom. Thank you, Jesus. The power of your name, the activities, Being, the Light, seeing things with freedom, with Life... Jesus, thank you for the secret of the fight, of prayer. Help me to fight tomorrow, to pray. The first thing on rising, prayer. Help me to live, fighting, with your name on

---

[229] Ps 31:14.

[230] Cf. Ps 31:20; 27:5; 31:3.

[231] Cf. Heb 12:2.

[232] Cf. Ps 45:8.

[233] Giuseppe (Pippo) Pappalardo (pb), pastor emeritus and member of the first community of the parish of *San Leone*, Catania.

my lips, Jesus, Jesus, Jesus, to drive away the ghosts, without yielding an inch. Away with you, Satan. Three-fourths are feelings, fantasies... what else? Jesus.

(Rome, April 15, 1980)

243. Vatican. Surprised by Tomko.[234]

The old times of incredible love like last night. My Jesus, most sweet, good, savior, don't abandon me later. Nothing is worth the effort. You are here for me, in the trial and in the pain, "the Only One." My Jesus, I love you, have mercy on me. All day without praying... Get me in the morning, with you, with my eyes fixed on You and fighting. I'm left with what is at the bottom of the depths, which is sin, like a terrible accuser. I love you, I believe in You, forgiver. Free. Help me fix my eyes on You. I love you.

(Rome, April 16, 1980)

244. At home. At night in the Crypt. How was the Easter vigil?

Lord, Easter is in danger. My Jesus, the crowd, the hardships, Holy Thursday... The terrible pastors, my Jesus. Faces of new responsibles. Everything leaves a bad taste in my mouth, bad, it's all dicey. At least you gave me the courage to speak, but I don't see things clearly. My Jesus, I see the itinerants happy, thank goodness. My Jesus.

(Rome, April 17, 1980)

245. Rome – Madrid – Valle. Three ancient communities.[235] Our Father.

After suffering, after preparing, what happens? Suddenly, you inspire Kiko so perfectly... Lord, you are great and work marvels. I'm so happy, called by this word of St. John, "Children of God."[236] When each letter becomes reality, life... You exist and the universe is magnificent, and your call to man is infinite. Children of God, Lord. That I may be able to shout to you, "*Abba*"! Lord, *Abba!*[237]

(Madrid, April 18, 1980)

---

[234] Cardinal Jozef Tomko (†) Secretary General of the Bishops' Synod, 1979-1985.

[235] First community of the Neocatechumenal Center, first community of *Tránsito* and the first of *La Paloma*.

[236] Cf. Jn 1:12.

[237] Cf. Mk 14:32; Rom 8:15.

246. I go to the mountain. I begin to resign myself to remain in silence. Kiko's charism for speaking is incredible. Lord, I wait for you in , when and how You want. I'm not interested in talking, but in your presence, your Love, freedom. My Jesus.

Eucharist in silence. I did not open my mouth for absolutely anything, Jesus. I'm in complete silence. And we finally finished.

Elisa's house. I'm only motivated by having to get up. It's already twelve-thirty. Tomorrow, Lauds in the Center at six-thirty.[238] Lord, wake me up.

(Madrid, April 19-20, 1980)

247. First day of prayer at six-thirty in the Center.

The telephone rings. Before I could realize what was happening, you woke me up. Miraculously, I spent the whole day without feeling sleepy. Happy, great joy, Jesus, like in the days of my youth. Wonderful, inexpressible, glorious, the sun has risen over life and how different it all looks. It's something else. Life, joy, grace, Love… Light! With no problems, no worries, no… Life, my Jesus. I entrust this night and tomorrow's waking to You. With you, my Jesus.

(Madrid, April 21, 1980)

248. Meeting with priests. On the dais. Difficult beginning. Finally, You appear, Strong. Gospel of the leper. My Jesus, thank you. Farnés has now changed his mind and is ready to go… My Jesus, mysterious, great, wonderful, I love you. Your promise is accomplished over time: Barcelona, Barcelona, Barcelona, Princesa, Sta. María del Mar, Tragura, Cathedral, Marés… My Jesus, miracle of Mattia, of communities in *Traditio*.[239] Blessed are you.

(Barcelona, April 22, 1980)

---

[238] During the last part of the step of the Our Father, the three communities celebrated Lauds in their community rooms first thing in the morning.

[239] Mattia del Prete from the first community of the parish of *Nostra Signora del Santissimo Sacramento e Santi Martiri Canadesi*, Rome. Communities of Sicily where Mattia is catechist (*San Leo* in Catania and *Sacra Famiglia* in Palermo).

249. "Ambushed" the Cardinal with a TV.[240] Lost sheep. Farnés. Pedralbes...[241] My Jesus, return to Madrid. I sleep in Narváez. Tomorrow, Lauds. Wake me up, My Jesus. It is already twelve-thirty a.m.

(Barcelona, April 23, 1980)

250. Prayer at the Center at six. Curia.
I'm half dead and rowing against the current all day long.
Mario goes to Portugal.

(Madrid, April 24, 1980)

251. Prayer at *Canillas* at six. The team from Colombia in the Center. Fr. Jesús. Those from Paris, *Canillas*...
My Jesus, I can do no more. Tomorrow, I'll sleep all day.

(Madrid, April 25, 1980)

252. Lake Alocén – In your house, "nature", all is free and everything lives, everything walks, Lord. I'm fighting. My soul runs away from things. People are drained, the catechumenate, life, and I fight in this tomb of death that is bland, chaotic, meaningless. You are, Lord. You are. Have mercy on me, fill this emptiness with life and meaning, navigating amid nothingness, sorrowful and helpless. My Jesus, resurrected, living, who ascends in your Passover, heal me, send your Consoler to fill my old bones[242] with holiness and spirit that are so devoid of energy and life. Jesus, Jesus, powerful is your name, my lips call to you in my heart. Help me fight these ghosts of the past and future that don't let me live.

Jesus, leave me to the Creator — *Abba*, Father[243] — to your will, that is always present, improvises, "creates." My Jesus, I want to plan things, and do, and I jot down small things that find no time, and I struggle in the impossible, paddling against the current of improvisation.

---

[240] Audience with Cardinal Jubany to which they brought a large television set to show him a video.

[241] Royal Monastery of Santa María de Pedralbes where Farnés was then chaplain.

[242] Cf. Ez 37:1-11.

[243] Cf. Mk 14:32; Rom 8:15.

Rome? Election? How?

Jesus, waiting for your unforeseen manifestation. You have always appeared without plans, and my incredulity makes rational plans, without knowing how. My Jesus, You, only You are. Come, Jesus, accompany this fight, have mercy on me.

Return. Lonely night in Elisa's house, seeking freedom and then I feel alone among ghosts. Jesus, Jesus, Jesus come to my head. Fill my heart with your presence. Yes. You are in all of this. You chose my life, you have walked in all my steps, and now I worry about the future… How foolish, how blind! Put confidence on my lips. That I may say "*Abba*" to God.[244] How difficult! Jesus, come, fill this house, this room, this night, tomorrow. Even the paintings make me nervous. Give me the joy of having nowhere to lay my head.[245] Jesus, Jesus, give me a word.

(Madrid, 27-29, 1980)

253. On the go since six in the morning. M-30.[246] Lost in the morning darkness. Everything is a symbol. The joy of Lauds, of getting up. Then tired, half-dead: worries, Rome… My Jesus, console me.

Afternoon, *Canillas*. Prayer. The One and only essential thing.

It's already two in the morning. Trip tomorrow. The consolation of Love, drowned. The children problem. This generation is escaping, my Jesus.

(Madrid, April 30, 1980)

254. Trip from Madrid to Rome – I feel free, eager to keep my eyes fixed on You, and free. I left Spain worried, feeling that the catechumenate, the Election are burdensome. Suddenly, I feel free from everything. Thank you, Jesus. I love you.

Desiring to not see bishops or priests or the Vatican… but yes to prayer and to getting up and running away and seeking you. I love you, Lord. Help me to fight.

(May 1, 1980)

---

[244] Cf. Mk 14:32; Rom 8:15.
[245] Cf. Mt 8:20.
[246] Ring road around the center of Madrid.

Carmen on the Mount of Olives

255. Arcinazzo again: Election.

We're blank, not knowing where we're going. My Jesus, your promised Spirit… we wait for You.

Thank you, Lord, that I'm serene today. Raise me up. Raise up Kiko. Inspire us.

(Arcinazzo, May 2, 1980)

256. Arcinazzo. Election – Well, Lord. Nunzio[247] and Stirati[248] make the Gospel present in their scrutinies, and that this moves and frees, my Jesus.

Night, Eucharist, dinner, children, and I feel mute and far away.

(Arcinazzo, May 3, 1980)

257. Return from Arcinazzo. Sad, worse off than when I left, but desiring to fight and to look for you, to pray.

(Rome, May 4, 1980)

258. I get up: straight to prayer. Quietude. My Jesus, I look for you because nothing keeps me occupied. You have surrounded me with suffering to hold me back, and I see that prayer is the only thing. Thank you, Jesus. You have put me in the nothingness — I am powerless — to bring me to prayer. You are great, Lord. See how stupid I am. How many years wasted, seeking so many things. My Jesus, wake me up tomorrow. I desire you, I seek you, I love you. Thank you, Jesus. You let me see it's all a game of love and I thank you. I desire only to be still, waiting for you. I love you. Jesus, Most sweet love of my youth, if you were to come… joy.

(Rome, May 5, 1980)

259. First *S. Luigi*. Scrutinies of the Election. Your presence envelops me, touching my heart with the Gospel, prayer. Headache. Heaviness. I am sick.

(Rome, May 6, 1980)

---

[247] Nunzio Chimens (†) from the first community of the parish of *Nostra Signora del Santissimo Sacramento e Santi Martiri Canadesi*, Rome.

[248] Giovanni Stirati from the first community of the parish of *Santa Francesca Cabrini*, Rome.

260. First *Natività*. Election. My Jesus, the huge parish, the crowd, seems to consume it all and it is meaningless. Where? Why? Everything seems useless. I'm mute. I don't open my mouth, my Jesus.

(Rome, May 7, 1980)

261. *Sta. Francesca*. My Jesus, far from everyone and everything. I cannot see, Lord, what everyone else sees as wonderful. I'm blind in the nothingness, Lord. Those from Israel are coming. Everything is so hard, impossible. But this brings me to my feet: to announce the Gospel well, to sustain it, structure it, leave it established. It seems impossible, My Jesus, that initial serenity of not defending anything, of not having anything.

(Rome, May 8, 1980)

262. Second *Martiri* – Morning in darkness, sad, very sad. Waking up with no objective, with no life. My Jesus, it's night and I feel the relief of living. Thank you, Jesus. Help me when I awake. It's already three. Three plus eight = eleven. The alarm set for eleven… My Jesus, help me.

(Rome, May 9, 1980)

263. Erasmo's house.[249] Easter video. Sadness. First *Martiri*. Scrutinies. Eucharist. "Let not your hearts be troubled…"[250] Jerusalem without temples. You encourage me, Lord, with the mystery of your works, Creator, improviser, consoler… I go to bed seeing that things are good and I get up without meaning, wandering in the nothingness. Lord, help me this day. Raise me up, my Jesus. Jesus, all day constrained by the nothingness and sadness. It seems impossible to understand at night, in serenity and normalcy. My Jesus, awaken me in You.

(Rome, May 10-11, 1980)

264. To be, to be, God is. You are. What do I care about anything in the nothingness. *Let nothing trouble you.*[251] Be violent with myself: move, pray, no smoking, <u>Live</u>.

---

[249] Erasmo Lionetti from the first community of the parish of *Nostra Signora del Santissimo Sacramento e Santi Martiri Canadesi*, Rome.
[250] Cf. Jn 14:1.
[251] ST. TERESA OF AVILA, *Poems*.

Firenze. Disastrous morning, black. No outlook for my life at the moment. Serene nights, normal. Life in life. Jesus, what a mystery. I believe in You even when I don't see you. Lead me not into temptation.

(Florence, May, 12, 1980)

265. Museum – Travel to Rome. Freeway. Hot. Scrutiny in *S. Luigi.* Battle.

My Jesus, to sleep. Love me tomorrow. You, Father of the light, pull me out of the night. Help me tomorrow. Infuse energy into me. Help me.

(Rome, May 13, 1980)

266. First *Natività.* Scrutiny of the Election. Agape. Maura is coming. It's two o'clock. I see everything as wrong, sad, far away, impossible and in the nothingness. I can't stand anything. My Jesus, dismal death. It all seems like a fairytale to me. No communion, far away, mute, blind, deaf, and like a block of ice. My Jesus, in the nothingness. What?

(Rome, May 14, 1980)

267. Rain, rain, rain – Jesus, if only your spirit were to descend into this dark night of my soul, that also weeps… my Jesus, I see it all dark, finished. I'm in a dark, sad, horrible death. My Jesus, I desire nothing, I have nothing except terror and the nothingness. Why? Of what? My Jesus, I see nothing except nothingness. Everything seems useless and fake, with no paths. My Jesus, only Holy One, the Only one, where are you?

I return from *Santa Francesca* reinvigorated. My Jesus, the door opens to possibilities and everything seems infinite: your presence in history, ten years, and the infinite future. Eternal Life.

My Jesus, shine your Face on this night that wants to swallow me up. Help me, my Jesus, have mercy. Do not let me suffer life like this, so miserably. I love you, help me.

(Rome, May 15, 1980)

268. Vatican. Second *Martiri*. Scrutinies.

Jesus, it's already two in the morning. In peace. By night I see things serene, peaceful. By day, I see everything depressing, dark and gloomy, in sadness. Why, Lord? Fear of what? That you might not exist? Fear of whom? Jesus, raise me up from being stupid because it embitters my life. I love you. Come, creator Spirit. Inspire me. Open my lips. Have mercy on me. Help me to fight, to live, to move, to be. The Gospel is life. Help me to live it, to <u>love</u>, to see the people. Jesus, to live, to live, to live!

(Rome, May 16, 1980)

269. First *Martiri* all day long. The community is doing well. It continues on its own.

My Jesus, your mystery, mystery. I love you.

Eucharist. Sweet Ascension. Thank you, Jesus, I'm jealous of your secrets, you shut my mouth. Thank you, Jesus. I love you.

(Rome, May 17, 1980)

270. The Ascension. *Sta. Francesca.*

Meeting with "the 18" at Giampiero's[252] house.

My Jesus, I'm sick of meetings. I see it on everyone's faces, they too are tired of meeting, dinners, everything. My Jesus, I see it all decaying, with no interest. I don't know if it's me or if it really is so. My Jesus, have mercy on me.

(Rome, May 18, 1980)

271. Prayer. First *Martiri*, end of scrutiny.

Lord, you have consoled me. A little gift: freedom! Jesus, it seems incredible. Thank you, Lord, you have opened my grave, heaven. Sweet Jesus, Consoler, the best, I don't deserve it. Do not try me at night, because I can deny you. Have mercy on me. I love you, most faithful, don't abandon me.

(Rome, May 19, 1980)

---

[252] Giampiero Donnini from the first community of the parish of *Nostra Signora del Santissimo Sacramento e Santi Martiri Canadesi*, Rome.

272. The people who walked in darkness have seen a great light. Great Light. Those who lived in the land of darkness, a great light has shone upon them. You have increased their joy, you have made their joy <u>great</u>. Joy for <u>your presence</u>, because the yoke that weighed on them, you <u>have smashed</u>.[253]

It is possible that the light may disappear from me in the morning; but in any case, through prayer, you have pulled me out of the grave, the only true satisfaction of the whole day, "prayer with you." My Jesus, don't stay silent. Do not leave me in the nothingness.

Today *S. Luigi*. My Jesus, wise, good, I love you, have mercy on my wickedness.

(Rome, May 20, 1980)

273. *Natività*. A new Pentecost. My Jesus, the itinerants console me. The day was cloudy and gray as usual, and when I awoke my soul was heavy, groaning, miserable, bound-up.

Prayer. You bring me to prayer. Thank you, Lord. Come, come, Holy Spirit. I don't know how to address you, as I'd like. I desire you, come. Come, Lord Jesus. Come, come, come Jesus, Jesus, Jesus, Lord Jesus, send your Holy Spirit, creator. I love you.

(Rome, May 21, 1980)

274. *Sta. Francesca*. They are all so impressed… They see everything so amazing. Only I, Lord, see everything dry. It all looks like exaggerated piety. My Jesus, the only thing I'm sure of is the memory of the beautiful times when You were a sweet, continuous presence. If it's like that for them, blessed are you.

Prayer. Yes, Jesus. I would wait for you until death, perhaps pretentiously. But You already know of so much pain, suffering, waiting… heal my unbelief, my Jesus. Do not continue your absence that makes everything agonizing. Jesus, interior emptiness. Jesus, nevertheless, today I owe you my serenity. Thank you, Jesus.

(Rome, May 22, 1980)

275. Poletti. Salimei. I'm exhausted. Lord, your Spirit is not chained to the Bishops. Thank goodness.

---

[253] Cf. Is 9:1-3; Mt 4:15-16.

Afternoon. Second *Martiri*. My Jesus, I'm serene, locked in silence. Inspire Kiko, my Jesus. All is well. You appear. The people follow obediently, miraculously. You appear and create love, communion, and life. Jesus, tomorrow is Pentecost.

(Rome, May 23, 1980)

276. CEI, Santoro,[254] Fr. Maximino, Trastevere… finally Pentecost. Open my lips. Sinai,[255] the Tower…[256] Thank you, Lord. Come, come, come, Holy Spirit, Consoler, Magnificent. Day of truce. Blessed are you, thank you. Lord, wake me up. Tomorrow "prayer."

(Rome, May 24-24, 1980)

277. All day at home. What boredom.

My Jesus, only in prayer does time seem to be well spent. Nothing else interests me. I feel like I waste so much time smoking and doing nothing else. My Jesus, wake me up tomorrow. Energy! Fill these days that seem empty with vitality. I so desire more time and then it feels like death. Jesus, my Love, visit me.

(Rome, May 26, 1980)

278. *Domus Mariae*…[257] Defend Easter against *rubricism*[258] to the letter… My Jesus, all things are in your hands.

Life, My sweet Jesus, Life.

Meeting with the ones from America. To travel… the big meetings horrify me, Lord. My Jesus, terror. Have mercy on us. You, You, only You.

(Rome, May 27, 1980)

279. I wake up surrounded by the waves of death. I am dragged by raging torrents. The bonds of hell surrounded me. Death's traps

---

[254] Mons. Pietro Santoro (†) Archbishop of Boiano-Campobasso, 1979-1989.

[255] Cf. Ex 19:16-25.

[256] Cf. Gn 11:1-9.

[257] Today the Church Palace Hotel.

[258] A term used by Carmen to denote following the letter of the rubrics but not the spirit – *Trans*.

lying ahead of me. In my anguish, in my travail I cry out to You, Lord. I love you, my strength, strong, liberator. Have mercy on me.[259]

All day long waiting like bullfighters.

Three hours with Martini.[260] We left at one in the morning. Incredible. He listens, he listens well. You have given us strong, inspired words, and in the end, disappointment: no sacraments... My Jesus, what a battle. My Jesus, inspire these Bishops, enlighten them.

(Rome, May 28, 1980)

280. Meeting with the *Cefalos* for the Synod in Maura's house (Pino,[261] Giuseppe,[262] Gregorio,[263] Mario, Diego,[264] Franco, Giampiero, Stefano).[265]

Tomko tomorrow. Inspire us, Lord.

Crypt: meeting with the five communities at the Election. It goes well. Dinner with the *Cefalos*. My Jesus, Kiko was right: being together is consoling, strengthens the union, the communion. Thank you, Jesus.

Prayer Vigil.

(Rome, May 29, 1980)

281. Impossible awakening. Kiko alive. Tomko. The Pope's address to Italian Bishops yesterday spoke of catechesis. It opens up my future in front of me, it consoles me, strengthens my soul, gives me energy. Thank you, Lord.

---

[259] Cf. Ps 18:4-6.

[260] Cardinal Carlo Maria Martini (†) Archbishop of Milan, 1979-2002.

[261] Giuseppe (Pino) Manzari from the first community of *Nostra Signora del Santissimo Sacramento e Santi Martiri Canadesi*, Rome.

[262] Giuseppe Gennarini from the first community of *San Luigi Gonzaga*, Rome.

[263] Gregorio Sacristán (pb) from the first community of *Natività del Nostro Signore Gesù Cristo*, Rome.

[264] Diego Martínez from the second community of *Santos Timoteo y Tito*, Bogotá, Colombia.

[265] V General Assembly of the Synod of Bishops, "Mission of the Christian Family in the Contemporary World" (October 1980).

The Pope in Paris. Everything gives me happiness. Meeting with the second of *Sta. Francesca. Traditio*. My Jesus, as soon as I feel the breath of life, I no longer know what to write. Yes, I love you.

(Rome, May 30, 1980)

282. I'm excited by the Pope's opportunity in Paris.

My Jesus, I go from everything to nothingness, from unity to incomprehension. What do I care? You. If You are, and Jesus Christ is, the Church is. Why, Lord, aren't we? My Jesus, draw me to You. Take us out of this world of lies. My Jesus, Jesus, you lead me to the nothingness to put me into prayer, secret prayer. Raise me up, Jesus. Your name... Revelation of your Unique name, Yahweh. Jesus, say to me, "I AM"...[266]

(Santa Marinella, May 31, 1980)

283. On TV: the Pope in Paris.

(Santa Marinella, June 1, 1980)

284. I wake up to the Pope's address to UNESCO. Many things...

I remain sad, scared, terrified and poor. My Jesus, there's nothing I can do. What is this papal hang-up of mine?

Lord, You, the Only One, wonderful God, You look over the world, your eyes watch every man.

Jesus, Jesus, Jesus, Jesus, Jesus... Name of Jesus. Your presence. Intimacy. Abandonment.

(Santa Marinella, June 2, 1980)

285. Santa Marinella – Rome – Maura's house. Meeting of the *Cefalos*. Letter to the Pope. Synod. It's all a mountain of confusion, of improvisation. If not outright chaos... You appear and give harmony, communion. Thank you, Jesus.

(Rome, June 3, 1980)

286. All day in the house. Visits. Letter to the Pope. My head spins. My Jesus, wake me up tomorrow. It's already two o'clock; plus eight,

---

[266] Cf. Ex 3:14; Mt 14:27.

ten. I set the clock for eight, no, for six. Lord, I feel sorry for myself… Come, Lord.

(Rome, June 4, 1980)

287. *Cefalos* again. Final draft of the letter to the Pope. Letter for the Synod. First meeting *Martiri*. Night shifts. Thanks to You, Lord! "Keep watch."[267]

My Jesus, I want to recite the Psalms to you all at once because I don't know how to speak, but every word of sorrow plays a psalmody on my heart strings. My God, don't be far from me. Raise me up, I love you.

(Rome, June 5, 1980)

288. Vatican. Fr. Maximino is happy. The letter for the Pope is left in the hands of Floriano.[268] Your will be done.[269]

Paris in the afternoon.

First time that I don't feel any fear. My Jesus, protect the community.

(Paris, June 6, 1980)

289. Eucharist with first community of *S. Pierre du Gros Caillou*.[270] Long, long, long. My watch stopped. Kiko never ends… *Corpus Domini*.

(Paris, June 7, 1980)

290. Convivence with the first of *Saint Honoré*. It reminds me of the shanty town. Only You create out of nothing. You elect what is worthless to confound the intelligent.

(Paris, June 8, 1980)

---

[267] Cf. Mt 24:42.

[268] Fr. Florian Pomykała, SI, the then responsible of the Polish section of Vatican Radio.

[269] Cf. Mt 6:10.

[270] The community was transferred to this parish from the parish of *Saint Germain des Prés*. It was later moved to the parish of *Saint Honoré d'Eylau* and finally to the parish of *Notre Dame de la Bonne Nouvelle*.

291. Paris – Rome – Mass. My Jesus! The bread, the wine… how much you have granted us.

(Rome, June 14, 1980)

292. Day off. At home.

Pushed to come out of the eternal mourning. My Jesus, everything is precarious and moveable. Set me in motion. Raise me up. What can man do to me?[271]

(Rome, June 15, 1980)

293. Dinner with Farnés. In the end, no lesson. It all seems silly, and yet it isn't. My Jesus, *Sta. Catalina*, the Pope, Easter, the Bishops… My Jesus, half-sad all day, far away, nothingness, and now… I love you. Who is this coming up from the desert leaning on her Beloved?[272] Set me as a seal on your heart.[273]

(Rome, June 17, 1980)

294. Rome – Porto San Giorgio – Itinerants Convivence.

My Jesus, you defend me from smoking and I am grateful. Help me.

(Porto San Giorgio, June 18, 1980)

295. Itinerants Convivence.

My Jesus, you appear and I'm afraid. Everything seems repetitious, with no emotion, and I feel like escaping. You withdraw your hand from me. Is it illness? Is it money? What is it, Lord? Are you trying me or do you not love me? Jesus, convert my heart to do your will. Give me strength. I have none.

(Porto San Giorgio, June 19, 1980)

296. Itinerants Convivence.

My Jesus, at night you come to me with serenity, like a dove that brings peace. Thank you, Lord, I'm moved by your unexpected visit.

---

[271] Cf. Heb 13:6.
[272] Cf. Sg 8:5.
[273] Cf. Sg 8:6.

I couldn't take it anymore, Lord. The suffering, on the verge of doubt, the disbelief, the apathy, and everything in darkness. My Jesus, why do I suffer? How is this helplessness possible? Thank you, Lord, don't leave me.

(Porto San Giorgio, June 20, 1980)

297. Itinerants Convivence.

Kiko speaks, and speaks, and speaks… and I'm mute, mute, mute. Oh, Lord, is it my fault? Is it your will? My Jesus, apathy, far from everything, I'm not interested in anyone or anything, and I see it all far from the ancient Christians.

Eucharist. I take refuge in You, only in faith.

(Porto San Giorgio, June 21, 1980)

298. The convivence finishes. Mute to the end. Dates. Mountains of convivences. Medical clinic… it's three o'clock in the morning. My Jesus, I feel better, more serene.

(Porto San Giorgio, June 22, 1980)

299. Free. Day off. The Philistine, armed, gigantic[274] is already there, first thing in the morning. I awake in terror.

My Jesus, put your name in my hands, this unique little stone.[275] The lion, the bear, the Philistine…[276] YOU, Jesus, victor… In your name, Jesus. The armor, the structures, the iron, the sword…[277] A stick, a little stone.[278].. In your name, Jesus, Jesus, I face every battle. You are. Your holy name. Come, Jesus.

I am afflicted all day,
chastened every morning…
My heart was embittered,
and my soul was deeply wounded…
Yet I am always with you;

---

[274] Cf. 1 Sm 17:4.
[275] Cf. 1 Sm 17:40; Rv 2:17.
[276] Cf. 1 Sm 17:36.
[277] Cf. 1 Sm 17:38-39.
[278] Cf. 1 Sm 17:40.

you grasped me by my right hand.[279]

My Jesus, dissatisfaction, boredom of existence. Is it possible to see life completely horrible, tedious, meaningless?

(Porto San Giorgio, June 23, 1980)

300. Have mercy on me, Lord. The aggressor always oppresses me. Day and night I cry to You. Help me. All day, incommunicable sorrow. Nothing interests me. To run away... where to? If You are not, nothing is. And if You are, there is no fear. My Jesus, leaning on your name... Jesus, Jesus, Jesus, only Jesus. Have mercy on me.

Visit to Loreto. Sweet Virgin Mary. "I am black."[280] "Who is this rising from the desert leaning on her Beloved?"[281] Most sweet one. Mysterious Christianity. Jesus.

(Porto San Giorgio, June 24, 1980)

301. Northern Italy... Pharaoh appears.

Jesus, I'm starting to savor solitude. The country reminds me of childhood, Ólvega. You call me.

Rome – Meeting first *Martiri*. Kiko inspired. I can't stand him. Life, impossible. Prayer. It's already three-thirty in the morning. Dinner. My Jesus, my only objective is prayer. You, Jesus, Jesus.

(Rome, June 25, 1980)

302. Rome – Madrid – My suitcase didn't arrive. Thank you, Lord, you lighten me.

Spanish Itinerants Convivence. El Pinar de Chamartín.[282] I feel serene, my Jesus, out of the tomb. Losing the suitcase, the books, frees me. Thank you, Lord.

(Madrid, June 26, 1980)

303. Leper. Purification. Bird in flight. Lord, you open my lips[283] and I feel like a different person. Lord, you are a mysterious God. Man, even more so. What a great mystery. How can a few words make

---

[279] Cf. Ps 73:14.21.23.
[280] Sg 1:5.
[281] Sg 8:5.
[282] Retreat house of the *Esclavas de Cristo Rey*.
[283] Cf. Ps 51:15.

me pass from death to life? Why, Lord? It is You, You who first change the interior and then, as a consequence, open my lips. My Jesus, thank you for allowing this tomb of death to open its mouth.

(El Pinar de Chamartín, June 27, 1980)

304. At the house, the paralytic servant who suffers so much…[284] My Jesus, the sufferings are good for me somehow. Thank you, Lord. Open my lips.[285] Do not let me turn back. Give me courage, bravery. Thank you, Lord. The teams, better. Freedom.

(El Pinar de Chamartín, June 28, 1980)

305. End of convivence at Chamartín – Elisa's House. Sleepy. Dinner. My Jesus, things pile up on me and there's no way out. Laziness, smoking… finally in Narváez. Jesus, help me tomorrow. You fill everything with light.

(Madrid, June 29, 1980)

306. My Jesus, the depression? Life appears gloomy, colorless… death. My Jesus, You are the Savior.

Center. Mountains of convivences and problems arise. Communities of the Center, routine Eucharists. Children. Jesús Blázquez. You. The Church. If You are not here, everything's impossible.

Night. Serenity, life takes on another color, and problems flee.

(June 30, 1980)

307. Madrid – Milan – Ivrea – Meeting with priests tomorrow. My Jesus, we never finish. I was hoping for something easier. My Jesus, You. Serenity, trips, outlook, calm. Today was the Gospel of the calming of the storm.[286] My Jesus, praying for my family does me good, it calms me down. My Jesus.

(Ivrea, July 1, 1980)

---

[284] Cf. Mk 8:6.
[285] Cf. Ps. 51:15.
[286] Cf. Mt 8:23-27.

308. Priests' meeting. Cave, cold, humidity. Dinner: Piedmont appetizers. Late. Bettazzi.[287] Document of the Piedmont Conference: Mass, Easter... My Jesus, it seemed impossible... Finally, I said a few words about Easter but wasn't happy with it, although the priests listened. Thank you, Jesus. But I see a fight looming on the horizon. I love you, My Jesus. Everything is in your hands.

(Castellamonte – Ivrea, July 2, 1980)

309. Arrows to my heart... Lord, what pain. All of a sudden, the dominion of darkness. Lord, have mercy. Piedmont, the Bishops, it hurts me. Consolation from the brothers, the community, the Word. Roll away the stone from the tomb...[288]

Tomorrow visiting pastors. The day after tomorrow, the Archbishop of Vercelli.[289] Lord, send your angels ahead. Inspire us.

(Ivrea, July 3, 1980)

310. Day of fasting, going around from parish to parish. My crucified Jesus, my love, most sweet one: foolishness and scandal.[290] They give you a farcical resurrection that doesn't pass through the cross. My Jesus, cornerstone of the building.[291] Poor priests, established on pseudo-wisdoms, by theologies with no faith. My Jesus!

(Ivrea, July 4, 1980)

311. Archbishop of Vercelli. My Jesus! Your church pains me. My Jesus, pain all day, Piedmont, the Bishops, the theologies.

Eucharist. Jesus, you console me with the Truth. You are not like those whose words are full of the leaven of the Pharisees.[292]

(Ivrea, July 5, 1980)

312. Ivrea – Bettazzi. At the door, but we leave a little better than when we woke up.

---

[287] Mons. Luigi Bettazzi, Bishop of Ivrea, 1966-1999.
[288] Cf. Mt 16:3.
[289] Mons. Albino Mensa (†), Archbishop of Vercelli, 1966-1991.
[290] Cf. 1 Cor 1:23.
[291] Cf. 1 Pt 2:7.
[292] Cf. Mt 16:6.

Travel to Venice.
My Jesus, teach me to live freely, easily. I love you. Wake me up.

(Venice, July 6, 1980)

313. Mario arrives with Kiko's parents. St. Mark's Square. My Jesus, nothing interests me. Silence. My Jesus, what should I do? I love you.

(Venice, July 7, 1980)

314. Apathetic, "*escorbútica,*" hateful. I don't know what to say. The world of evangelization is incompatible with the family. I don't know what to do. I put up with it all day. My Jesus, I don't know if I should go to Ólvega…

(Venice, July 8, 1980)

315. The Biennale. Rain. Empty paintings… My Jesus, rain, rain, rain. There's no way to escape from Venice. No energy. I sleep, eat, get fat, and feel lifeless. July, the time of vacation, passes in the nothingness. It seems like we're wasting time.

(Venice, July 9, 1980)

316. Murano: glass. Burano: food. Torcello: church, baptistry. The net… the sea… My Jesus, I'm alone, surrounded by people. Nothing interests me and everything seems fake. My Jesus, tomorrow to Le Vignole again. This Venice… it's inescapable. Where can I flee? Only smoking…

(Venice, July 10, 1980)

317. Like a prisoner. No escape. Le Vignole. Paella again. Pictures from last year… how awful. My Jesus, don't make me come back. I don't know how to live, I can't live, everyone bothers me. Nobody and nothing interest me. And we don't pray. Everything seems like a farce. We're acting. What? Lord, the only purpose of this life is evangelization.

(Venice, July 11, 1980)

318. My Jesus, vanity of vanities.²⁹³ Laziness. Nothingness. Tragedy. Tragedy of a Eucharist: I explode. Kiko in his own world. My Jesus, one is alone before You. For You, Lord, better, thanks to You. Have mercy on me.

(Venice, July 12, 1980)

319. We leave Venice. Finally in the mountains. Cortina. My Jesus, my selfishness… The mountain. Thank you, Jesus, for the echo of joy that resounds in my heart.

(Cortina, July 13, 1980)

320. My Jesus, to me everything seems like selfishness and losing one's life not for the gospel but for nonsense. Jesus, where can I escape? Seeking you. I feel essential in combatting this disaster, and it all makes me suffer.

(Pieve di Cadore, July 14, 1980)

321. The lake. Crossing. Mountains, mountains, mountains. The Only and great God, Lord, I love you. Freedom, prayer, consolation. I come back feeling better. I didn't want to go, my Jesus.

(Pieve di Cadore, July 15, 1980)

322. Virgin of Mount Carmel. My saint. No one remembered. I gift myself a blouse…

Prayer, Lord. Reading by chance: Isaac, the Promise, your Faithfulness. I love you.

We climb the mountain. I was cold. Lunch in a shelter. We descend. Eucharist. Dinner, farewell to Kiko's parents.

My Jesus, sorrow, and freedom. You are powerful. Blessed are you.

(Pieve di Cadore, July 16, 1980)

323. *Mary, little Mary,*²⁹⁴
daughter of Jerusalem,
mother of all peoples,
Virgin of Nazareth.
You are the "place near Me" (Ex 33:21)…

---

²⁹³ Cf. Qo 1:2.
²⁹⁴ Song *Mary, Little Mary* composed by Kiko that year.

says the Lord to Moses.
In this intolerable absence,
in this devouring fire of the Lord who passes by
and takes his hand away from the rock: his back.[295]
Terrible yearning for God
that makes us want to die.
You, Mary, help me,
protect me, have mercy on me.
Let the Lord come with us,
if we have truly found favor in his eyes,
even though we are a wicked and sinful people.
Let the Lord come with us
so that he may replace our evil with his glory.
Forgive our sins
and welcome us as your heritage.[296]
A ragged people,
a people cursed by the world,
of evildoers, of sinners, of miserable ones,
a stiff-necked people,
a people from far away.
"Your people, Lord."
You, little Mary,
in this song,
you are the refuge of sinners.
Help us, build a house of prayer,[297]
of forgiveness for the scoundrel,
of liberation for the crazy and oppressed.
Help us!
Gentle breeze of Elijah,[298]
whisper of the Spirit,
burning bush of Moses,
that bears the Lord of glory
without being consumed.[299]

---

[295] Cf. Ex 33:22-23.
[296] Cf. Ex 34:9.
[297] Cf. Mt 21:13.
[298] Cf. 1 K 19:12.
[299] Cf. Ex 3:2.

Cloud that protects.[300]
Thunder, lightning, thick cloud,
powerful trumpet blast.[301]
"Glory of Yahweh,"
that rests on Mount Sinai.
Tent of the gathering.
Dwelling of God in the desert.
Arc of witness.
Decalogue of the covenant.
Sanctuary of God among men.
"Glory of Yahweh" who passes.
Unbearable absence of God.
Cleft in the rock
that God covers with his hand.
"A place near Me" (Ex 33:21).

"Look, here is a place near me where you shall station yourself on the rock. When my glory passes, I will set you in the cleft of the rock and will shield you with my hand until I have passed by. Then I will take my hand away, so that you may see my back; but my face will not be seen."[302]

The forgiveness of sins.[303] It is not only a way to lighten, relieve, unload, reassure a guilty conscience *(although it also has this effect)*. It is rather the inexhaustible capacity for new growth, or better, it is a creative act of the living God, who is not satisfied with passing over the shipwreck of past failures, but transforms them and uses them. Man's stinginess gives God a new occasion to create. It's why evil is condemned to be conquered. Consequently, forgiveness opens the possibility for a new beginning when we are the most hopeless. His

---

[300] Cf. Ex 13:21.
[301] Cf. Ex 19:16.
[302] Cf. Ex 33:21-23.
[303] This passage was written by Carmen in another diary from 1978 on the page of August 5. The content seems to have been taken from some text that she must have been reading. Since there are no references of when Carmen wrote this, it has been included here because of the affinity of ideas.

infinitely great <u>power is effectively manifested</u> in the power that he has bestowed in Christ by raising him from the dead.

To recreate the other. "It was necessary that Christ…"[304] "<u>TESHUVÁ</u>."

(Pieve di Cadore, July 18, 1980)

324. My Jesus, the housework, service, the tortillas… console me, as if I were actually doing something… My Jesus, I love you, help me, don't let the night consume my soul.

The Eucharist. My sweet Jesus, I believe in You, help my unbelief,[305] my doubt. My Jesus, your Word is true, your love is true. Come, Jesus. Have mercy on my wretched, miserable poverty.

Word.[306] To be <u>God's chosen people means to be directly exposed to his Word</u> with all the capital consequences of "discontent" that come from listening to Him. No one can presume to explain the mysterious motives behind the predestination that this particular people has <u>for listening to the Word of God</u>. The liturgy of the Word is essentially the <u>actualization</u> of the <u>Word of God</u> in the <u>liturgical assembly</u> where Christ the Lord is present in the midst of those who believe in Him and gather in his name.

Israel is the permanent witness in the eyes of the nations of the One God and of his Revelation.

Peter, "You have been <u>born anew</u>, not from a perishable seed but from an imperishable one <u>through the living and enduring Word of God</u>."[307]

(Pieve di Cadore, July 19, 1980)

---

[304] Cf. Lk 24:46-47.

[305] Cf. Mk 9:24.

[306] Written by Carmen in another diary from 1978 on the page of August 6. Also this content seems taken from something she may have been reading. There is no date but the writing has been included here because of affinity of ideas.

[307] Cf. 1 Pt 1:23.

325. José Miguel[308] calls and tells me that María Ángela Sagristá[309] is looking for me. My Jesus, you make the mystery of your action present in my life. I love you, Lord. How can I not believe in You? Your holiness is limitless with regard to me, as it has let me know my helplessness and pettiness. My Jesus, My sweet Jesus, I love you. Alone in the mountains... I love you. Consolation. Sweet Jesus, it's been so long since I felt this way. Alone, the mountains, the clouds that blanket, the rain... so beautiful. It is You, my God, You are.
(Pieve di Cadore, July 20, 1980)

326. On the way back from praying in the mountains, an idea for collaboration and renewal comes to me. Javier... when? Come, my Jesus, I love you. I was doing so well, desiring to be holy and now I've exploded, raging and mean. My Jesus, I will seek you tomorrow. I love you.

Cortina – the river, the guards, the money, my unrelenting, despicable stinginess. I am ashamed. I'm an impossible burden, I'm impossible. Only your presence opens my heart and my hand, and I hope for this miracle from You, your works. You do it, my Jesus. You, You. I'm obnoxious, hateful, *"escorbútica."*
(Pieve di Cadore, July 21, 1980)

327. Kiko wakes up suffering. Ghosts. A sunny day. Fighting with the ghosts. Desert monks.

Prayer on the mountain. My Jesus, "you who dwell in the gardens where my companions are listening for your voice: let me hear it!"[310] My Jesus, you console me. The good memories from my youth console me. That María Ángeles Sagristá would look for me... I see the history You are leading. I love you, my Jesus. I've suffered so much this year, terrible sorrows, the inability to speak. My Jesus, You free my soul from everything. You have let me know my stinginess to its very depths so I don't lift my head over anyone else. I'm ashamed of my miserable stinginess. I don't know how they put up with me. You surround me with marvels and I am ungrateful, an imbecile. My God,

---

[308] José Miguel Romero (†) from the first community of the Neocatechumenal Center in Madrid.

[309] One of Carmen's companions from the *Misioneras de Cristo Jesús*.

[310] Sg 8:13.

immense, listen to me. The enormous mountains... and the Earth moves... "Your voice. Let me hear it!"³¹¹

(Pieve di Cadore, July 22, 1980)

328. High mountains. Three peaks of Lavaredo. Everything is magnificent, Lord. I am saturated with mountains, beauty, your infinite generosity, my Jesus. Time flies.

(Pieve di Cadore, July 23, 1980)

329. At the house. Last day – The night. The mountains seem flat, the Earth, like nothing. Lord, You, awesome, awesome God. I am afraid. Darkness, nights, sufferings, terrors, anguishes... My Jesus, what a terrible mystery of existence, life, death, and "man" are. My Jesus, thank you for your free gifts that I don't know how to appreciate. Have mercy on me.

(Pieve di Cadore, July 24, 1980)

330. Pieve – Cortina – Fishing – Travel – Mestre (Mario stays behind) – Bologna – Rimini – Ancona.

Porto San Giorgio – what joy. It's like coming home. And there's no convivence tomorrow... Thank you, Lord.

Fr. Maximino's document,³¹² Lord, encourages me.

Word. Exodus. Full steam ahead. Defeat the enemy. My Jesus, thank you. Encourage me. Help Kiko.

A night of temptation. My Jesus, you change the coordinates. Thank you, Lord, you defended me.

(Porto San Giorgio, July 25, 1980)

331. Raise me up, Lord. Have mercy on me, poor, miserable, sinful, unworthy. Cover the evil of my heart with your mercy. My sin pains me. Do not let me succumb to it. Holy, most sweet one, may your

---

³¹¹ Ibid.

³¹² Perhaps she is referring to the Instruction *Postquam Apostoli* by the Congregation for the Clergy. Fr. Maximino Romero de Lima was then secretary for the Congregation. The document of March 25, 1980 establishes directives for the collaboration between particular churches, especially for a better distribution of the clergy around the world. The document underlines the *pressing urgency to evangelize*.

most precious blood purify my iniquity, my lips, my life. My Jesus, holy one, take me from death to life, from sadness to rest. I confess to You my sins. Hide me in your tent.[313] Have mercy on me, My Jesus. They lie in wait for me to devour my life. You alone are strong, Lord. Come, raise me up.

(Porto San Giorgio, July 26, 1980)

332. My Jesus, fear, interior fear. Sodom-Gomorra.[314] Sin. Your mercy. Thanks be given to you for Jesus Christ, the just one, the only one. My Jesus, you cover the multitude of my sins.[315] The mystery of man... Come, Jesus, I am in the dark.

(Porto San Giorgio, July 27, 1980)

333. To wake up – why? I struggle in the nothingness, in living for nothing. My Jesus, I hear your voice and my existence is filled with meaning, the day, the night. Let me hear your voice.[316] You are. Speak to me.

Where can I escape? And with whom? I can't be with anybody anywhere. Lord, where are you? I don't know how to live. Let me hear your voice. Lord, heal me, I have sinned against You. I love you, Lord.

(Porto San Giorgio, July 28, 1980)

334. Why, Lord, this nothingness that envelops me? Everything seems like nothing. Life... everything is threatened by the nothingness. With no life, no energy. Prayer is laborious. When I read, nothing interests me. Thank you, Lord, for this breeze because it makes me think of the Holy Spirit, who exists, who is here, who will lead this convivence, that the Pope... that... That your voice, Lord, that your voice may sound in my ear. Revive the life of your servant.[317] Come, Lord.

(Porto San Giorgio, July 29, 1980)

---

[313] Cf. Ps 27:5.
[314] Cf. Gn 18:20.
[315] Cf. 1 Pt 4:8.
[316] Cf. Sg 8:13.
[317] Cf. Ps 86:4.

335. Porto San Giorgio – Travel to Rome, with Kiko and Patricio.[318]

Lord, how distant everyone is. I want to leave. Where to? And why? They're speaking and what they say seems impossible. I am frightened by how much they trust us. Lord, I am nothing, from nothing, in nothing.

(Rome, July 30, 1980)

336. Lord, what pain. The ghosts haunt me, gnawing at my soul in the nothingness all day long.

Santa Marinella – Finally, night. I have no interest in anything. The cat smell wakes me up. At least I fight to clean… My Jesus, I wait for you here, come, Jesus!

Sleepless night.

(Santa Marinella, July 31, 1980)

337. First day. Thank you, Lord.

Psalm 37 [38].

Your arrows have pierced deep into me,
your hand has pressed down upon me.
There is no soundness in my flesh,
my sin has left no health in my bones.
My sins stand higher than my head,
they weigh on me as an unbearable burden.
I have stinking and festering wounds
thanks to my folly.
I am twisted and bent double;
I spend my days in gloom.
My loins burn with fever,
no part of me is unscathed.
Numbed and utterly crushed,
I groan in distress of heart.
Lord, all my longing is known to you;
my sighing no secret from you.
But I hear nothing, as though I were deaf,

---

[318] Dr. Patrizio Astorri (†), of the first community of the parish of *Sacra Famiglia*, Porto San Giorgio.

as though dumb, saying not a word;
I am like the one who, hearing nothing,
has no sharp answer to make.
For in you, Lord, I put my hope,
Lord, do not desert me;
my God, do not stand aloof from me!
Come quickly to my help,
Lord, my Savior![319]

Thank you, Lord, You are near. First day of rest for my soul. Activity, zest. Lord, I feel like I'm dreaming. I sense You. I only want You to exist, that I not doubt it. Enkindle my faith in You. Lord, I love you, even if you did not exist. You, Lord, I love you.

(Santa Marinella, August 1, 1980)

338. Rift over money. I sink in the discommunion, the loathing, the sadness. Everything is collapsing like the Station at Bologna,[320] like a bomb of destruction and death. Jesus, my Jesus, there is nothing healthy in me. "Vanity of vanities, everything is vanity."[321] Where are you? What do you want? Run, Lord, You are the Liberator. Come, Lord, help me.

(Santa Marinella, August 2, 1980)

339. I have no energy. Too lazy for anything. Lord, finally a swim in the sea.

The Pope worries me… We set the longline.

(Santa Marinella, August 3, 1980)

340. We get up at five to reel in the longline. One bream. And the line breaks. What's wrong with it? The sea gets rough.

We read Bouyer's article and it prompts endless discussions. Symbolism, sacraments.

My Jesus, I'm comforted. Thank you, Lord, for granting me a respite amid days of suffering. It's incredible how one can suffer this way, with this oppression, this darkness inside. Without anything

---

[319] Ps 38:2-9.13-15.21-22.

[320] On this day there was a terrible massacre at the Bologna train station (85 dead).

[321] Cf. Qo 1:2.

changing, everything changes and acquires direction, meaning, life. My Jesus, I want to make a few resolutions: to wake up early…

You, my Jesus, are the only purpose for things. Even my worrying over the pope vanishes. And You calm my soul. Thank you, Lord. "Why did you doubt?"[322] Truly, Jesus, You are Lord. Save me! Say to my soul, "It is I. Do not be afraid."[323] Remember, Lord, my brothers and sisters. Show yourself to them with Life.

(Santa Marinella, August 4, 1980)

341. Sadness seated in the center of my heart. My Jesus, why this sadness, this lethargy, this nothing of wanting nothing, absolutely nothing in nothing? I don't move, like a motor that has been shut off. Rather a body without a motor, without a "spark" or without a "soul," Jesus.

Abraham, *"Tout est soudain remis en question."*

Jacob, *"C'est donc la veille angoissante d'un lendemain incertain. Reste seul."*

Absolute disinterest. I can't see. Why these sufferings, Lord, these spiritual ghosts? With no rhyme or reason.

The Pope… today is the anniversary of the death of Paul VI.

Jesus, don't abandon me in the morning when I awake. Give me freedom this night.

(Santa Marinella, August 6, 1980)

342. Day of truce, serene. "Peace."

Jesus came and stood among them and said, "Peace be with you. As the Father sent me, so I am sending you."[324]

Thank you, Lord. The extreme positions become more moderate. Serenity in the soul. Thank you, Lord, Alfredo's[325] visit helped me, as did swimming, and moving about. Lord, I don't know… all interpretations. You, Lord. The Lord is my Shepherd, I lack nothing.[326] You surround

---

[322] Cf. Mt 14:31.

[323] Cf. Mt 14:27.

[324] Cf. Jn 20:19.21.

[325] Alfredo Cholewinski, SJ, (†) from the first community of the parish of *Nostra Signora del Santissimo Sacramento e Santi Martiri Canadesi*, Rome. He alternated his time between teaching at the Pontifical Biblical Institute in Rome and itinerant evangelization in Poland and in other Eastern European countries.

[326] Cf. Ps 23:1.

me with everything: swimming in the sea, this house, money. When your Spirit does not blow, everything else becomes chains. Thank you, Lord, for serenity. Thank you, Lord, teach me to be good like You.

(Santa Marinella, August 7, 1980)

343. Set the longlines and badly. Rough sea. I sleep.

(Santa Marinella, August 8, 1980)

344. We reel in the longline. Nothing.

Jesus, raise us up, have mercy on us. Keep us from falling in the storm. Have mercy.

Sea. Eucharist: unknown journey… wisdom… Abraham does not know where he is going…[327] "Do not be afraid"…[328] "Sell…"[329]

My Jesus, my life is in your hands. Have mercy on me. You have shown me already that I'm worthless. Show that You are. Thank you for this truce of Peace.

(Santa Marinella, August 9, 1980)

345. Cholewiński consoles me. My Jesus, the sea and still nothing. I am more serene, fighting. Thank you, my Jesus.

(Santa Marinella, August 10, 1980)

346. Morning… pain. Lord, help Kiko. I suffer less. My Jesus, my soul is serene. Thank you, Jesus. Origen… poor thing… uneasy as well. Make me good, Lord. Teach me to forgive from the heart. Good night, Jesus.

(Santa Marinella, August 11, 1980)

347. Leviathan… My Jesus, joy. You see our weakness: a little thing makes us suffer so much and a little sign lifts us up. I love you. Last day spent with the cry of the longline. Afternoon in Fregene. Free me, Lord! I'm up and it's two in the morning. Peace. Thank you.

(Santa Marinella, August 12, 1980)

---

[327] Cf. Heb 11:8.
[328] Cf. Acts 18:9.
[329] Cf. Mt 19:21.

348. No sea, no swimming. Maura comes. We watch "Brothers Karamazov"… blah… blah… Jesus!

(Santa Marinella, August 13, 1980)

349. Vigil of the Assumption.

Sweet Virgin Mary, now and at the hour of our death intercede for us.

My Jesus, Resurrection, consolation, *kerygma*, a serious miracle of the Resurrection. A Eucharist with the multitudes. My Jesus, I love you. Thank you, Sweet Virgin Mary.

(Santa Marinella, August 14, 1980)

350. Assumption.

Sweet Virgin Mary, thank you for this Word: a long, tempered, beautiful sword that You have kept in your heart.[330] You lift us up with your signs. Drive away the Ghosts. Graces, and Blessed. The way is long, stronger than the enemy. Flaming sword, let me not forget your signs, your grace! Most sweet one, help me.

(Santa Marinella, August 15, 1980)

351. In the heart of this vacation, I see no future. My Jesus, where will we escape? Free us. Escaping in sleep, almost 24 hours straight… Free me, Lord! I love you.

Longline: bream.

(Santa Marinella, August 16, 1980)

352. Storm at sea. Third longline lost. Lord, Eucharist! My sweet Jesus, free me from the terror that seeks to envelop me. The ghosts want to arise. Do not leave me! I love you, my Jesus.

(Santa Marinella, August 17, 1980)

353. Fishing: another swordfish, smaller.

Lord, don't torment me. You know I'm a miserable sinner, but I love you. Have mercy on my bone-deep stinginess. But, in any case, this kind of sinful neurosis, like the cats, still gets on my nerves more than my stinginess.

---

[330] Cf. Lk 2:35.

In any case, Lord, I'm happy the ghosts are going away. You give me indifference to pull the blanket over my head. And so? Help me, don't let me enter the darkness. Thank you, Jesus, for the sea, swimming, all your graces, your light, when You want.

(Santa Marinella, August 19, 1980)

354. The one who shared my table has betrayed me.[331] My sweet Jesus, you, alone, are the only Lord in my heart. Thank you for instilling a deep serenity in me, eradicating my heart's perverse anger. I love you, my Jesus. Forgive me. Lord, forgive Kiko, forgive each sinful man.

My Jesus, it's all in your hands: the mystery of every path, of man. It's all a mystery. My Jesus, have mercy. Help me, help all those in temptation. Have mercy. I love you. Thank you, My Jesus. Jesus, wandering about at night, seeking your mysteries. My Jesus, have mercy, have pity. Help us. Jesus, have mercy, have pity. But then, will I turn out like a cliched conversion, my Jesus, as if nothing had happened?

(Santa Marinella, August 20-21, 1980)

355. Turbulent Sea.

My Jesus, show me what I must do. To go on like this, on the razor's edge of insanity… my heart has become restless, my Jesus.

Terrible day, Lord. Have mercy on us. Give me mercy down to my depths. Take pity on me. Show me the road to follow.[332] I've had a crazy day. Finally, the situation was resolved. Night. Bed. A day of vigil. Thank you, my Jesus, that you've been faithful. Thank you, Jesus. Show me what to do. Help me.

Night of prayer in the garden. My Jesus, it's already five a.m.. Night of prayer, of sorrow, of insomnia, of suffering, of energy. I also thank you, Lord, for being so close to me in all the craziness of this pain, for reviving me.

My Jesus, prayer. I was up at seven. My Jesus, a quieter day.

(Santa Marinella, August 22-23, 1980)

---

[331] Cf. Ps 41:9.
[332] Cf. Ps 143:8.

356. Problems at sea. The engine won't start. The police. Conger eels… and finding a lost net.

My Jesus, your readings are terrifying. My imagination's killing me. Agonizing Eucharist. I give in and am sad. Free me, Lord. Let your will be done.[333] Dread, dread… Mercy, Lord. Thank you, Lord. You have visited me. Thank you, Lord. Do not leave me. Pull me out of so much suffering.

(Santa Marinella, August 24, 1980)

357. My Jesus, serenity, energy. When I feel well, I don't feel like writing. But I do, to thank you, Lord.

I feel like I'm coming out of a grave illness. It's incredible how one can suffer in a tide of imaginings, ghosts and pain.

All of a sudden, everything changes, Lord: the temptation, the Way, everything seems possible, my Jesus. The night, the loneliness. Just the memory of suffering keeps me enclosed here. Help me, my Jesus. The Pope, the convivence, the itinerants… Lead me not into temptation.

(August 25, 1980)

358. Your power is victorious at night, my Jesus. Thank you, Jesus.

Except… I'm restless all day. I'm haunted by the idea of hypocrisy. I'm terrified. My Jesus, free me. Do not leave me. Hide me, terrifying fears are coming for me. "The abyss."

My Jesus, sweet, generous, savior. I begin to understand now that you are the savior, that you have descended, that you have risked everything, my most sweet possession. I love you. Save me from the ghosts of terror, from this crazy imagination. Give me rest, Jesus. I love you. Simplify the way I see things. I love you. Quiet me down.

The trap of being scandalized[334] so as not to confess and not come to the light. The confession of sin never scandalizes. It instead edifies everyone (Bible). The devil deceives to prevent change, because

---

[333] Cf. Mt 6:10.

[334] Written by Carmen in another diary from 1978 on the page for June 28-29. There is no date but the writing has been included here because of the affinity of the ideas.

confession is a help (it humbles, changes one's perspective, clarifies) in the decision to break with sin. God lives in the humble heart.[335]

Whoever thinks he can save himself, come out of sin by himself, and is silent, deceives himself. It is a deception that leads him more and more to hypocrisy, which is the ferment of corruption. Confession strikes down the deception, and through the work of the Lord in our freedom, transforms one's own evil into "light." The truth, confession, make man free.

(August 26, 1980)

359. My Jesus, you are recreating me in serenity, goodness. The Pope on the horizon for September.[336] Jesus, my Jesus, thank you. You are the defender of my life. Whom will I fear? You are my light and my salvation. Whom should I fear?[337] My Jesus, "peace" in my heart. Sweet Jesus, help me to run after it, not to lose it. Drive off the satanic ghosts. Jesus, Jesus, Jesus. So sweet is your name. Savior. I love you.

(August 27, 1980)

360. My Jesus, it's August 28th. La Princesa, Barcelona, departure… Thank you, My Jesus, for accompanying me with so much love. You carried me on eagle's wings.[338] Thank you, Jesus. "Your presence" on that day, in those days, comforts me like a memorial. Thank you, my Jesus. Tonight I felt the security, the joy that You are mysteriously in my life. And even in the midst of the storm, with all the lightning and noise, You are there, You are there, and you are immutable, faithful. Thank you, my Jesus. I want to go to communion to be close to You, as in the times of my old devotions. My Jesus, so much love. I love You, too. Help me.

My Jesus, I went to Carmel[339] to receive communion. How many things I now understand, that You will defend, my Jesus. Help me.

(August 28, 1980)

---

[335] Cf. Is 66:2.
[336] Possibility of the first audience with St. John Paul II.
[337] Cf. Ps 27:1.
[338] Cf. Ex 19:4.
[339] *Nostra Signora di Monte Carmelo* Carmelite parish in Santa Marinella. – *Trans.*

361. Lord, You are, if not, everything is impossible. What am I looking for in so many books? Help me, Lord, to live. Enlighten me. Come. The convivences, the Pope: mountains. The enemies, sin... Lord, if you keep a record of it,[340] what sadness! Jesus Christ, blessed are you.

(August 29, 1980)

362. Many visits. Dancing from one thing to the next, all day long. Not one free minute. Better. Anxiety, angst... Calm me down, Lord.
Eucharist, Restlessness. Jesus, I love you, calm me.

(August 30, 1980)

363. Turbulent sea again. Lost longline. How terrible the strength of the sea. My Jesus, so many visits... "marriage counseling"...

(August 31, 1980)

364. Anxiety for Fr. Maximino. Kiko says that the sea bream, the sea bass, and the document are fantastic?
"I will make you an object of eternal glory and you will know that I, Yahweh, am your Savior."[341] Jesus, Savior!

(September 1, 1980)

365. Sleepless Night. Why? Dinner, restlessness, My Jesus. Kiko leaves with Patrizio... Peace, day of activity, of serenity, of work. My Jesus, how is it possible to live a life so full of surprises... of You? My Jesus, peace. Thank you, Jesus. I love you. Help me. Help Kiko, my Jesus.

(September 2, 1980)

366. Peaceful sunrise. Kiko suddenly goes to pray...
Fears. I'm going crazy, with a broken heart.
My Jesus, finally peace. Wonderful longline in peace.
Lord, I search for you like this, frantically. Help me. Thank you, Jesus, for sustaining me all summer. Do not let my feet stumble.[342] Defend me. You, Faithful, Holy One, my Jesus.

(September 4, 1980)

---

[340] Cf. Ps 130:3.
[341] Cf. Is 60:15-16.
[342] Cf. Ps 66:9.

367. Morning. Sea. Empty longline. The sun rises, it's magnificent. My Jesus, Lord, only one, great in all your works,[343] I love You. Bicycle ride to Civitavecchia: wonderful, easy, fantastic memories, especially of your love.

Franco and Margherita come. Plans: Pope, Poletti, Tomko... Lord, your will be done.[344]

Tomorrow travel to Spain. Come, Lord.

(September 5, 1980)

368. Empty longline. Depart Santa Marinella. Fiumicino. Madrid.

Heat. Eucharist in the Center. Narváez, empty without my mother. Nothing in the house. I'm in bed. My Jesus, I love you, mysterious, incomprehensible. Spirit of Wisdom, come.

(Madrid, September 6, 1980)

https://www.twitch.tv/videos/1569574575?t=0h15m2s

369. Eurobuilding. Synod of Families Convivence. My Jesus, what joy to see you present in everything, even before starting. Lauds. Letter from Javier.[345] Tarancón. Experiences. All a miracle of your presence. Lord, I begin to understand the sufferings of the summer. Lord, I love you. You are.

(Madrid, September 7, 1980)

370. Flight to Rome. I get anxious over small things, for nothing. My Jesus, I'm happy. The joy of the convivence lingers in me, your presence. You are great in everything, so sweet.

Answer from Castel Gandolfo. Return to Santa Marinella. Good night, my Jesus, I love you. My Jesus, yes, the foundation of everything is the Mount of Beatitudes, the Lake... You, Jesus.

(Santa Marinella, September 8, 1980)

371. Last day in Santa Marinella. Rush. Restless. To Arcinazzo with Salimei.

---

[343] Cf. Ps 92:5.

[344] Cf. Mt 6:10.

[345] Javier Sotil, from Brazil where he was itinerant catechist, 1973-1982.

Thank you, my Jesus. Already in Arcinazzo. What energy. I feel free, my Jesus. Let your will be done.[346]

(Arcinazzo, September 11, 1980)

372. Penitential. Inspirations. My Jesus! Questionnaire, experiences. Night: pastors. Lord!

(Arcinazzo, September 12, 1980)

373. Sermon on the Mount… new, Sweet Jesus.

(Arcinazzo, September 13, 1980)

374. Arcinazzo – Eucharist. Exaltation of the Cross. Sweet Jesus, St. Paul moves me.

Merkaba. Miracle of miracles, until 12 midnight.

In Santa Marinella. It's almost dawn.

(Santa Marinella, September 15, 1980)

375. You have consoled me. Sweet one, your sweetness pours out. Thank you, Jesus. My heart races from the consolation.

Jesus, you snatch from Hell. Thank you, my Jesus. Suffering opens my heart to generosity. Thank you, Jesus.

(Santa Marinella, September 15, 1980)

376. Magnificent September. I'm going a mile a minute: family, planning and planning, and Rome, and alone, and architects, and Fr. Maximino, and so many telephone calls, and sleepiness… my Jesus, You console me to the depths of my heart. Thank you, Jesus.

(Santa Marinella, September 16, 1980)

377. Santa Marinella – Last swim. Wonderful.

Always leaving. My heart breaks from all the hurrying. Flight. I'm happy, my Jesus.

Madrid – Home. Government. Television. My Jesus, give me courage, detachment. I love you. The convivence… My Jesus.

(Madrid, September 17, 1980)

---

[346] Cf. Mt. 6:10.

Carmen in Jerusalem

378. Madrid – Zaragoza – Spanish Catechists Convivence. Technical College. My Jesus, serenity, hoping for your manifestation.

(Zaragoza, September 18, 1980)

379. Penitential. My pride stings from Kiko's encroachment. Thank you, Lord, for allowing me to yield to him and go to confession. Joy. I already see your manifestation.

Teams, questionnaire. Your presence, Lord, has brought wonderful communion. The demons submit.[347] Fight, my Jesus. Priest from Navarra... My heart races: "history"... thank you, Lord.

(September 19, 1980)

380. Saturday. Lauds. I speak bluntly and all over the place, but I speak: *Yom Kippur*. Thinking of Jerusalem, the sound of the *shofar*. Sweet one, Jesus, Lamb of God... Your people.

Afternoon. Experiences. Pastors, my Jesus.

Eucharist. Money, my Jesus! I wait for you, I love you, help me.

(Zaragoza, September 20, 1980)

381. Sunday. *Merkaba*. End of convivence. From miracle to miracle. Thank you, My Jesus for the courage you give me.

(Zaragoza, September 21, 1980)

382. Zaragoza. "El Pilar." Travel to Pamplona *(seminary)*. Merche Goicoechea.[348] Memories... history... Hotel food: Rosario Montagut,[349] General; María Ángel Sagristá,[350] Vice general. Miguel Flamarique.[351] Javier. History... memories...

We continue our trip toward Madrid. Ólvega. Cemetery. My Jesus, Castilla in the evening, Sierra, Moncayo.

Madrid. Night. Meeting at the Center. "The 18." You are always present. Blessed are you.

(Madrid, September 22, 1980)

---

[347] Cf. Lk 10:20.

[348] Carmen's companion in the *Misioneras de Cristo Jesús*.

[349] Carmen writes "Montserrat Montagut."

[350] From the *Misioneras de Cristo Jesús*.

[351] Presbyter from the first community from the parish of *San Jorge* in Pamplona.

383. Narváez. We leave for Alocén. Always departing in a rush.

Evening. Lake of Entrepeñas. My Jesus, calm my excitement. You console me like you did when I was young. You renew my strength, courage, joy. Thank you, my Jesus. Iran-Iraq war.

(Alocén, September 23, 1980)

384. In Sacedón.[352] Sweet one, you wake me up full of energy. Always departing.

Madrid. Already three when you begin to calm me down. Calm me down, Lord. Shrink this mountain of papers and books. I love you.

(Madrid, September 24, 1980)

385. Paris. Hotel. You preceded us there, My Jesus. You make everything perfect. Is it France's hour? Thank you, Jesus.

(Paris, September 25, 1980)

386. Penitential. My Jesus, you give me courage. You inspire Kiko in French. Thank you, Jesus for freedom. You are powerful, the Only one. Thank you, Lord.

(Paris, September 26, 1980)

387. Sermon on the Mount in the open field. Experiences. Eucharist. My Jesus, you console me, you give the wild ox's strength.[353]

(Paris, September 27, 1980)

388. So tired. The *merkaba* revives me. My Jesus, I love you. Collection. Miracles. Very late dinner.

(Paris, September 28, 1980)

389. Day off. My "engine" is racing. I get up early and go non-stop. My Jesus, calm me down. I love you. Thank you, my Jesus. You have freed me. I love you.

(Paris September 29, 1980)

---

[352] Township of the Province of Guadalajara, near Alocén.
[353] Cf. Ps 92:10.

390. "While you are sleeping, the wings of the dove are covered in silver, and its feathers with sparkling gold."[354] My sweet Jesus, your love resounds in my heart, the consolations of your indescribable presence. My Jesus, it is indescribable how you revealed yourself to me in the depths of these many years of suffering. Sweetest Jesus, your Spirit covers with silver your mysterious, secret, powerful, great actions. Great, eternal, your Love. I prostrate myself before You, Lord. You have convinced me of sin. You are stronger. You love me. I love you too, Lord. Don't leave me.

(Paris, September 30, 1980)

391. You wake me up, full of vigor. My Jesus, I would like to be alone with you. I love you.

So many visits… phone calls… my Jesus, mighty, with power, I love you.

Travel to Madrid – Alocén. My Jesus, thank you. Sweet one, I love you.

(Alocén, October 1, 1980)

392. You are wonderful, generous, limitless in everything: the figs, the tomatoes. My Jesus, I love you.

(Alocén, October 2, 1980)

393. I'm still 'running', like the green car that the motor keeps running even when you turn the key off. October 3rd. Javier in my heart: history, memorial of your presence, of your action, of your election, of your faithfulness. Holy, Holy, Holy. You are, Lord. You are. Your most sweet love, my Jesus. You console me like in the days of my youth. The darkness, the gloom, the sin, haven't been able to cancel your great covenant on that day I went out the window and your sweet Ascension of life and Life eternal.[355] My Jesus, everything is possible for You,[356] and I love you because your Love is as strong as death.[357]

---

[354] Cf. Ps 68:13.

[355] She is referring to the dream she had, of a mystical nature, during the month-long spiritual exercises in Javier.

[356] Cf. Mt 19:26.

[357] Cf. Sg 8:6.

I'm going to Sacedón with Diego.³⁵⁸ I've told him about the thousand things that are bouncing around in my memory like a volcano of your love. I love you, My Jesus. Calm me down, help me. I love you. It's almost six already. Night is falling. I love you.

(Alocén, October 3, 1980)

394. St. Francis of Assisi.

Jesus, at dawn you awaken me with your most sweet and consoling presence. You are and life awakens to eternity, and detaches from everything with freedom, with uncontainable joy. Thank you, Jesus. Your grace is worth more than life.³⁵⁹ I praise you. Blessed are you! You have visited me. I'm moved, my Jesus. I'm not worthy. Truly it's right to sing that you are holy. I love you, my Jesus. You did not let my feet stumble.³⁶⁰ I love you.

José Agudo and Josemari Garciandía³⁶¹ come. You give me the strength of a wild ox,³⁶² my Jesus. I'm a pathetic person who doesn't deserve you. Thank you, Jesus.

Good news: Dadaglio³⁶³ at Worship. You are great, Lord. You lead this catechumenal history as you do your people.

(Alocén, October 4, 1980)

395. Leaving already. Always on the move, my Jesus. To Rome.

(Alocén, October 5, 1980)

396. Convivence of married couples at the Ergife. My Jesus, I'm hurt a bit by the day, which was one of frustration, or rather, of incomplete triumph.

(Rome, October 6, 1980)

---

[358] Diego Martínez.
[359] Cf. Ps 63:3.
[360] Cf. Ps 66:9.
[361] José Mari Garciandía (pb) from the first community of the Neocatechumenal Center in Madrid.
[362] Cf. Ps 92:10.
[363] Cardinal Luigi Dadaglio (†), Apostolic Nuncio to Spain, 1967-1980. Secretary of the Congregation for the Divine Worship and the Discipline of the Sacraments, 1980-1984.

397. Ergife. Big mob of people, my Jesus, I almost get really angry, but I feel free. My Jesus, this "fever" has passed. My soul is serene. Help us. Let your Word be fulfilled,[364] Lord, my love.

(Rome, October 10, 1980)

398. Ergife. Fifty Bishops. My Jesus, almost a parallel Synod… I'm moved by your faithfulness. How your promises are fulfilled. You are faithful, great, Lord. You are. Sweet Lord, I love you for your great name. Lord, I love you.

(Rome, October 11, 1980)

399. Mass for the families in the Vatican. My Jesus, rain, rain, rain. Happy.

Pope Paul IV hall (Sala Nervi): "parade" of "wonderful" married couples… my Jesus, have mercy on the Church, on the Pope… my Jesus, you allay my passing daydreams with reality. Better. Jesus, You are. I wait for You, I love you. Thank you, Jesus, for so much Love.

(Rome October 12, 1980)

400. They're all happy. My Jesus, I'm very happy. You anoint me with new oil; you give me the strength of a wild ox.[365] You fill me with consolation, my sweet Jesus. Battle-ready, alive. The night of anguish seems but a dream to me. My Jesus, remember those who are sad. Shine your life on us. I love you. Thank you, Lord. I would sing to you my joy; which is yours, Lord. I feel like I'm dreaming. I love you. Piazza Trastevere all day. Thank you, my Jesus. Night.

(Rome, October 13, 1980)

401. Phone call to Magee.[366] The Pope in meetings with Central America.

Anxiety, phone calls, preparations… Is disappointment coming? No. I'm so happy. My Jesus, your ways always surpass our ways.[367] Thank you for the joy you are giving me. I love you, My Jesus.

(October 14, 1980)

---

[364] Cf. Lk 1:38.

[365] Cf. Ps 92:10.

[366] Mons. John Magee, MSF, Bishop of Cloyne, Ireland, 1987-2010, then second personal secretary of Pope St. John Paul II, 1978-1982.

[367] Cf. Is 55:8-9.

402. St. Teresa.

Turmoil, unbridled inspirations, smoke... My Jesus, my head is exploding. I'm disappointed and pretentious, ridiculous. To me, this Church looks like a terrible, monolithic, dogmatic wall... Lord, I love you, have mercy on me, heal me. Return my soul to your peace.[368] I love you, Lord.

(October, 15, 1980)

403. Italian plus European Itinerants.

My Jesus, freedom, consolation, your presence... Sweet one, I love you. I'm moved by your love, your manifestation, faithfully fulfilling your promises from my youth. My Jesus, Lord, my God, immense, great. Lord, I love you too, Sweet one. Your sweet promises, enlightenments from youth come to light for me as I see them being realized. And You exist, You are. Blessed forever.

(Porto San Giorgio, October 16, 1980)

404. European Itinerants.

You open my lips, Lord. Penitential. You come with power.[369] Blessed are you, my Love, sweet one, liberator, Lord! Thank you.

Lord, St. Ignatius, martyr. Martyrdom... My Jesus, only one, powerful, Lord, I love you.

(Porto San Giorgio, October 17, 1980)

405. European Itinerants.

Lord, when I am in your presence, I see you so magnificent, Sweet one, powerful, strong. My God, holy.

"The Lord announces a good news.
The messengers of victory are an immense army.
The kings flee, the armies flee.
Even the women share in the loot."[370]

(Porto San Giorgio, October 18, 1980)

---

[368] Cf. Ps 116:7.
[369] Cf. Is 40:10.
[370] Cf. Ps 68:11-12.

406. Eucharist.

Amalekites.[371] You are powerful, wonderful, Lord. I love you. Thank you for your invincible power.

(Porto San Giorgio, October 19, 1980)

407. *"The messengers of victory are an immense army.*
While you were sleeping within the fences of the sheepfold,
The wings of the dove are covered in silver,
Its feathers with sparkling gold."[372]

My Jesus, David went with all who found themselves in trouble. All those who were in distress, all those in debt, and all those who had a grievance gathered round him and he became their leader. There were about 400 men with him.[373]

After a delay, the *merkaba* departs. So full, and so happy. Lord, you have blessed us with peace.[374]

(Porto San Giorgio, October 20, 1980)

408. Finally free but spent all day on the telephone. Two hours with Amadei.[375] Lord! My sweet Jesus, I stand like a sword, ready for whatever comes on my right or on my left. In your humility, calm me down. I love you.

You console me, Lord, with your being. You, You, You are, wonderful. Lord, faithful to your promises, to your manifestations, to your works. Lord, St. Teresa's fourteen years...[376] Numerically, the same as mine... I love you. Since you consoled me, I no longer know how to write. You are enough. I love you.

(Porto San Giorgio, October 21, 1980)

---

[371] Cf. Ex 17:8-16.
[372] Cf. Ps 68:11.13.
[373] Cf. 1 Sm 22:2.
[374] Cf. Ps 29:11.
[375] Fr. Guglielmo Amadei, SSS (†) presbyter from the first community of the parish of *Nostra Signora del Santissimo Sacramento e Santi Martiri Canadesi*, Rome.
[376] ST. TERESA OF JESUS, *Autobiography*, 2, 4-10.

409. Strength, my Jesus. Truly you renew my youth.[377] Your power is unbelievable energy.

Leaving already; always leaving, without having rested in You for enough time. I love you. I desire it as the only thing,[378] but you shake me up with insights, fights, Bishops, your Church… my Jesus, I love you. How? And the Pope? Should we go, yes or no?[379] Enlighten us. Poor Kiko!

Rome. It's already four in the morning. My Jesus, I love you. Alone…

(Rome, October 22, 1980)

410. Leaving the Synod, Poletti. He takes us in his car to Piazza Campo dei Fiori. My sweet Jesus, so visibly sweet.

Hurry up, my Jesus.

Finally, Fiumicino. To Madrid.

Valle. Itinerants Convivence of Spain and Portugal, and others.

The Samaritan woman.[380] Inspiration flows because of your beauty; your word is gentle and powerful. Yours, Lord, is the inspiration, the Power, the Glory. I'm speechless. My Jesus, don't abandon me, inspire me, help me, so that I may announce your Word without competing with Kiko. So many sufferings lived in this house, and today it's like new. I love you.

(Valle – Madrid, October 23, 1980)

411. Itinerants Convivence – A huge increase in boys, priests. Lord, American panorama. My Jesus, uninspired, presumptuous… humiliated. Jesus, my Jesus. My only interest is you, You. I love you. Have mercy on me. Help me. The inspiration from my delusions of grandeur is gone. Kiko has crushed the few ideas I had and I feel deflated, yet I feel a strong desire, Jesus, to be alone with you, to see you, to love you. Jesus, You. I love you. Help me, inspire me. Come, my Jesus.

(Valle – Madrid, October 24, 1980)

---

[377] Cf. Ps 103:5.

[378] Cf. Lk 10:42.

[379] To the pastoral visit of St. John Paul II to the parish of *Nostra Signora del Santissimo Sacramento e Santi Martiri Canadesi*.

[380] Cf. Jn 4.

412. An intense day. The priests speak. Consolation, my sweet Jesus. Inspiration! The two-edged sword.[381] Strong, powerful, the only one. Eucharist. So full, Jesus.

(October 25, 1980)

413. My Jesus, it's been a day of inspirations against politics. And listening, listening to the girls. What a painful disappointment. My Jesus! All of a sudden all is dark, painful and I don't see anything. Help me. The girls don't seem to have their hearts in it.

(October 26, 1980)

414. Itinerants. It's daytime again. The *merkaba* enlightens me, the teams. The room is of one heart. Lauds, serenity, inspirations. Spain, more enlightenment on many things. My Jesus, finally the *merkaba*: Samoa, Korea, Chicago… I love you, My Sweet Jesus. I love you. You console me deeply. I love you. I'm tired, so happy. Thank you, my Jesus.

Ideas about Itinerants.[382] — Start from St. Paul (it's not me that is saying this): do not change state.[383] Evangelization. It is the encounter with the Risen Christ. There is nothing greater. It cannot be fathomed.

"Standing up"; courage, boys: for celibacy, to incarnate Jesus Christ.

Girls: virginity; not the delusions of feminism. Exclusion? No. Importance. Not the same as men. We are something else. We women possess "the secret of life." Man is at the service of this, and consequently, of the woman. From there we dominate and hold the key: the first ones to let sin in; the first ones to let in the Resurrection, through the announcement. The Samaritan woman, Jesus Christ… the Apostles enter the pagan and heretical world through women.

An exhortation about stability with teams, both within and with those they interact. Without this, Jesus Christ as an experience and a true call is impossible. Also necessary is a well-circumcised heart.[384] And even with it, a team must be for evangelization, not for this life.

---

[381] Cf. Heb 4:12.
[382] Written by Carmen in a diary from 1978 on the pages for June 9-10.
[383] 1 Cor 7:20. 24.
[384] Dt 10:16.

Nothing can be above the evangelization. If it isn't like that, it will be impossible because they will be seeking their daily bread by the sweat of their brows.[385] Good intentions are not enough. The "accidents" of the *merkaba* are serious and painful, for them and for the brothers. And if they recover, they need years of healing and recuperation, with much suffering.

(Valle – Madrid, October 27, 1980)

415. From Valle to Madrid, greatly consoled by the power of your presence in the convivence. Browbeaten all day long: defense, the Pope at *Martiri Canadesi*,[386] phone calls, fighting…

My Jesus, how right you are, "Do not resist evil",[387] and so many apologies, my Jesus…Fr. Antonio Varela,[388] and Calahorra… and running, Lord. Come, come, come. Help Kiko, Jesus, Jesus, Jesus, have mercy on me.

Eurobuilding. So hot. Horrible room. Kiko inspired, but no, we don't leave happy, at least I don't: beaten down, my Jesus.

(Madrid, October 28, 1980)

416. You give me the strength of a wild ox; you anoint me with fresh oil.[389] "Do not resist evil."[390] My sweet Jesus, the denials you suffered.[391] I love you. Sweet Lord, victor over Pharaohs[392] and Hamans.[393] I love you. Your wonderful, powerful presence. You put your power into the Word. Thank you, Lord.

Meeting at the Center. You give me grace, generosity, joy, strength. I love you, Lord. It's late. Two a.m. already. Hyper, joyous. I love you. Good night.

(Madrid, October 29, 1980)

---

[385] Cf. Gn 3:19.
[386] Cf. *infra*, November 2, 1980.
[387] Cf. Mt 5:39.
[388] Mons. Antonio Varela Verástegui (†), pastor of the parish of *San Roque*, Madrid, for 56 years. At the time he was also the episcopal vicar.
[389] Cf. Ps 92:10.
[390] Cf. Mt 5:39.
[391] Cf. Mt 26:34.
[392] Cf. Ex 14:28.
[393] Cf. Est 7:10.

417. My Jesus, miraculously, you wake me up. I love you. Burial of Jose Luis' father.[394] My Jesus, I feel familiar with sister death. Serenity. Morning of uncertainties, combative phone calls, the Pope's visit....[395] My Jesus, you console me. They set a snare for me and fell into it themselves.[396] Luke 7....[397] The Lord catches the wise in their own craftiness.[398]

I love you. Most sweet one, You make justice. *Martiri Canadesi* is neither the beginning nor the end. The boycott… I see how gently you allow things to happen to show your glory and your power, my Jesus.

(Madrid, October 30, 1980)

418. Jesus, how sweet to sing of your faithfulness at dawn. You anoint me with the oil of youth; you awaken me strong as a wild ox.[399] Wonderful in holiness, faithful, invincible, Lord, my Love. I wake from this purifying night as if from a dream. My Sweet Jesus, I love you. I love you, I love you. Because of your grace, I would eternally and tirelessly sing of the faithfulness of your love for man.

I went down to the *Sacramentinos*. Those times with Fr. Baigorri,[400] leaving the university campus after having received you! I love you.

All day battling with a two-edged sword from your hand…[401] Lord, I love you. Everything is possible with you.[402]

At night, with Bellido, in Alocén.

(Alocén, October 31, 1980)

419. In this wonderful panorama, like a lightning flash, "Centro Vallecas", "Palomeras", future parish!

---

[394] José Luis del Palacio, from the first community of the parish of la *Virgen de la Paloma*, Madrid, former Bishop of Callao, Peru.

[395] To the parish of *Nostra Signora del Santissimo Sacramento e Santi Martiri Canadesi*, Rome.

[396] Cf. Ps 57:6.

[397] Cf. Lk 7:35: Wisdom is justified by all her children.

[398] Cf. 1 Cor 3:19.

[399] Cf. Ps 92:10.

[400] Fr. Luis Baigorri, SSS (†).

[401] Cf. Heb 4:12.

[402] Cf. Mt 19:26.

Lord, you anoint us with peace. Blessed are You! You enlighten my life, like illuminating memorials of your magnificent presence. You are, you are here, you are, you are. Blessed are you forever, great, awesome, wonderful. I love you.

Feast of All Saints. You are Holy, the only one, blessed forever.

(Alocén, November 1, 1980)

420. The Pope at *Martiri*. At dawn, glorious with the stars, Alocén – Barajas – Rome. You are more powerful than anyone, Holy, Blessed, and you kept the Pope seated with us for an hour, and you made Kiko speak with holiness, humbly. Jesus, I was acting a little crazy, but free. I told the Pope in his ear, "We love you very much." And he began his speech like this, "I love you." Applause. My Jesus, You are the victor and I love you. Help me.

Holy Father, "May I say a word?"[403]

We love you very much. Father we are in deep communion with You. The same one who gives You power and grace to lead his Church, and who sustained Paul VI in his difficult time, and has led the Second Vatican Council, is also giving you the power and dynamism to carry all this, which is nothing more than the Second Vatican Council in action amongst the people: a new catechumenate, "neocatechumenate," revitalizing the faith – looking toward the atheist world that surrounds us – which is nothing other than the Church plunging into her own Baptism, into the Death and Resurrection of Jesus Christ, and opening an Exodus, a way of Eternal Life.

We are in deep communion. We are nothing more than useless servants,[404] witnesses of the Lord's work.

Paul VI used to say, "They tell me… But they say so many things…" Father, the Accuser exists, Satan,[405] and he passes through the Vatican walls, and tries to separate us with accusations. But the Holy Spirit is the Advocate, the Defender.[406] We hope your guardian angel tells you, "Do not be afraid to take with you 'the catechumenate',

---

[403] Written by Carmen on another diary from 1978, on the page for August 27.
[404] Cf. Lk 17:10.
[405] Cf. Rv 12:9-10.
[406] Cf. Jn 14:16.

Mary, that which has been born in her is the fruit of the Holy Spirit."[407]

We are not a parallel Church.

(Rome, November 2, 1980)

421. Jesus, one in the morning and I'm still trying to pray. All day on the phone. Enthusiasm. You console me deeply. I love you, I love you, most sweet one, incredible. Subdue me, make me gentle, you are wonderful. Put your Word in my mouth. I love you, I love you, I love you. Help me not to smoke. Stop me by contemplating you. The pictures with the Pope...my Jesus, Javier... What a joy, what a pleasure from you of the Resurrection, of life. I love you.

(November 3, 1980)

422. The Pope's saint day. Address to the Cardinals: post-council.[408] Bravo!

Lord, you are great in your works, faithful. I meditate on your promise, I see it in action. You are. My bones rejoice.[409] I love you. My Jesus, you give me the strength of a wild ox.[410] My Jesus, I'm dying to sleep.

(Rome, November 4, 1980)

423. You, My Jesus, are the only one and are always new. I love you.

Afternoon. Center *S. Salvatore* with the communities of the *Traditio*.

My Jesus, tomorrow the trip to Paris. The mess in the house is overwhelming, without rest. I love you.

(Rome, November 5, 1980)

424. Order finally. A terrifying flight from Rome to Paris.

---

[407] Cf. Mt 1:20.

[408] "May the post-conciliar period, so rich in fruits and perspectives, which Providence has also granted us to live through, find us to be far-sighted and intrepid ministers in daily ecclesial service, for the benefit of the People of God, for whom Christ died and is risen."

[409] Cf. Ps 51:8.

[410] Cf. Ps 92:10.

Japanese movie. I like it very much. I see you in everything, You, the Eternal one, immortal, holy.

I'm dying to sleep.

(Paris, November 6, 1980)

425. Convivence. The Samaritan woman at midnight. Inspiration… isn't it coming? My Jesus, without preparing anything. You are wonderful. I love you.

(Chantilly – Paris, November 7, 1980)

426. Lauds. Penitential. Lunch. The Samaritan woman,[411] questionnaire. New will to work. I'm so drowsy. The Eucharist starts at twelve. I've been awake for 18 hours. I complain: the Eucharist is supposed to begin at night fall, it's to enter into the feast, into rest. My Jesus, it was already twelve thirty; I was being stupid: proud, haughty, unbearable, resistant, onerous, unbearable. My Jesus, help me.

(Chantilly – Paris, November 8, 1980)

427. Lauds. Catechesis of the *kerygma*. We finished very happy. Hurray! Lord, I love you. Deeply happy, free. Calm me down. So much happiness, smoking… I love everyone. I love you.

(Chantilly – Paris, November 9, 1980)

428. You are great, Lord, wonderful, the only one. How can I give thanks to your name for your power, your faithfulness, your immense love? Thanks be to you in Jesus Christ, sweet Lord. Through Him, with Him, in Him, all glory and power are Yours forever and ever. I love you, Lord, for your immense love. I will raise the cup of salvation…[412] with your Church. Help the Pope, Lord. Thank you for the great communion you have so graciously provided. Help me. You know the enemy. Strengthen Kiko, help him. You alone are. Blessed are you.

(November 10, 1980)

---

[411] Cf. Jn 4.
[412] Cf. Ps 116:13.

429. Most sweet Consoler. Blessed be your holy name. Sweet Jesus, before you all knees shall bend.[413] I love you, my Jesus. It is sweet to tell you: I am a sinner. It is like singing of your great love, so sweet, faithful, Lord, Savior. You, crucified. Your love is so sweet, powerful, unfathomable, infinite. Thank you, Jesus, thanks be given to you. In him, in your Love, everything is amazing, unfathomable. And You are Eternal. Blessed are you. Good night.

I love you. Thank you, my Jesus. You anoint me with new oil and truly, like the wild ox, I feel an inexplicable strength.[414] You. You are. Blessed are you.

(November 11, 1980)

430. Thank you, Lord. With the earthquake,[415] you make present the deep, deafening sound of the *shofar*, Sinai, and with it, Eternal Life and eschatology. The beginning: Advent. Sweet and terrifying Lord, Just Judge, Loving. The world passes. You, Love. Blessed are you for all time. Eucharist.

(Arcinazzo, November 29, 1980)

431. St. Andrew – you are always present. Blessed are you. I love you. Lord, help me. Keep your hand on my head. Blessed are you. You have brought me so much good… You did it for *me*, You, loyal, with no deceit, discoverer. Thank you, Lord.

(Arcinazzo, November 30, 1980)

432. Meeting at the Center *S. Salvatore*. Northern sector. Advent. Kiko Inspired. New language. Eschatology. Justice. My Jesus, most sweet, I love you.

(Rome, December 1, 1980)

433. Rome – *Firenze* – Highway: amazing views. Your work, Lord, the Creator, the "Only One." I love you.

---

[413] Cf. Phil 2:10.
[414] Cf. Ps 92:10.
[415] On November 23, 1980 there was an earthquake the region of Irpinia in the south of Italy, causing almost 3,000 casualties.

Meeting at the Center. "Shofar", Advent, eschatology, "acorn."[416] Lord, I love you. The years are passing. These Florentines... You are, Lord. Blessed, great. My life is serene in You, Holy, unmovable rock. I love you.

Today I finished reading the encyclical *Dives in Misericordia*.[417] You, Lord. I love you.

(Florence, December 4, 1980)

434. Good meeting with the pastor of *Martiri*.[418] Operation "earthquake."[419] I never stop and am happy. I love you. Sweet Jesus, I love you.

It is already late at night. I love you. If you would free me from this tobacco... I love you. Wake me up in you. I love you.

(Rome, December 10, 1980)

435. Rome – Madrid – You, wonderful in history. Lord, Only One, I love you.

The Madrid Center. You are great in all things, splendid. Thank you, Lord, I love you. Prayer. Wake me up. I love you.

(Madrid, December 11, 1980)

436. Madrid – Rome – Waiting, anxious. Why? Lord, defend us. *Gaudete* Sunday. Joy, my Jesus, I love you.

(Rome, December 13, 1980)

437. The Pope at *Natività*. Consolation, Jesus. He treats us with love, with deep understanding. We are happy. Blessed are you, Jesus, Holy.

(Rome, December 14, 1980)

---

[416] Analogy: acorn = the current reality; oak = the eschatological reality.
[417] Published November 30, 1980.
[418] Fr. Paolo Sirio, SSS (†).
[419] After the November 23 earthquake in Irpinia (Italy), Kiko and Carmen formed a team to bring a word of hope and evangelization to those hurt by the earthquake (Fr. Ezechiele Pasotti, Fr. Elia Pitozzi, Fr. Giuseppe Giuli and Antonio Voltaggio).

438. Jesus, Wise, poor, the only one, I love you. You know all things and You gladden our hearts. You are here. You are here and are the Victor in history.

(December 15, 1980)

439. Order in the library. I am happy, I'm even free of books, of the house, of everything because I feel You, Sweet One. "Your hearts will rejoice."[420] Sweet Jesus, the hoped for, prophesied, most sweet Lamb of God. I cling to your salvation, I hope. I love you. Thank you, Jesus Savior. The Only One. You, the Eternal One.

(Rome, December 16, 1980)

440. Your great generosity. My Jesus, between the phone and other things… Prayer. Sweet Jesus, so generous, great, the only one, I love you.

(Santa Marinella, December 18, 1980)

441. All day running after things, without praying, without reading… My Jesus, as if you had abandoned me. I am left with no consolation, insipid. Anyway, my Jesus, come, come, come, return. I love you.

(Santa Marinella, December 22, 1980)

442. You anoint me with strength, with activity. Thank you. Rome: chancery, Poletti, Riva. I was terrible. Lord, I love you. Stronger than everyone, the Holy Spirit. Fr. Maximino, excellent. Tomko, fair. I attack… my Jesus, I run around like a crazy person. And faith in your victory… Beware.

(December 23, 1980)

443. Diego, Stefano, Gregorio. All day running around. Preparations. A new color TV. I'm crazy, the generosity makes me "*escorbútica*"…

My Jesus, I love you. The sweetness of Christmas deeply resounds in me. It moves me interiorly. I see everything like this, like it is,

---

[420] Jn 16:22.

believable. Incredible, because you are so wonderful, wonderful prince.[421] Your love, so sweet, eternal, Lord.

(Santa Marinella, December 24, 1980)

444. Message from the Pope. Brave. I love you, Lord. Fr. Maximino and "the 12" come. My Jesus, I love you. Great dinner. I attack: Israel is alive today, the Church, terrible... we almost come to blows...

(December 25, 1980)

445. St. Stephen. My Jesus, I'm moved by St. Stephen. You, great in your Church. I love you. You free me. Sanctify me.

(December 26, 1980)

446. We welcome the year overwhelmed by your blessings, by your generosity, by your splendor, sweet Lord, Alpha and Omega.[422] Midnight in the middle of the anaphora. Sweet Jesus, I love you. You surpass time, Jesus, faithful and sweet one, one who fulfills promises. I love you.

(Santa Marinella, December 31, 1980)

---

[421] Cf. Is 9:5.
[422] Cf. Rv 1:8.

1981[423]

---

[423] On the cover of the diary from 1981, Carmen wrote, "Difficult year up through September. October, November, December: consolation." She continues on a separate piece of paper making a summary of the year 1981: January: some sparks [of serenity]; February: some sadness, Jerusalem – a place; March: tight; April: terrible mornings, peaceful nights; May – June – July – August – September: bad; October: good, energy; November: good, courage.

447. I enter the new year in the Liturgy with the earthquake team and Kiko, Stefano, Gregorio and Diego.

This is how you must bless them:
the Lord bless you and protect you;
the Lord make <u>his face</u> shine upon you and be gracious to you;
the Lord turn <u>his face</u> toward you and give you peace.
This is how they must invoke <u>my name</u> ... and I shall bless them (Nm 6:23-27).

Sweet "Jesus." Sweet is your name, your power. You... teach me to bless, put your name and your sweetness on my lips, in my heart. I love you, most sweet, wonderful one, splendid in everything. Thank you, Jesus, for your Love. Year of liberation through your power, and you repropose it to me in the middle of the night. Thank you, faithful, present, Savior, Jesus.[424]

(Santa Marinella, January 1, 1981)

448. You anoint me with strength, with courage, with life, and I love you. Thank you, my Jesus, for secretly calling me to prayer. You calm my life, the future, with the fullness of your loving presence. I love you. Clothe me with the deepest recesses of your mercy, of blessing.

"Blessed the man who cares for the weak. The Lord will sustain him on his bed of pain. He will relieve him of his illness."[425]

I'm hateful, attacking everyone and everything. Have mercy on me. Clothe me in the depths of your being, my Jesus. I love you.

---

[424] On a loose page of a third diary from 1981 on the page for January 1, Carmen wrote the same texts with some variations: "My Sweet 'Jesus.' Sweet is your name, your power, You. Teach me to bless, put your name and your sweetness on my lips and in my heart. I love you, most sweet, wonderful one, splendid in everything. Thank you, Jesus, for your Love, for this past year's sufferings of my powerful liberation, in this house. You have given me a way out to freedom; *and tonight, you present it to me again, in the middle of the night.* Thank you, Jesus, faithful, present, Savior. Jesus."

[425] Cf. Ps 41:1.3.

Since your visits, I'm no longer interested in writing. Thank you because you have pulled me out of the pit of *Sheol*, of anguish. How incredible the darkness, the suffering. Thank you, Jesus, Savior, Savior. Jesus, put your name in my heart.[426]

(Santa Marinella, January 2, 1981)

449. My Jesus, I love you. I would sing your name all day long. Blessed are you. Why, Lord, this vitality, and at the same time, I'm being hateful? I'm exasperating Kiko. Terrible attack. Always icons. I'm horrified. Lord, have mercy. The mystery of each one of us is in your hands, Jesus!

I'm going to Rome. Books, books, books… for what? My Jesus, you are my surroundings, my life. In you, the only book I need, the only love. Powerful, holy, improvisor. The Lord is the Spirit.[427]

(Rome, January 3, 1981)

450. Return to Santa Marinella – Lord, I sleep, sleep, sleep… Sleep treatment: 10 uninterrupted hours. I'm surrounded by papers, books, all kinds of things, mountains, with nothing but time now, so many things that I would like to dive into with you, and suddenly you so cleverly free up my time. You cannot be contained in any interesting book or magazine. I feel like throwing it all out and contemplating you in the sweetness of existing, of being, of living, of loving you in your most sweet name. Jesus, mysterious, unique, holy, I love you!

(Santa Marinella, January 4, 1981)

451. Engrossed in *La Maison-Dieu*[428] all day. Happy. Jesus, I want to sell everything. Many things overwhelm me. Why? I love you.

(Santa Marinella, January 5, 1981)

---

[426] On a loose page of a third diary from 1981 on the page for January 2nd, Carmen wrote the same texts with some variations, "I am hateful when I attack. Have mercy on me. Wrap me in the deep recesses of your mercy, my Jesus. I love you. Since your visits, I haven't been interested in writing. Thank you for pulling me out of the anguish of the pit of *Sheol*, unbelievable. The darkness, the suffering. Thank you, Jesus, 'Savior', 'Savior.' Jesus, put your name in my heart."

[427] Cf. 2 Cor 3:17.

[428] *La Maison-Dieu*, a monthly periodical on liturgical pastoral care.

452. Epiphany in the Vatican, and for me, here in Santa Marinella. The star. Jesus, they adored you. That is what I want: to prostrate myself before You, mysterious, "a child." Sweet Virgin Mary, why do I worry, why do I agitate myself, why am I "*escorbútica*"? All day I look like a muleteer, stupidly poking. Why? Sweet Virgin Mary, sweet Jesus.

Meeting of "the 18." Jesus, for you, everything is possible.[429] Jesus, help me.

(Santa Marinella, January 6, 1981)

453. Almost time to leave. I start working at four with enjoyment. *Eucharist,* Bouyer.[430] The star glimmers sweetly. My Jesus, I get serious right when I'm about to leave. What I wanted to do the entire vacation, you only allow me on the last day. Why?

"Lost sheep," phone, directories, meetings, guests… My Jesus, like a muleteer, goading with the whip all day long. Why? And smoking… Jesus, put your name, your blessing in my heart. And prayer? I'm so stupid, no time… My Jesus, the only one necessary,[431] help me.

(Santa Marinella, January 7, 1981)

454. Last day in Santa Marinella. Always leaving. Hurry, mountains of things, of bags, hoarding, and no time. Books come and go, waiting… for what? My Jesus, you are free, the only one! Lord, I love you.

Travel to Porto San Giorgio. Itinerants convivence. Snow, snow, storm. The car breaks down. Taxi. Already here. Porto San Giorgio, so beautiful. The "*conventino*"[432] is beautiful. Free. Freedom and grace are in the air. My Jesus, You are so gracious. My back hurts so much… and I love you. Help me to bless, not to make life impossible and difficult.

(Porto San Giorgio, January 8, 1981)

---

[429] Cf. Mt 19:26.

[430] L. Bouyer, *Eucharist: Theology and Spirituality of the Prayer of the Eucharist* (Indiana: Notre Dame Press, 1968).

[431] Cf. Lk 10:42.

[432] Complex of small cells at the International Neocatechumenal Center.

455. Italian-European Itinerants Convivence. Kiko turns 42.

My Jesus, peace. I bless you with blessings, blessing people without attacking them. Grant me the serenity of heart in the face of all this mess that You lead and that proceeds on its own, in communion, in obedience, in freedom. Lombardy without the Eucharist, the sterility of Denmark ... you know all things. You direct it all with a wisdom that surpasses us. All things are in your hands. Blessed are you. I love you, my Jesus.

(Porto San Giorgio, January 9, 1981)

456. The convivence of itinerant teams continues.

My Jesus, mysterious. Kiko, inspired. In your presence, I become nothing, I disappear. Suddenly without any grace, sunk into devastating muteness. Why? How? Now I'm incapable of opening my mouth for anything, my Jesus.

Eucharist. I want to escape alone with you. And I can't stand Kiko. My Jesus, how is this possible? Come, come.

(Porto San Giorgio, January 10, 1981)

457. I get up, going against the current. The convivence never ends. I'm absent, mute and sad; not sad, but hollow, with no enthusiasm and as one to whom none of this pertains. Jesus, You alone interest me. Where are you? My Jesus, mysterious, holy, only one, have mercy on me. And it's one in the morning. Turin. Everything is possible.

(Porto San Giorgio, January 11, 1981)

458. Leave Porto San Giorgio – Travel to Turin, parish of *S. Francisco de Paola*, meeting with priests.

Night. Ivrea. My Jesus, we build castles in the air: priests, persecutions, Bellestrero.[433] It all seems like smoke to me, ghosts, nonsense. You are. You and only You. Blessed are you.

(Ivrea, January 12, 1981)

---

[433] Cardinal Anastasio Ballestrero, OCD (†), Archbishop of Turin, 1977-1989. President of the Italian Bishops' Conference, 1979-1985.

459. Ivrea – Milan – Seminary. Pastors. You allow me to speak: Eucharist, Council, "take, all of you, and drink."[434] My Jesus, most sweet one, a covenant in your Blood. Holy, blessed are you.

Night in Milan. I feel itinerant. Joy, my Jesus.

(Milan, January 13, 1981)

460. Milan – Curia. Kiko makes me rush like crazy, with no time. My Jesus, it makes me so angry, but I feel free.

Travel to Ivrea. Return. Bettazzi. Lord, You close eyes and You open them. So obvious, and I see nothing. When You want. Blessed be your name and power.

It is necessary to form small communities (essential today as we are confronted with individualism, mass society and the weakness of the family), an integral nucleus for action and realization, in everything. To make love and communion visible.

How to create the community? The Eucharist is essential to the community and vice-versa. The Eucharist in its fullness: Wine, Chalice, Covenant. Why was the wine lost? Practical reasons, contagion, etc. The Chalice, the signs, the participation are very important, this is the refrain of the whole Constitution:[435] to better and actively participate in the Mystery.

Why do you say it's a parallel church? What makes it the Church? What makes it parallel? Would it not be better to say "ferment of renewal, of creation, of communion, of truly communitarian relationships among each other (people) and with the head (presbyter)?"

(Ivrea, January 14, 1981)

461. Ivrea – Milan, airport – Spain.

El Escorial. Spain-Portugal Itinerants Convivence – It's like a blessing, my Jesus, the communion, waiting for your presence. Holy gospel: a leper.[436] Your hand, most sweet, holy, sanctifying, unique.

---

[434] Cf. Mt 26:27.

[435] *Sacrosanctum Concilium*, Constitution on the Holy Liturgy, Vatican Council II.

[436] Cf. Mk 1:35-45.

You don't want to inspire me. Kiko goes into orbit and now I I feel left out. Jesus, how long? Leprosy. Jesus!

(El Escorial, January 15, 1981)

462. Itinerants Convivence – I cannot drag myself out of bed. Suddenly you open my mouth, you defend me in Kiko's domain. You allow me to announce your Word. Thank you, Jesus, I don't deserve to utter your name. Holy, blessed are you. Day of peace, of inner fullness. Your presence, blessed are you. Jesus, everything is possible to you.[437]

(El Escorial, January 16, 1981)

463. Itinerants Convivence – Team after team. Death of the Capuchin from Asturias.[438] Heart attack. My Jesus, listening all day. You act in Jacob.[439] I feel peace, freedom in your works, my Jesus.

In the morning, the Word enlightens me like a light saber, a sharp edge that sweetly cuts me and then calls to me. In the evening, stuffed from dinner.

The Eucharist. You. Everything can be seen without color or charm, or mystery… my Jesus, I see how everything is charming when you want.

(El Escorial, January 17, 1981)

464. Itinerants Convivence – Sunday. Lauds. Re-make the teams. The Pope's news. Argüelles. House of the Sacred Hearts. History… You are always surprising. You take the seed to the Orient, to the farthest islands. Mighty Jesus, I love you. Everything seems decadent, except You in our midst.

(El Escorial, January 18, 1981)

465. Curia. *Palomeras* plans. In any case, they've lost control of the Church. Lord, I see many things that would be terrifying, were You

---

[437] Cf. Mt 19:26.

[438] Fr. Luis Dueñas de la Torre (†), pastor of the parish of *Nuestra Señora del Rocío*, Huelva, presbyter for the itinerant team in Asturias. He died November 1, 1980.

[439] Cf. Ps 59:13.

not the Victor and already Victorious. My Jesus, mysterious, holy. If you would free me from cigarettes… my Jesus, Peace. Come.

(Madrid, January 19, 1981)

466. Elisa's house. Books, folders… I sleep alone, but You fill this heart with your most sweet presence. Thank you, Lord, liberator, wonderful, holy. Everything is possible for You.[440]

(Madrid, January 20, 1981)

467. I wake in Elisa's house. Happy. My Jesus, I waste so much time smoking and spend so little being with you. You are always with me. Jesus, since everything is possible for You,[441] free me from smoking! I love you.

Night. Meeting at the center. Communion. Dinner. Joy. Thank you, my Jesus, I love you.

(Madrid, January 21, 1981)

468. Travel from Madrid to Rome with a stop in Barcelona. Forced change of routes… In Barcelona we missed the plane to Rome because of Ignacio.[442] They were waiting for us in Rome at *Martiri Canadesi* at 9 p.m. And so? You, Lord, direct life. Blessed be your power.

Barcelona. Meeting because of the forced landing. Lord, You love each sheep.[443] You see the wolf and defend them.[444] Blessed are you. The assembly of the people… Jesus, how much patience…

(January 22, 1981)

---

[440] Cf. Mt 19:26.

[441] Cf. ibid.

[442] In order to speak with Ignacio Baixeras from the first community of Barcelona. After many years in the parish of *Maria Auxiliadora* in Barcelona, the community is today in the parish of *Santas Juliana y Sempronia*, San Adrian de Besós.

[443] Cf. Jn 10:11.

[444] Cf. Jn 10:12-14.

469. Barcelona. Morning, sword in hand: Isidoro, Carlos, Ignacio[445]… You, present, strong and holy. My Jesus, your outstretched arm.[446] Confronting all this terror. Merciful. Blessed are you.

Rome. Maura's house.

Arcinazzo. Sudden change: the man blind from birth.[447] My inspiration, many brothers, the itinerants… you console me. Blessed. Thank you, Lord.

(Arcinazzo, January 23, 1981)

470. *Traditio* Convivence. Ivrea, third *Firenze*, *S. Giovanni*, *Lourdes*, *S. Ireneo*,[448] etc.

Morning, Lauds. You release me and console my heart. Sweet one. Afterward, *kerygma*. Scattered in too many points. Exhausting day. I can't go on. Eucharist. Bland for me… and distant. I desire to escape with you in a blessed ascension, Jesus.

(Arcinazzo, January 24, 1981)

471. *Traditio* Convivence.

Lauds. Kiko inspired, and I'm glad. Jesus…. so long. Very tired. Can't believe it: the end of the convivence. Excellent collection. You console me. Then problems and problems… My Jesus, you are holy, so generous in mercy, holy. My Jesus.

(Arcinazzo, January 25, 1981)

472. Free. Joy upon waking. You console me with your presence. Prayer. The sweetest of my goods, free. You know all things. You are Eternal and you love me, what do I care about the rest of the world or of any future? You are my present and my future. I love you. Lord, strengthen my frailty, my head. Come Jesus.

(Rome, January 26, 1981)

---

[445] Isidoro Duran (†), Carlos Olive, Ignacio Baixeras, from the first community of Barcelona, today in the parish of *Santas Juliana and Sempronia*, San Adrian de Besós.

[446] Cf. Acts 13:17.

[447] Jn 9.

[448] Parish of *San Ireneo* in Centocelle, Rome.

473. I wake up unsettled. I'm not here. Nor are the books, nor anything stable. I am sad, my Jesus.

Travel to *Firenze* for the dialogue on the blind man from birth with the third community. The sadness of the ghosts grips me and makes me sad. You teach me what faithfulness is, what sin is, deception, hypocrisy. My Jesus, You, Faithful, forgiving, the only one, the Faithful One. Everything is possible for You.[449] Resurrection. Life. My Jesus, set my feet upon the rock,[450] in You.

(Florence, January 27, 1981)

474. Jesus, I wake up looking for you. In You alone is regeneration, serenity, the future. You alone are. Help me, make my life happy. Teach me to forgive and to recognize my body of slavery and sin.[451] I love you. You who put up with my infidelities. You, always faithful. I love you. Help me. Meeting in *S. Martino*[452] with the third community in *Firenze*. My Jesus.

(Florence, January 28, 1981)

475. I get up with no desire to return to Rome, like someone who doesn't have a place to stay and as if my axis has shifted. Why? Only You Lord are the axis, the equilibrium, the life of my existence. Make me happy with injustice, open my eyes, Lord!

Travel to Rome. Viterbo. Duomo of *S. Lorenzo*. Restaurant. Lord, You love each and every man. I don't understand them.

(Rome, January 29, 1981)

476. My Jesus, all day long running from home and worried. The itinerants, the teams, the Way all come toppling down. I don't trust anyone or anything, and the sadness enters my heart and comes out of my eyes.

Center *S. Salvatore*. I breathe a little easier, my Jesus, faithful. Help me have faith in your faithfulness. I hope in You. Come.

(Rome, January 30, 1981)

---

[449] Cf. Mt 19:26.
[450] Cf. Ps 40:2.
[451] Cf. Rom 6:6.
[452] Church of *San Martino alla Palma* in Scandicci, Florence.

477. Visit to the first of *Sta. Francesca*. History. Argüelles. Eucharist. Dinner.

My Jesus, fighting in the morning. Ghosts and distrust. You, Lord, the only answer for the storm, calming one, free. Jesus, liberator, the only one, my love, dispel my fears. And so? You command the waters.[453] Thank you, my Jesus, help me. Your voice quiets, mutes, Jesus.

(Rome, January 31, 1981)

478. Sunday. Pope's Angelus. My papalism is passing: broken radio, less interest. All of a sudden, the tiniest suspicion rises up like a ghost of death, of pain, of irreparable pain. Jesus, it's not possible to live in distrust, heal me, free me. And then that community... All terrible. But to sustain so many people in communion is your wonderful work, sweet Lord. I love you. Help me.

(Rome, February 1, 1981)

479. In Maura's house. Like in a telephone prison, my Jesus, faithful, unwavering. I love you. Free me, my Jesus, have mercy.

(Rome, February 2, 1981)

480. I seek you in the morning, my Jesus.[454] Savior, ever faithful, deliver me from the present and the future. Life and Love are in You. You are, Lord, and your name is Jesus, Savior. My Life, I love you. Let your name shine upon me. Consoler, free, help me.

Parish of the *Natività*. Surprises, sadness. Lord Jesus, what a failure, what pain. Dark outlook. You groan powerfully within me. I love you. My Jesus, your power is in the Church. Let it be done according to your will.[455]

(Rome, February 3, 1981)

---

[453] Cf. Mt 8:27.
[454] Cf. Is 26:9.
[455] Cf. Mt 6:10.

Carmen at the Holy Sepulcher

481. Travel Rome – *Firenze* – with a broken heart. Sorrows of defeat. *Natività*… as if everything crumbled. Lord, you no longer march with our armies.[456]

Florence meeting good, excellent. Your presence encourages me, the spirit of the Way with which you have always accompanied me. Blessed are you. Sleeping so late… my Jesus, blessed are you.

(Florence, February 4, 1981)

482. I could sleep all morning, my Jesus. Those wonderful, free mornings. Come! I'm sleepy. Fr. Dino. Car broke down. Meeting with the found sheep. End of the scrutiny. Good. We will return for the rite.

Travel to Rome. Arrive in Rome at five in the morning. Help me in this house, do not torment me. Come, my Jesus, help me, forgiver, holy. Tomorrow *Natività*. Help me.

(Rome, February 5, 1981)

483. Sleepy. My Jesus, dragged out of bed to go to the *Natività* to meet the priests. We get there late. All of a sudden, a possibility in the impossible. My Jesus, this house makes me sad. *S. Luigi* in the evening. Difficult, it's all difficult, poor, impossible. My Jesus, everything is possible for you.[457] Manifest your presence. Come, Jesus. Everything seems stalled, with no hope, finished. My Jesus, I love you, come.

(Rome, February 6, 1981)

484. First *Martiri*. My Jesus, mysterious. What will you do here? Dispersed? Jesus, your ways are not ours.[458] You, Lord. Eucharist. The community is happy, in communion. My Jesus.

(Rome, February 7, 1981)

485. Rest. Day off. My Jesus, it flies by. Tomorrow, Jerusalem. Nothing interests me. A sadness comes over me. I feel swollen and sad, my Jesus, like one who doesn't exist. Death. Sweet one, my love,

---

[456] Cf. Ps 44:9; 60:10; 108:11.
[457] Cf. Mt 19:26.
[458] Cf. Is 55:8-9.

come, You. Let your face shine,[459] joy, on my poor heart that is lonely, rich. My Jesus, liberator, love of my youth, nothing does anything for me.

(Rome, February 8, 1981)

486. Travel Rome – Jerusalem – Sleep in Notre Dame. My Jesus, You alone know all things. The old times of your unique and wonderful love... My Jesus, the old times seem better when I had nothing in my hands. It was a promise. And today I walk around with so much financial support, and I'm sad. Nothing interests me, not even Jerusalem. How is this possible? My Jesus, come, wake me.

(Jerusalem, February 9, 1981)

487. New Custodian: Mancini.[460] Delfinato.[461] Holy Sepulcher. Wailing Wall. Armenian quarter...Wow, Lord, this Jerusalem has changed. Architectural tour. Mount Scopus. Abuna Butros.[462] Facing the desert, a voice to my disillusioned heart. My Jesus, it's half past midnight. I can't sleep and I'm hungry. My Jesus, all this land...

(Jerusalem, February 10, 1981)

488. Nighttime crisis. Crisis on top of crisis. The stinginess of my heart. The pain of money, of life. My father.[463] The impossible. Here, wildly spending unearned money. My Jesus, architects, lawyers, the languages, the Arabs, the market from 300 to 100, the deceit... My Jesus, to escape... where to? All your land seems like hell...

(Jerusalem, February 11, 1981)

---

[459] Cf. Ps 80:3.7.19; 119:135.

[460] Fr. Ignazio Mancini, OFM (†), Custodian of the Holy Land, 1980-1986.

[461] This is what Carmen called Brother Delfín Fernández Toboado, OFM (†), her friend since 1964.

[462] In 1974, as a presbyter in Bethlehem, he accompanied the first Neocatechumenal community, then 2001-2008, he was the Syriac Patriarch in Antioch under the name Ignace Pierre VIII (Grégoire) Abdel-Ahad.

[463] Antonio Hernández Villar (†).

489. Jerusalem – Jericho – Nazareth – Lake.

I take rest from my worries in the peace that surrounds the Lake. The Mount.[464] My Jesus, and so? You know all things. You know, and you are able. Come, my Jesus. Show yourself, Jesus.

(February 12, 1981)

490. Nazareth – Tiberias – the Mount once again. Return. Ramallah: team of catechists does me good. Balance. Good. Exhausted arrival to Jerusalem. Notre Dame. In the street with the boxes... my Jesus, give me perfect joy in the depths of my being. My Jesus, what you say is the truth, truly.

(February 13, 1981)

491. My Jesus, Jerusalem, difficult. Everything becomes almost impossible. Running around senselessly. Difficult. Sun. Climb up the Mount of Olives. Descend. Dizzy... all tragic. Finally, Eucharist in the house of Abuna Butros. My Jesus, dinner, 14 children... as soon as the sun is out the heat is unbearable. I am sad.

(Jerusalem, February 14, 1981)

492. Lauds on the terrace of the YMCA.[465] Jerusalem. It doesn't seem impressive to me, white, like it's covered in powder. What a desert. Jesus, pacify my heart a bit. The mystery of your presence in history. My Jesus, money pursues me painfully, constricting me with stinginess... and thieves pursue me... Symbolic! I take refuge in the Holy Sepulcher and at the foot of the Cross. My Jesus, liberator, holy, I love you, help me. King David.[466] Jesus, I'm an obscene penny pincher.

(Jerusalem, February 15, 1981)

---

[464] The Custody of the Holy Land offered the Neocatechumenal Way the possibility to build a formation center to facilitate studies and retreats on land located on the Mount of Beatitudes. This was a project of particular interest for both the Church and Israel. Today it is a miraculous reality called the *Domus Galilaeae International Center.*

[465] Jerusalem International YMCA.

[466] King David Hotel, Jerusalem.

493. Jerusalem – Tel Aviv – Airport – Rome – four in the morning. The house seems like a paradise. My Jesus, priceless things. My Jesus, a comforting bath, but I'm still under pressure, struggling, afraid. My Jesus, everything crumbles into the absurd. If You are not here, the meaning of everything disappears.

(Rome, February 16, 1981)

494. My Jesus, smoking… Meeting with the presbyterate of *Martiri Canadesi*. Meeting with "the 18" in Giampiero's house. Communion, relaxation, my Jesus.

(Rome, February 17, 1981)

495. Rome – *Firenze* – Restlessness. Prepare, why? Kiko improvises. You follow irrational ways, your amusing manifestations, free, loving, Jesus. Rite. Happy. I'm frustrated: you don't allow me to act. But your presence makes me rejoice. Blessed are you. I don't know how to live. Help me to abandon myself.

(Florence, February 18, 1981)

496. *Firenze* – Rome. Restless. Problems. So many lost sheep, my Jesus. I feel overwhelmed. I have no life. I want to live. Gladden me, my Jesus, teach me to live. I smoke like an idiot. Jesus, I love you. Lost in the nothingness. I fall asleep in the car, I arrive exhausted. Rome at three in the morning. Jesus.

(Rome, February 19, 1981)

497. Rome – Madrid – Elisa's house. Valle. It's already three in the morning. My Jesus, I am relieved seeing your presence in the preaching that you give Kiko. I'm mute in the darkness. My Jesus, I woke up bland today, as if I had the measles, and I struggle all day in the dark, without the Star,[467] without direction. My Jesus, at nightfall I can finally breathe. Blessed are you.

(Valle – Madrid, February 20, 1981)

---

[467] Cf. Mt 2:2.9.

498. *Traditio.* My Jesus, you don't inspire me, but I feel freer. Your holiness. You make me want to return to your holiness, to your love. Thank you, Jesus.

(Valle, February 21, 1981)

499. Kiko's catechesis was interminable, but with authority.[468] My Jesus, I look down on this people with distrust. The women seem old, the problems, insurmountable. No time, my Jesus. If You were in everyone, my Jesus, how each thing would change: Barcelona, the sins, the future. Everything overwhelms me as if you didn't exist. Come, Jesus.

(Valle, February 22, 1981)

500. Day off. Alocén. My Jesus, last night I was serene. My Jesus, I'd like to prostrate my heart to you and lift up my eyes to You. Oh, immense creator, oh, immense creator, Lord, Jesus, creator, creator, have mercy on my muteness, my foolishness, my nothingness. Let your creating Spirit come over me. Have mercy. Help me. Everything seems like it's over and impossible. I cannot see the love with which you have blessed and accompanied my life. Open my eyes, Lord. Show yourself. Come, come, come. Gladden my sad life of misery.

Six thirty in the evening: coup in Parliament; military.[469]

(Madrid, February 23, 1981)

501. Radio, TV, repetitive, all saying the same thing, without giving real explanations. How can things like this be possible? My Jesus, I calm myself down recounting my worries to Kiko, which later prove unfounded. The preaching is not a doctrinal program. Your presence comes, and it's always a "manifestation", not a program. Let me take risks in the present. "*La Paloma*" parish. I'm consoled that You have wanted it to be so significant. "*Palomeras*"[470]… The nothingness. You,

---

[468] Cf. Mt 7:29.

[469] There was a failed coup d'état perpetrated by some military groups in Spain on February 23, 1981 ("23F").

[470] Carmen highlights the coincidence of the two names: "Palomeras" was the shanty town where the Way began, and the parish of *Virgen de la Paloma*.

my Jesus. Peace. Look on my sufferings. Let peace rest in my heart. The sufferings make me look for you. Come, Jesus!

(Madrid, February 24, 1981)

502. After the night of joyful insomnia, waking up is impossible, painful, without daylight. All day hobbling in impotence, in nothingness, in smoking, in suffering.

Convention. Catechists of Madrid. I don't see anything. Nothing has any future, navigating through the absurd, poor routine. Thank you, Jesus, that you always appear in this risk of Kiko's. My Jesus, the cross that shines. My Jesus, wake me up to live.

(Madrid, February 25, 1981)

503. Third *Sacramentinos*. My Jesus, the day goes by in sorrow, dark sorrow, suffering, like the foggy outlook of a fatal ending. My Jesus, as if you were not here and everything were impossible, burdensome. Is Christianity impossible? My Jesus, I'm going to Elisa's house to flee from Narváez as if from a tomb. Jesus, deep down I feel a tiny bit of freedom, and yet no, everything overwhelms me. I don't even know how to tell you anything. You know of this dark night. What is happening to me, my Jesus, that all your gifts burden me like condemnations? Jesus, the preaching… I'm mute, mute and graceless. Jesus, come.

(Madrid, February 26, 1981)

504. Valle – *Redditio* first *S. Roque*, first and second *S. José*, etc.

I awake in Elisa's house with thoughts of terror. My Jesus, thoughts of the people in the community overwhelm me, their sins after so many years, and I think that the Way has been of no use. My Jesus! Why? Let your voice resound in my heart, "It is I, do not be afraid."[471] Tell me that you're here. Everything looks like the moment of failure, of passion when everything disappears as if Christianity were of no use to anyone. You, Jesus, Christ… returning to the law, to the terror of Hell, as if your freedom and love only lead backwards.

---

[471] Cf. Rv 1:17.

How difficult men are, Lord. Each one a mystery. Hypocrisy? Jesus, the darkness. Who will give me wings to fly away.[472]

My Jesus, nothing remains standing, only your Cross, under which I take refuge in your cleansing blood.[473] My Jesus, mysterious, holy. Let the dawn of your resurrection rise over this discouraging darkness.

Night in Valle. All of a sudden, I feel free and nothing matters to me. Not even Kiko seems inspired to me. All is old and trite, and You don't appear… but suddenly I feel free and can breathe.

(Valle, February 27, 1981)

505. 28: my father.[474]

My Jesus, dark dawn as usual. A ray of peace at the end, in the penitential. I see everything as super-poor, and everyone with old, helpless eyes.

Finally, the Eucharist. I open my mouth and then my eyes, my heart, and the burdens also change. Lord, peace, seek peace,[475] banish the accuser[476] who buries me. Money… You are, Lord, you will give me the day, the opportunities… It is Yours. Help me.

Jesus, if You wanted… The inspiration… what to do? It depends on You, Holy Spirit, to open the Scriptures. I look for books, ideas… Oh, Holy Spirit, you burst in and are Lord[477] without me calling you. Let your will be done.[478] I want You to come over me. Come, Holy Spirit, sweetest consoler. Your holy gifts… Come, come, come.

(Valle, February 28, 1981)

506. Valle – Madrid. My Jesus! Return from Valle, problems upon problems. Pastors… my Jesus, to each day its own worry.[479] Say it to my heart. My Jesus, I am hurt by the sins of the older brothers who

---

[472] Cf. Ps 55:6.
[473] Cf. Rv 7:14.
[474] Carmen's father, Antonio Hernández Villar, died in Madrid February 28, 1970.
[475] Cf. Ps 34:14.
[476] Cf. Rv 12:10.
[477] Cf. 2 Cor 3:17.
[478] Cf. Mt 6:10.
[479] Cf. Mt 6:34.

live as if You did not exist. My Jesus, powerful, holy, only one. You have profoundly enlightened my muteness: "brazen since infancy." Jesus, my love, I'm not alone in this house. You are with me. Come, come, Jesus, enlighten my awakening. Jesus, my Jesus, holy, good, consoler, I love you.

(Madrid, March 1, 1981)

507. Problems. Pastors, my Jesus. Elisa's house. I wake up overwhelmed by time, feeling like I have none. The problems pile up: the pastors, sin… my Jesus, crucified, liberator, holy, faithful, show your power. It seems like the whole Way doesn't work. The community consoles us.

My Jesus, four in the morning… and then five, no sleep. My Jesus.

(Madrid, March 2, 1981)

508. I can't wake up. I awaken half dead. It's already two. No energy to go out.

Counseling room. One by one… To the monastery to pray… my Jesus, I see everything colorless.

Eucharist. Second *S. Sebastián*. My Jesus, how tedious. It is as if everything lacks appeal without your presence, with no energy, without novelty. I even feel sorry for Kiko. What a mystery. I see it all without creativity and I don't know where to escape to, my Jesus.

(Madrid, March 3, 1981)

509. Weighed down. Restless in spirit, choked by time. My Jesus, with no creativity, with no inspiration, with nothing. I'm horrified as the catechumenate seems to fall like a house of cards. My Jesus!

S. Roque. You console me, my Jesus. It seems impossible. Jesus, my Jesus, the suffering. Everyone notices, my Jesus.

Two-thirty in the morning. I can't fall asleep but I breathe, my Jesus. Everything seems easier. An organized chaos… my Jesus, I love you. Help me in the morning. The early rising gives me joy.

(Madrid, March 4, 1981)

510. Prayer at six at the Center. Miraculously I wake up without even having slept and I feel joyful, strong. My Jesus, holy one, savior,

I feel untethered, help me. Thank you, Jesus, I begin to see things with freedom, without distress. Thank you, Jesus.

S. Roque. First *Redditio*, always surprising. Everything surprises me like a show. Lord!

(Madrid March 5, 1981)

511. Prayer at six in *Canillas*. My Jesus, the peacefulness. Sleepy… couldn't open my eyes…

My Jesus, all day in a sorrowful grief, pressed for time and unmotivated. I do nothing. St. Augustine. My Jesus, You inspire, You show yourself. I flail about in absolute helplessness, in the nothingness, of nothing in nothing. My Jesus. Everything is disconnected, my Jesus.

(Madrid, March 6, 1981)

512. I wake up at six thirty. I go at eight by myself. Prayer. You surround me with suffering and there is nothing else I can do, my Jesus. The burning bush.[480] I move about in grief and pain. Everything feels like pain, dark, terrible. My Jesus, have mercy on me.

Night. *S. José. Redditio.* In front of the chapel of the Blessed Sacrament, sweet memories of youth. Thank you, my Jesus, my love. Lord! You raise me up, Jesus. Escaping when I finally start to breathe. Jesus!

(Madrid, March 1981)

513. Madrid – Rome. Voltaggio consoles me, waiting for us and accompanying us.

Canadesi, everyone, and *Firenze.* My Jesus, the world is not collapsing. My Jesus, you know everything about each one. You are Lord, infinite[481] God, Father. Blessed are You. My Jesus, I'm moved by the sacrifice of youth, the battle. Help me to fight in the morning. Lauds… I'm so sleepy!

(Rome, March 8, 1981)

---

[480] Cf. Ex 3:1-5.
[481] Carmen uses ∞.

514. Lauds at seven at *Martiri*. You open my lips to prayer. Hellish day, sufferings, ghosts. Distraught from head to toe, my Jesus.

"Man hastens the arrival of his end. His anxieties do not allow him to rest. He gives himself over to bitterness because of his hatred and envy, and so he saps his strength; he carries within himself his own destruction."[482]

My Jesus, all of a sudden, peace. Thank you, my Jesus, freedom, grace, and light seem like a dream. My Jesus, You fill everything. You remain the only one, always. I can't find one book to read. Only You. Thank you, Lord.

(Rome, March 9, 1981)

515. At *Martiri* at six. Hard to wake up – Counseling room in Maura's house. And so the terrible day begins. All day suffering, suffering, unable to do anything but suffer. Tragically suffering. Fears… and boom: in the end, Him, Jesus. Thank you, Lord. Tenderness…

Ideas for Easter, the itinerants… Finally, in creative orbit once more. Jesus, I am serene. Help me to live.

Victorious.[483] St. Peter says: new heavens, and a new earth in which "Righteousness" will reside.[484] It is the faith in the Resurrection and the Church — water and blood from the side of Christ…[485] – that brings us together this night, that makes us await "the righteousness", that calls us to <u>Easter</u>, to go through a transformation, and we are united already from the first reading: the origin, *"bereshit"* "in the beginning, God created…."[486] To be at peace with our own origin (Second Scrutiny)[487] and in the happiness, to live and contemplate the marvels of the power of God, in which we live, we move, and have

---

[482] Carmen writes in quotation marks only at the beginning of the quote. Reference unknown. Or are these Carmen's words?

[483] Carmen wrote this in a different diary from 1981, on the pages for January 1-2.

[484] Cf. 2 Pt 3:13.

[485] Cf. Jn 19:34.

[486] Gn 1:1.

[487] A step of the Neocatechumenal Way.

our being.[488] Open your heart to the Lord who speaks for us here tonight, and awaken your hearts; open your eyes so that you may see how well He has made everything, that everything was good.[489] Their eyes were opened, leaning on Him, on Jesus Christ risen.[490]

The <u>night of Easter</u>[491] comes from the very first Word that we will hear, that impels us to immerse ourselves in the immensity of the power of the Creator. There is One Creator. One who has known Israel and has given it the eyes (faith) to contemplate the universe. With this light it has seen the Light.[492]

I'm excited by the thought that we are traveling on a "marvelous spacecraft" in space;[493] on a spacecraft with its own highway in the infinite universe where everything is moving, spectacular. Lift up your eyes: I am the Lord your God, One.

First, the light. A Word of God can shine a light on the chaos that you have lived this year, and help you to see that everything is good, very good.

(Rome, March 10, 1981)

516. *Martiri* at six.

Adrift all day, with no destination. The darkness, the plagues.[494] My Jesus, not even one book, nor an idea, or an aspiration. St. Teresa… disappointment… I don't even like it. TV is boring. Nothing says anything to me in nothingness, my Jesus. Sleepy. Ten and it feels like it's late at night. Jesus.

(Rome, March 11, 1981)

---

[488] Cf. Acts 17:28.

[489] Cf. Gn 1:31.

[490] Cf. Lk 24:31.

[491] Carmen wrote this in a different diary from 1981, on the page for January 5.

[492] Cf. Ps 36:9.

[493] Carmen wrote this in a different diary from 1981, on the pages for January 7-8.

[494] Cf. Ex 10:21-23.

517. At six, *Martiri*. Taking a bath cheers me up. Jesus, my heart tightens. My Jesus, an intriguing mistrust eats away at my soul. Jesus. *Natività*, distrustful about that, too. Fr. Maximino, distant. The Vatican, dark. I see everything without color, without perspective, without enthusiasm, in the nothingness. Jesus on the Cross. Yes. Your resurrection enlightens my life, my Jesus. Eleven at night. Now, serene. Thank you, Lord.

(Rome, March 12, 1981)

518. Six, Lauds at *Martiri*. Running after the pastor like an idiot. My Jesus, wandering, drifting because of dread, the darkness. At the house: sleep, dark, terrifying. My Jesus, how sad I am, how helpless. What can be done? Jesus, on my knees.

Finally, Arcinazzo. *Redditio*. The paschal candle enters,[495] and in its light, I read the gospel. It seems insignificant. Not to call anyone crazy and not to make of anyone a saint. The gospel, to believe the gospel, that You are, Lord. Something else, different from all our ideas of justice. Let your light shine.

(Arcinazzo, March 13, 1981)

519. *Redditio*. My Jesus, these neuroses... In the center, in the heart, only one thing: You, Lord of the Resurrection and of life. Transfiguration today.[496] You leave me nostalgic for unforgettable past encounters, my Jesus, sweet one. Suffering puts me on the threshold of holiness, with no other desire than to be yours in everything. My Jesus, help me.

(Arcinazzo, March 14, 1981)

520. *Redditio*. My Jesus, distress, tightness... So much suffering, my Jesus, obsessions, depressions. Do we live as ghosts? My Jesus, it's like I'm in a police car, with the sirens constantly going. Unbearable Saturday dinner. Everything looks gloomy, colorless, threatening.

---

[495] Celebration of the *Lucernarium*.
[496] Gospel of the Sunday Eucharist: Mt 17:1-8.

The Pope at *S. Giovanni*...[497] It doesn't say anything to me. Only You, My Jesus, and wanting to run after your Cross by myself, without opening my mouth.[498] You, despised, man of sorrows, you who know every kind of suffering.[499] My Jesus, help me. I take refuge in You.[500]

(Arcinazzo, March 15, 1981)

521. Rest. My Jesus, reading the past year, 1979, as one continuous night, and the year 1980 is the same... is it illness or is it You in all this suffering? Glimmers of calm in the midst of this darkness.

My Jesus, free my heart! Jesus! Jesus, my Jesus, let your voice cross over the waters to my heart.[501] You, victorious over the waters, invincible, speak to me. Come, let your face shine[502] on this night of my life. Unbind me.

Jesus, peaceful day, incredible. Don't let me recreate ghosts around me. The quiet of this morning was good for me, my Jesus.

The life of man is short.[503] Just a few yards away from death and I'm worrying about the things of this life. How stupid I am. Help me. You are, Lord. Let your voice resound in my heart. Help me.

(Rome, March 16, 1981)

522. My Jesus, *Redditio* at *Sta. Francesca*. My Jesus, the suffering leads me to rest[504] in your most sweet and painful Cross. My Jesus, You will open my mouth.

(Rome, March 17, 1981)

523. Saint Teresa and the Virgin Mary. A woman in Scripture, in history, before the feminists. Nightmares of accusations. Looking for

---

[497] In reality, this was the pastoral visit of St. John Paul II to the parish of *Nostra Signora di Coromoto*, Rome. This parish welcomed the communities that used to belong to the parish of *San Giovanni di Dio*.
[498] Cf. Is 53:7.
[499] Cf. Is 53:3.
[500] Cf. Ps 143:9.
[501] Cf. Mt 14:25-27.
[502] Cf. Ps 67:1.
[503] Cf. Ps 37:36; 39:5.
[504] Cf. Sg 1:7.

the "enemy." The feeling is like entering a hostile Sanhedrin.[505] Terror! No protection? My Jesus, I am consoled by the second of *S. Luigi*: your healing work, of maturation, of life. My Jesus, to each day its trouble.[506] Let your gospel resound in my heart, your voice when I awake. My Jesus, help me!

(Rome, March 18, 1981)

524. Fighting with life and with my bed when I wake up. Prayer. St. Teresa's method consoles me. You are close, inside me, my Father.

Redditio S. Luigi. Consolation: your powerful, holy action. My Jesus, help me. Open my lips. Come. Wake me tomorrow.

(Rome, March 19, 1981)

525. Six in the morning, Lauds in *S. Luigi*.

Arcinazzo again: *Traditio Natività*. My Jesus, I desire death. I desire to die as much as to sleep. Dead tired. Happy because I remember your gospel with all its newness. Lord, You are unique in love. Come, Jesus. I'm like a mute person, I don't open my mouth.[507] Condemned. Is it my fault? Is it your will, Lord? Well, then don't let it make me suffer like this, gloomily. I would like to disappear, Sweet Virgin Mary, hidden in your tent.[508] Jesus!

(Arcinazzo, March 20, 1981)

526. What pains, my Jesus, of labor, of kenosis, of suffering! Why? How, My Jesus, is this interior pain so terrifying? Jesus, Jesus Crucified, mysterious, awe-inspiring, we announce your Resurrection. Lord, show yourself. You understand helplessness, the nothingness. My Jesus, don't abandon me in this loneliness, in this terrible darkness. My Jesus, faithful, holy, savior, show the power of your holy name. Jesus!

Peace, finally. Incredible peace. Listening to people, seeing you act, has freed me. Thank you, my Jesus.

---

[505] Cf. Acts 4:5-22.
[506] Cf. Mt 6:34.
[507] Cf. Is 53:7.
[508] Cf. Ps 27:5.

Eucharist. Serenity, facing the problem in peace. Jesus, to battle! Yes. Help me. Remind me of the history of when you appeared.

(Arcinazzo, March 21, 1981)

527. Prayer in the dark night. Lord, "defend me from the wicked foe."[509] You are, Lord, awaken my ear to your voice, "I Am, I am. Do not be afraid."[510] You are, Lord. I have seen you. Remind me of history, your presence, your manifestations, your Word incarnated so many times in all its richness and power. If You are not here, then everything is a lie. If I forget you, Jerusalem, let my right hand wither.[511] Defend Kiko, my Jesus.

(Arcinazzo, March 22, 1981)

528. Rome – Hard to wake up. Rest in Santa Marinella. The ghosts, the fear… finally, prayer, serenity. Thank you, Jesus. You have proclaimed your word even in my exhaustion, so much love, so much mercy. My Jesus, how can I forget the opened sea, the desert, your wonders, your inspirations?[512] Lord, don't allow me to separate myself from You.[513] Protect Kiko. Away with you, Satan![514] Don't frighten me with ghosts. Lord, your love for the sinner, your forgiveness… Teach me to forgive, to forget sins. Give me a heart of mercy, of freedom. Set my feet on your holy rock.[515] Defend me. My life is yours. You have given me everything I have, and all that is mine is in your hands. You fulfill everything in its time.

(Santa Marinella, March 23, 1981)

529. Fourth *Martiri*. *Redditio* scrutiny. I have a critical eye. My Jesus, deep down, it all seemed objectionable, terrifying. Fear. My Jesus, everything looked bad. I was embarrassed of Kiko and it all left me cold. My Jesus, my terrors, ghosts all day long. The sliver of hope

---

[509] Cf. ST. IGNATIUS OF LOYOLA, *Anima Christi* (prayer).
[510] Cf. Ex 3:14; Mt 14:27.
[511] Cf. Ps 137:5.
[512] Cf. Ps 136:13.16.
[513] Cf. Jn 15:5.
[514] Cf. Mt 4:10.
[515] Cf. Ps 40:2.

from the Pope calms me.[516] My Jesus, the Paschal night, You. Only at nightfall do I see things with peace. Help me.

(Rome, March 24, 1981)

530. In this prison, in the hands of the enemy. My Jesus, this pain stings my heart all day. At *Martiri*, fourth community. Lord, your authority, your power has appeared, and you have reconciled me. Your presence in Kiko frees me from the terrors. My Jesus, at night, serene, free, after these days of hell, doubt, mistrust, that prostrate me on the ground, without being able to see you. My Jesus, wake me, my eyes fixed on You.[517]

(Rome, March 25, 1981)

531. I haven't gotten up yet, and this house is already unbearable. My Jesus, you throw me out on the street. Better than here, my Jesus.

(Rome, March 26, 1981)

532. Vatican. Noè:[518] we showed him pictures of baptism by immersion. Silvestrini consoles us. Thank you, my Jesus: the Pope finally says yes to the cantors meeting. Sliver of satisfaction that wards off the anxiety.

My Jesus, I'm going to run away from this house. It makes me sick. Help me, Jesus, to look at things with mercy, not with loathing or fear. I trust in You, Lord. To transcend these neuroses of wanting to help like I'm a criminal accomplice. Free. Lord, help me, calm these fears and awaken me to your closeness. Jesus, my Jesus, everything unravels spontaneously, without time to calm things down. My Jesus, a house, a place of freedom. Where?

(Rome, March 27, 1981)

533. Jesus, it's always hard to wake up, the house... my Jesus, as soon as I feel a little normal again, I no longer feel like praying with you.

---

[516] See *infra* March 31, 1981.
[517] Cf. Heb 12:2.
[518] Cardinal Virgilio Noè (†), then Undersecretary for the Congregation for Divine Worship and the Discipline of the Sacraments, 1975-1982.

Fourth *Martiri*. My Jesus, it's already four in the morning. This action of yours that seems impossible... You are. You act in Jacob.[519] Lord, make my night serene. Shed light on my existence. So much suffering!

(Rome, March 28, 1981)

534. My Jesus, all day with imagined sufferings, terrors, trials, crazy women, anxieties, defeats, rejections, denials, condemnations. My Jesus, your luminous footprints through suffering.[520] Have mercy. The terrors and the danger eat me up, attacking my heel.[521] This dark, dark valley... gripping my heart all day long. Why, Lord? You are in all of this. Teach me to fight. The communion, dinner, being with others gives me serenity in this lonely solitude of abandonment.

The 31st, cantors... everything is improvised. Everything is like the races in the backyard. How will it be? You, Lord, are impromptu, spontaneous, my Jesus.

(Rome, March 29, 1981)

535. Monduzzi,[522] Fr. Maximino. Courtyard of *S. Damaso*.

Only at night do I see things normally, with serenity, life, life. My Jesus, all day struggling with restlessness, suffering, anxiety, like a bullfighter. Spending my time like a robot. My Jesus, thank you for giving rest to my heart at night. My Jesus, tomorrow, the Pope. Night. Calm me down, everything is in your hands. Allow me to place the future, the persecution, the criticisms, the imaginings in your power. Come, Holy Spirit, come.

Ideas regarding the Pope.[523] – To oblige all the churches in the center of Rome, devoid of worship, to open for the Easter vigil. Allow them to be used by the communities to celebrate in vigil, all night long. Wake Rome up. Jesus Christ lives.

Send 500 itinerants. Pentecost.

---

[519] Cf. Ps 59:13.

[520] Cf. 1 Pt 2:21.

[521] Cf. Gn 3:15.

[522] Cardinal Dino Monduzzi (†), then Secretary and Regent of the Apostolic Palace. Later Prefect of the Prefecture for the Pontifical Household, 1986-1998.

[523] Written by Carmen in a different diary for 1978, on the page for June 18.

The Word. It is good to prepare, but then speak, not read. Forget philosophers and doctrines and infallibility. St. Paul, St. Clement, St. Augustine, St. Leo, they didn't speak from writings. It's the difference between reading and preaching. Not to limit the work of the Holy Spirit out of fear of making mistakes, and thus not giving space to the creativity of the announcement and to the Holy Spirit who builds through speaking. Especially today.

On the retirement of bishops: the Church is an anti-witness.

Kierkegaard: the Church is bound to the State because of money.[524] The most serious problem in Germany: the perversion of lay counsels and pastors. The deception of *Adveniat* and *Misereor*.[525] The wealthy Church.

(Rome, March 30, 1981)

536. The Pope with the Cantors in the courtyard of *San Damaso*.

The Paschal Praeconium, better than a well-prepared, hour-long catechesis. The rain. The Pope, alone on the balcony. My Jesus, my lonely heart. We stormed the Vatican en masse with the Easter Vigil. Symbolic? Real. Thank you, Jesus. Dance in the courtyard. Assembly: with one heart.[526] Jesus, Jesus, my Jesus, lift up my heart.

Serenity at night. I see life normally, things in their proper place, without fear. My Jesus, I think of You, don't make me suffer looking for you. Come, You, Consoler, Savior.

(Rome, March 31, 1981)

537. Poletti. Afterward, the highway to *Firenze*. I sleep, sleep insatiably. I want to escape through sleep to another planet, my Jesus. Kiko's endless catechesis. He throws himself, tired, repetitive, uncoordinated, unbearable. Lord, it's as if you were no longer with us. Is it only I who am seeing things like this? My Jesus, I neither see nor hear you. Have mercy on us. My Jesus, mysterious and holy, come.

(Florence, April 1, 1981)

---

[524] Cf. the last work by S. KIERKEGAARD: *The Instant (Øjebblikket)*.

[525] An organization of the German Episcopal Conference whose purpose is to collect money to help the Church and Catholics in South America (*Adveniat*) and in Africa, Asia, Oceania and also South America (*Misereor*).

[526] Cf. Ez 11:9; Acts 4:32.

538. From *Firenze* to Rome – Meeting in Rome for Easter is cancelled. Thank God. I can't go on. Yesterday was like a bad afternoon at the bullfight. Lord, only one thing. In so many, many things, You are always present, Creator, Holy. Jesus, will You return to give us life? I have no interest in anything, not even in papalism. Everything seems like nothingness to me, my Jesus. "Passover." I wish I could escape with you by myself. Sustaining Kiko holds me back. My Jesus!

(Rome, April 2, 1980)

539. From Rome to Madrid – On a flight while in absurdity, pain, fear. My Jesus, in the Convención Hotel with the itinerants. The Spanish Bishops console me. My Jesus, I don't want to return to Rome… My Jesus!… far!

Narváez. I go to bed seeing things with joy. Wake me up, my Jesus, with the light of the resurrection. Come, Jesus.

(Madrid, April 3, 1981)

540. Day: the night; night: serenity. Jesus, who can understand the mystery of this suffering, so unreal, unheard of, terrible? Everything is suspicion, nothingness, darkness and absurdity.

It's already two thirty in the morning. Return from the Eucharist in the Center, and I see with serenity that everything is normal. My Jesus, I love you, don't complicate my existence, give me joy to live, to wake up, to love the others. Unbind me, make me live. You are the resurrection and the life.[527] I believe in You. Say to me, "Come out, out, out!"[528] Pull me put of the tomb of death.

(Madrid, April 4, 1981)

541. Sunday at home, with my mother and her needlepoint. Thoughtful: she would like to give me something for staying with her… It has done me good. Without love, my Jesus, the nothingness. I don't see life. Everything is the gray of the nothingness, without a reason for being. My God! Two-thirty in the morning. Alocén. Nothing. Everything feels like the nothingness. My Jesus, have mercy

---

[527] Cf. Jn 11:25; 14:6.
[528] Cf. Jn 11:43.

on my life that has no meaning, no life. My Jesus, what's happening to me? What do you want? Where are you? Wake me up.

(Alocén, April 5, 1981)

542. Alone in the mountains. You remind me of my childhood, Ólvega, the solitude, your presence. Who am I, Lord? Where are you? The field, the earth, the trees, the rain, Lord, the universe, all of it... Where are you? Who are You? My Jesus, calm my uneasiness. The rain... balm for my nothing in the nothingness. My Jesus! You trample on my life in the nothingness. Make me one with this wonderful earth in its adventure. Lord, the Resurrection, the transformation. Everything is an impossibility. Night. Serenity of the night, my Jesus.

(Alocén, April 6, 1981)

543. All of a sudden, the ghosts, like maddening lions, rummaging through the details, burrowing in lies, in suspicions. Restlessness, disloyalty, mistrust that makes me put everything in doubt in the nothingness of the darkness. It's like I'm in the shanty town, with nothing to hold on to, between nothingness and everything. You are here, Lord, and everything becomes infinite. You disappear, and what is left is insanity, nothingness. My Jesus, what suffering!

(Madrid, April 7, 1981)

544. Madrid – Rome. Paschal trip, truly paschal, from death to life, from terror to courage, from darkness to light, from fear to joy, from sadness to exultation. Blessed are you, Lord, who make me anticipate victory. My Jesus, my Jesus, the suffering... what a mystery. The night, the darkness, the hate, the loathing, what pain. Blessed are you, Lord. Thanks be given to You. Faithful, Holy, Lord, don't let the night close around me. Help me when I awake. I love you. Thank you, my Jesus.

(Rome, April 8, 1981)

545. Chancery. Nothing. All in the mystery of contradiction. Each man, a unique and incomprehensible whole. My Jesus, *Natività*, what pain, those overwhelming sins. Sin has crucified you. My heart is crucified. My Jesus, crucified, expelled, rejected... intrigues... mysterious pain that makes it all present for me, terrible, real. My

Jesus, it's a prophecy, a preparation. My Jesus, free us from the evil one.[529] Help me!

(Rome, April 9, 1981)

546. Lauds at *Martiri*. Communion. I'm in paschal pain. My Jesus, You move this people, who cannot be controlled. My soul hurts, my Jesus, Fr. Maximino, the Vatican, the controversies… why? Are you really above all things? My terrible life. My Jesus, draw me to you, protect me, resurrect me.

My Jesus, from oppression to liberty, freedom. My Jesus, what a mystery oppression is, how surprising freedom is. Blessed are you. To be able to hold this key! You, my Jesus, free, most sweet, free me.

(Rome, April 10, 1981)

547. Rome – Madrid. My Jesus, liberator from oppressions, from ghosts, Holy, Lord. Plane. Sleep, sleep, sleep. Tomorrow, procession. My Jesus, since it's like I'm doing nothing, come, let us experience this Palm Sunday by going out. I remember in Barcelona. Holy in your passion, transcendent. Lord, I love you. Let us flee, beloved.[530] I love you.

(Madrid, April 11, 1981)

548. Palms. From the Seminary to *La Paloma*. Better than last year's. Rapidly, without chocolate and the vicar. The clerical ghost has taken hold of my heart, tormenting me all day, and I didn't know where I could escape. Home. *S. José*. Fleeing from people, from everyone. Finally, at night, I am enlightened.

I make relative things absolute, making an all in all or total death. Suddenly, Life, Eternal Life. My Jesus, help me to see with serenity, to downplay problems, things. Three-quarters are fantasies, feelings. But this interior terror… there's nothing I can do about it. What is it, Lord? How can I fight? It is You. What is the point of prayer? It's the devil who torments me. Help me! Staying in my house just a few hours makes me see everything obsolete. One day, and already I feel more normal. Thank you, Lord.

(Madrid, April 12, 1981)

---

[529] Jn 17:15.
[530] Sg 1:4; 7:12; 8:14.

549. Free. Where are you, my God, so that I may look for you? Are you here? I'm in the nothingness, where nothing is. When my life is without meaning, I cannot live. Walking in death, everything feels like death to me and I haven't the slightest interest. All day full of neurotic doubt. My Jesus, how is it possible that everything is not being, darkness, sadness? I'm mute, blind, and dead, my Jesus, You, dead. Nobody can accuse you. Your face is the only thing that speaks to me in this horrible night. Move me, Lord, revive me, resurrect me. How can the world navigate like this, so calmly? How mysterious everything is. If You are here, come.

(Madrid, April 13, 1981)

550. My Jesus, travelling. Parceled land, my Jesus. I arrive tense, which is usual now, subjected, oppressed. At night, Easter resounds: suddenly, freedom and everything changes without anything changing. Everything in its place, its beauty, its... Painless, my Jesus. Nothing matters to me. If everyone could wake like this, with you! You are here and everything changes. Thank you, Lord.

(Paris, April 14, 1981)

551. Paris provokes joy in me. How far from everything. The itinerants, happy. I'm floored by it all. My Jesus, why?

Rome – They attack. It's foreign to me. I don't want to stay. How? Where? Without laying my head.[531] My Jesus, I'm "hungry": I left my bag with the Bible and breviary inside it in the airport... My God!

(Rome, April 15, 1981)

552. Holy Thursday. Coming out of the tomb, as usual. More. You have been encouraging me and bringing me out into the sun, outside, to the little things. Thank you, Lord. Around Rome, a blouse for Easter, some time alone, café, and a window of freedom opens up for me. My Jesus, that I may not take things too seriously.

Franco's house. Washing of the feet.[532] The pastor is worse off than I am.... Disillusionment. From what? The entire community.

---

[531] Cf. Mt 8:20.

[532] In addition to participating in the parish Mass *In Coena Domini*, the Neocatechumenal communities meet community by community at a

Lifeless, but it's here. A mystery. Jesus, I want to fly away.[533] I love you. Thank you, Jesus, for these moments of peace. Help me.

(Rome, April 16, 1981)

553. Good Friday. Vatican. Passive crowd. Rite. I fall asleep in the car. My Jesus, *Martiri* the same: standing crowd with no participation. My Jesus, the spirit of participation, of communion… all impossible. Nothing is authentic, not the kissing of the cross, the prayers, nor the songs. Like this, neither is the Passion. The vast assembly. Another tactic, no spontaneity, sincerity, or communion. My Jesus!

(Rome, April 17, 1981)

554. Easter. Easy fasting. Night in *Martiri*, big church. I hide myself. Vast assembly. My Jesus, participation: yes, fashionable, too fashionable, desacralized. My Jesus, it almost scares me. Liberating Word. Essential: Creation, Abraham, Exodus. My Jesus, everything is simpler than one imagines it to be. This way, essentially, the rite proceeds by itself, with its signs, its life, communion. My Jesus, mysterious, holy, and I suffer, suffer. My Jesus. You.

(Rome, April 18-19, 1981)

555. Easter Monday. Feast. My Jesus, You free me. Mysteriously free, a gift I cannot repay. But what boredom, Lord, and what a burden all of life is, being. Everything and everyone bore me. Where are we going? How? My Jesus, it is Easter. Help me.

(Rome, April 20, 1981)

556. Tuesday of Easter. All day in the house. Reconciliation with this house, with books, with life? My Jesus, I leave tomorrow. Come with me.

(Rome, April 21, 1981)

---

separate time. They have a celebration of the Word in order to foster mutual reconciliation and brotherly love, meditating on Jesus' words at the Last Supper (Jn 13-16) and obeying his words, "I have washed your feet, you too ought to wash one another's feet" (Jn 13:14).

[533] Cf. Ps 55:6.

557. Rome – Madrid – Alocén. It's raining. It's cold and I'm happy, snatched from the Roman nightmare. It seemed like a crazy trip and now I laugh at the whole world and its ghosts. My Jesus, my love, free me from the evil one.[534] I feel I have no faith in You, and yet I believe in this damned satan, torturer, accuser,[535] ghostly. My Jesus, don't let me fall into temptation; free me from evil.[536] Thank you, my Jesus, because I can see things in freedom. I love you.

(Alocén, April 22, 1981)

558. All day in the car. Quiet? Passivity. My Jesus, in any case, it's the only thing that calms me, and I love you even amid the doubts of my troubled heart. Jesus, the crucifixion. You, crucified. How can I not love you? Crucified One, how can it be that my heart weeps? My Jesus, mysterious, holy, only one. I feel like there is nothing but death. It is Easter, Lord, have mercy on me. The power from on high...[537] Don't leave me.

(Alocén, April 23, 1981)

559. If You, Lord, said to my heart that You are, and are here... The disbelief, the meaninglessness, the wandering... fighting, Lord, with existence, with the day, with living, because it's all nothing to me. How can this be? Lord, wake me because I sleep in the tomb of nothingness, sad, dead with powerlessness.

(Alocén, April 24, 1981)

560. Quiet day in my cell. Work. I worry about the catechesis for the Our Father, but I'm almost happy, I am alive. Prayer, I hope, mysteriously. The Bellidos edify me, their faith, my Jesus.

(Alocén, April 25, 1981)

561. Terrible day. Truly as if taken by the devil himself, with no way of escape. Destroyer, accuser.[538]

---

[534] Cf. Jn 17:15.
[535] Cf. Rv 12:10.
[536] Cf. Mt 6:13.
[537] Cf. Lk 24:49.
[538] Cf. Rv 12:10.

My Jesus, it seems impossible, and all of a sudden, "this relief." It's already nine o'clock. Night has already fallen and I begin to live, emerging from the nightmare that transforms everything into the nothingness, into destruction, into death. My Jesus, peace. Thank you, Lord, I believe in You. Do not pay attention to me when I doubt You. I'm a poor imbecile, stupid. Lead me not into temptation,[539] don't allow me to deny you, help me.

(Alocén, April 26, 1981)

562. Wake me, Jesus. Last night, a tragedy because of the ghosts. The devil is really unleashed. But this morning I didn't stir until eleven or twelve. And then prayer, study, radio. My Jesus, finally moving. An exchange of words, communication, gives me life, activity.

Leave for Rome. My Jesus, how different it is to see things normally, away from the deadly nightmare, destroyer: the nothingness. Free me, Lord. Don't let me fall into the nothingness.

(Rome, April 27, 1981)

563. *Natività*. The CEI? Doctrine of Faith?[540] My Jesus, it's all in your hands. Your wisdom is life. I see the gospel working with the novelty of it being free. My Jesus, free me from the Roman ghosts of this house. Wake me, love me, help me.

(Rome, April 28, 1981)

564. *Natività*. Better. We finished at three in the morning. Sleepy, my Jesus. Fears of the future, Lord?

(Rome, April 29, 1981)

565. *Natività*. My Jesus, after seeing impossible mountains, you simplify life with your manifestation. The CEI thing, good. Your presence in the telling of history. Poletti on the phone: consolation. And at the *Natività*, miraculously, everything is fixed. My Jesus, you drive off my fears. And tomorrow, open my mouth to your name, my Jesus.

(Rome, April 30, 1981)

---

[539] Cf. Mt 6:13.
[540] Congregation for the Doctrine of the Faith.

566. At the airport. May 1st. The traffic jam on Via Aurelia makes me get into the car with the enemy. My Jesus, I've suffered so much today. Deaf to my cries, terrible hardship, inner bitterness, pain of life and death, fear.

Rome – Madrid – Valle.

Our Father. My Jesus, on my knees. Thank you, my Jesus. Peace has come to me and with it, freedom. My Sweet Jesus, faith, to believe in You, how beautiful. My Jesus, don't abandon me in temptation. You lead me to pray through suffering. Have mercy on me, my Jesus.

(Valle, May 1, 1981)

567. Our Father. First and second from the Center, first *Canillas*, first *Paloma* and first *S. Sebastián*. My Jesus, all day suffering in the nothingness. At nightfall, normality, life is visible, the people. My Jesus, how strange this powerlessness is, the nothingness, the disbelief, the disillusion. What is happening to me? In the morning, almost nauseated, powerless. Raise me up, Lord, resurrected, holy, mysterious. Do not abandon me, raise me up.

(Valle, May 2, 1981)

568. Same awakening in death. Dark day. Misery. Return to Madrid with sadness, misery, without joy. Fourth or third time that I leave Valle sad, my Jesus. Problem of the old itinerants… time…

My Jesus, communion, life. I return to life. Thank you, my Jesus. Give me back the joy of living, of the gospel, of the mission, of your presence. Thank you, Lord. Lift me up when I awake.

(Valle, May 3, 1981)

569. Narváez. You who have seen my misery and have witnessed the miseries of my soul,[541] You who are close to the brokenhearted.[542] My life is worn out with sorrow, and my days with sighs. My strength gives way under my misery.[543] Powerless. Since I have no meaning, I do nothing. Not to the dentist, nor go anywhere. Indolent because I

---

[541] Cf. Ps 31:7.
[542] Cf. Ps 119:151; 51:17.
[543] Cf. Ps 31:10.

don't want to see anyone. So much restlessness, I don't even read, and today I almost didn't pray. My Jesus, at night, when things return to normal, calm returns. I'm going to have to change how I work. My Jesus, every moment of my life is in your hands.[544]

(Madrid, May 4, 1981)

570. Narváez. Waking up without being awake, the agony of living, and fighting, fighting. Miseries, sorrows, ghosts, anxiety.

Meeting at the Center: *La Paloma* and *S. Sebastián*. And at nightfall, serenity, my Jesus. I have to get up tomorrow. I'm even looking forward to it, like when I was young. Help me.

(Madrid, May 5, 1981)

571. Wake up at six. Lauds at *La Paloma*. For how long, Lord? These days spent in anxiety, restlessness, sorrow… I got up feeling good. Lauds at *La Paloma*, good.

My Jesus, what powerlessness in everything. Jesus, at nightfall peace, serenity, everything in its place. Incredible. What's happening to me? Tomorrow the same, you'll see. Jesus, what can I do?

(Madrid, May 6, 1981)

572. Terrorism in Madrid.[545] Father, my Father, better today, the heavy clouds are exiled, more serenity. The Cardinal,[546] excellent. Patino.[547] The Rector of the Seminary.[548]

To sleep. Jesus, how terrible it is to sleep in the afternoon. *S. Sebastián* again. Father, my Father,[549] in the fight. My Jesus, help me in this dark battle. Help me.

(Madrid, May 7, 1981)

---

[544] Cf. Ps 31:15.

[545] On May 7, 1981, at 10:30 in the morning ETA assassinated three soldiers in the center of Madrid.

[546] Cardinal Vicente Enrique y Tarancon (†), Archbishop of Madrid, 1971-1981.

[547] Fr. José María Martín Patino, SJ (†), then personal secretary of Cardinal Tarancón.

[548] Juan de Dios Martín Velasco, Rector of the Conciliar Seminary of Madrid, 1977-1987.

[549] Cf. Mt 26:39.42.

573. Lauds at *La Paloma* at six a.m. Bishop from Peru.[550] All day holding on to "Father, my Father."[551] It helps me: less anxiety and fear, more indifference.

Colorless catechesis. Kiko, uninspired, at least that's how I see it. My Jesus, freedom. I smoke like an idiot. Help me, Jesus.

(Madrid, May 8, 1981)

574. Incredible, Lord, this serenity I have at night, after this dark, arduous day, full of dread, apprehension, hidden fears and disinterest. All meaningless. The human psyche is mysterious, Lord, the helplessness, lack of love, doubt, mistrust. My Jesus, love, trust, community, the Eucharist, being able to speak are all good for me. Sweet one, tomorrow, once more… I'm going to the doctor…

(Madrid, May 9, 1981)

575. Snatched from the house. My Jesus, I don't know how to live. The peacefulness at night helps me see how I make the day difficult with my contradiction between my judgmental thoughts and the reality of the present. My Jesus, what should I do? Not look ahead, my Jesus. Strengthen my present in your presence, trusting in You, in You, Lord, present so many times, always unexpected. My Jesus, I love you. Help us.

(Madrid, May 10, 1981)

576. Pastors at the Center. I'm late and have no desire to go. Well, desire for nothing, distanced from everything and everything like an impossibility of impossibilities, apprehensive and scared. Consolation from the people: they are kind, consoling, trusting. How is it possible, Lord? In this nothing of nothingness. My Jesus, calming sunset. Things recover their proper perspective, my Jesus. Everything returns to its place. You, Lord, defender, holy. I love you.

(Madrid, May 11, 1981)

---

[550] Archbishop *ad personam* Ricardo Durand Flórez, SJ (†), Bishop of Callao, 1975-1995.

[551] Cf. Mt 26:39.42.

577. At six, Lauds in *S. Sebastián*. The Church, my Jesus, back then! I move with enough courage, free from the mental web. My Jesus, have mercy. Lord, Pharaoh… How long? My Jesus, for You, everything is possible.[552] Your Kingdom come.[553] Help me. You are Lord, show yourself in your mercy.

(Madrid, May 12, 1981)

578. I don't get up. My Jesus, all my bones ache. My mother is in bed. My Jesus, everything is ending.
ATTEMPT TO ASSASSINATE THE POPE.[554] Jesus, terror, terror, inside and out. My Jesus, faith, where? Come, my Jesus.

(Madrid, May 13, 1981)

579. Fr. Resta[555] calls Elisa's house. Again, nothing can be done. Meeting in the Center with "the 18." Disconcerted. It feels like we're adrift, rudderless. My Jesus, where are you? I suffer, I suffer.

(Madrid, May 14, 1981)

580. Madrid – Rome – Maura's house. I'm like clockwork. Anguish, sufferings, dread.
At Collevalenza.[556] Our Father Convivence. *Firenze*, third *Martiri*. My Jesus, moments of serenity, to push forward. Everything looks different.

(Collevalenza, May 15, 1981)

581. Anxiety, misery upon waking. Always into the unknown, without knowing what or how, my Jesus. Kiko's catechesis was good. I calm down.

---

[552] Cf. Mt 19:26.

[553] Cf. Lk 11:2.

[554] Assassination attempt on Pope St. John Paul II on this date in St. Peter's Square in Vatican City. Mehmet Ali Agca shot the Pope four times as he was entering the Square.

[555] Fr. Vincent P. Resta (†), then pastor of St. Columba in Chelsea, Manhattan (New York). There he welcomed the Neocatechumenal Way in 1976.

[556] *Santuario del Divino Amore* at Collevalenza (Todi, Perugia).

Afternoon. The countryside. I'm always skeptical, always alone. I'm scared.

Late Eucharist, unbearable. I don't know what to say and I see everyone as neurotics.

(Collevalenza, May 16, 1981)

582. I wake up super anxious. Catechesis on the Sermon on the Mount. My Jesus, a light: let this mountain be thrown into the sea…[557] Thank you, my Jesus. Misery comes and goes like a mystery.

Return to Rome. Speaking with Kiko calms me: also to see him better. New changes. My Jesus, I feel freer. My Jesus, wake me. Help me fight. Come, my Jesus.

(Rome, May 17, 1981)

583. At the house. Restlessness. Prayer. Work. Somewhat serene. I escape.

Martiri. Our Father. I suffer through the catechesis and am inadequate. My Jesus, always waiting, terrified, for your manifestation. The itinerants and everything else terrify me. If I don't pray. My Jesus, why? St. Teresa, prayer. Father, my Father.

(Rome, May 18, 1981)

584. I even wake up early, and always terrified. At ten o'clock, *S. Luca*:[558] barricaded, my Jesus, in the battle…You are the victor.

Natività. Seems impossible: the traffic, the cars; seems like madness, my Jesus.

Third *Martiri*. Our Father. Father, my Father, I wait for you. Come, Jesus. All is made possible. You, my Jesus. Everything changes peacefully, my Jesus.

(Rome, May 19, 1981)

585. *Firenze* – My Jesus, I'm sick of being idle. What would I like to do? Follow a schedule: one hour of peeling potatoes? I complain about not reading and, when I have time, it feels like I'm wasting time

---

[557] Cf. Mt 17:20.
[558] Parish of *San Luca Evangelista*, Prenestino, Rome.

and reading no longer interests me. Why? I cannot grab hold of anything, anxious like a bullfighter. Kiko is "intangible", my Jesus.

St. Teresa seems wonderful one minute and a wild hoax the next. And we are the same, either all or nothing. I'm like a crazy woman, idle, stupid, selfish, sick, depressed, with no faith whatsoever. My Jesus, I'm invaded by dread, fear, terror, restlessness.

(Florence, May 20, 1981)

586. Restlessness… itinerants, communities, pastors, Bishops. The Church, my Jesus, and the world, all is terror, terrorism, terror, terror, powerlessness, impossibility, distrust. My Jesus, my Jesus, if I had faith in You, if my feet were on your holy rock… But I don't see your face, I don't see anything, I suffer, I suffer, and I suffer in the helplessness of death and in a visceral silence. My Jesus, I lament… I cry out to You, answer me. Have mercy on this unbelief of death.

Rome. After this day of sorrow, my Jesus, prayer at night. Serenity, freedom. Help me to fight tomorrow, give me energy.

(Rome, May 21, 1981)

587. Is this creation really better? So what? Acting as if nothing affects me and as if God exists. And if He is not does not, what do I lose? Rejecting outright all depressing thoughts of family, Kiko, the Way, Bishops, itinerants. So what? Out… out… empty my thoughts. Jesus, I love you. You. Now I pray on my knees, detached, quickly. Help me, infuse me with energy. Help me remember my youth when I fought, together with your grace, with more fervor.

Natività. Rite of the *Traditio*. Poletti. Jesus, I'm surprised at the courage you have given me. Thank you.

(Rome, May 22, 1981)

588. Chapter 20 of St. Teresa.[559] My Jesus, the miracle of speaking with Poletti yesterday at the Rite. How? Suddenly St. Teresa and prayer all seem like a game of psychological highs and lows. I analyze history. God seems like a refuge to me. All the effect of illness. My Jesus, You are the only one left. I see myself and everyone else as ill, and prayer as a danger. My Jesus, I only want to close my eyes and

---

[559] Surely from *The Way of Perfection*.

run away with you. To where? It doesn't matter. Only with you. Everything is bland and I suffer all day long.

(Rome, May 23, 1981)

589. Nunzio's house. My Jesus, it's as if I'm alone, apart, nothing. Kiko, distant. Where? I'm not interested. My Jesus, a little light and everything changes. My Jesus, I'm always tense, always on the defensive, terrified by St. Teresa, by prayer. Terrifying. You make me see everything normally and they seem like lies. I don't want justifications. Everything is possible for You.[560] Your holiness, Lord. Hallowed be your name.[561]

(Civitavecchia, May 24, 1981)

590. Hallowed be your name, my Jesus. The world isn't ending. Free all day for anything tragic, terrified, scared, scared, scared, anxiety, anxiety, anxiety. Why? Gladden me, my Jesus, let me live. I'm sick. Accept it as an illness. No, my Jesus. Nothing matters to me now. Everything is simple. So what? Always foreseeing, like in a bullfight with no way out. Either life or death, Jesus.

(Rome, May 25, 1981)

591. Your kingdom come.[562] My Jesus, these troubles, this not-living, like a continuous agony, troubled, mute, helpless, distrustful, with no interest, and the terrors… my Jesus, the night, the rain… Serenity comes only at nightfall. All day, afraid, even of prayer. It seems like madness to me. My Jesus, raise me up with you.

(Rome, May 26, 1981)

592. Vatican. My Jesus, Fr. Maximino, itinerants, nothing consoles me. Nausea, terror, fear. My Jesus, where can I escape? Serenity.

Firenze. My Jesus, it's incredible that on the same day one can feel so differently about things, from fear to serenity, from difficulty to indifference. My Jesus, how mysterious the human psyche is. Help me.

(Rome, May 27, 1981)

---

[560] Cf. Mt 19:26.
[561] Cf. Mt 6:9.
[562] Cf. Mt 6:10.

593. I wander about the shops in *Firenze* like a sleepwalker, disinterested and sad. My Jesus, always anxious and distant.

Lunch. I'm going to bed.

Catechesis. I am revived during the prayer. My Jesus!

Return trip to Rome. Night in the tomb.

(Rome, May 28, 1981)

594. I sleep but it feels like I didn't. The TV is like a demon! Restlessness.

S. Luca parish. My Jesus, suffering all day. Why, my Jesus, so much suffering? I don't want to go to Arcinazzo for anything in the world. My Jesus! Pain!

Arcinazzo. Our Father, the first and second *Martiri, Natività, S. Luigi, Sta. Francesca*. Kiko's catechesis, good. Thank goodness. I suffer. Tear me away from this suffering, my Jesus.

(Arcinazzo, May 29, 1981)

595. I feel good when I wake up. Kiko's interminable catechesis calms me down. My Jesus, on the eve of your Ascension. Thank you, my Jesus, for calming my restless, stunned, and unbelieving heart. Thank you, my Jesus, heal me. Today serenity, life. My Jesus, it seems impossible that I could ever deny you. The suffering... Help me, if it returns, to be more faithful, better, and to believe in You even in the suffering. Lead me not into temptation.[563] May your sweet Ascension defend me, without letting me forget you. Thank you, Lord.

(Arcinazzo, May 30, 1981)

596. The mystery of suffering and grief. People overwhelm me. I want to escape. Kiko terrifies me with his crazy prayers. My Jesus, the mountains: ghosts of the *Gran Madre di Dio*,[564] the accusations...

Finally, peace. Incredible freedom. St. Teresa, prayer, call to me once again. My Jesus, sweet company. These things that St. Teresa speaks about, we have sweetly lived for so many years. Come, accompany me. I love you. Say it to me. Come, Jesus.

(Rome, May 31, 1981)

---

[563] Cf. Mt 6:13.
[564] Parish of *Gran Madre di Dio*, Rome.

597. As always, it's difficult to wake up with my mountains of anxieties. An anxious day.

Our Father catechesis at *Martiri*. Serene, peaceful night, without problems, laughing to myself about my anxious awakenings. How is this possible? Help me, Lord, to fight, consoler, holy defender. Come when I awake. Jesus, my love, fill me with your spirit.

(Rome, June 1, 1981)

598. Chancery. Poletti. Heat. Misery. Where to escape?

Our Father catechesis at *Martiri*. My Jesus, all day long with a bag of books, dismayed about Kiko's catechesis, and then it was surprising. You are better than any father: your inspiration, presence, the living gospel. My Jesus, this guy is a mystery of "intangible" craziness. Better than my analyzing. My Jesus, teach me to live freely, trusting in You.

(Rome, June 2, 1981)

599. Overwhelmed as usual. St. Teresa says it clearly, but sometimes she seems so crazy and so sickly…

Our Father catechesis at *Martiri*.

Dinner with the Gennarinis. Mimmo consoles me. Vacation. Blessed are you!

(Rome, June 3, 1981)

600. *Firenze* – Our Father. My Jesus, a miraculous day: unburdened, without suffering. It seems incredible. Besieged by books, plans, meetings, dates, problems… all of a sudden, free. My Jesus, holy, holy, holy. Thank you, Lord. Everything is different: free, peace, life, my Jesus. You. Blessed are you. It is an illness that has passed, it's a demon that has fled… it's your blessing. Blessed are you. Help me when I awake.

(Florence, June 4, 1981)

601. My Jesus, drowsy, drowsy, and I can't sleep, and I can't get moving. A day without great sorrow, but also without glory, wanting to return to being busy with preparations, things to do… and nothing to do. My Jesus, I live in the nothing of the nothingness.

The catechesis, surprise: forgiveness. Lord, yes, to live doing nothing, to be yours. Say these things to me in the morning. Jesus!

(Florence, June 5, 1981)

602. Benelli.[565] The Way. My Jesus.
Travel to Rome. A bit overwhelmed. My Jesus, Pentecost. Free, unattached. My Jesus, I create burdensome mountains for myself.

(Rome, June 6, 1981)

603. Jesus, nevertheless, you have consoled me; with freedom. The day is still sorrowful. Meeting with "the 18." It all works itself out and I suffer like a bullfighter in preparations that are impossible, my Jesus.

(Rome, June 7, 1981)

604. Another painful awakening. Painful day.
Finally, Porto San Giorgio. Itinerants.
Night, serenity. Thank you, Jesus, not having plans relaxes me, accepting not doing anything, to be, to be. What? In You, because You are almighty. You are: enough. Good night.

(Porto San Giorgio, June 8, 1981)

605. First day of convivence. Calm. China, Samoa, Madagascar… Everyone is doing better than me, Lord, they are determined, good. My Jesus, I have no energy. Thank you, for giving me serenity upon seeing that You carry everything on your own. My Jesus, I wait for you. St. Teresa intrigues me: so much doubt, so much work, so many visions. My Jesus, the pain tells me strongly that it's all like an illness. And You? Tell me, "I Am."[566] Lord, only this I ask. Come.

(Porto San Giorgio, June 9, 1981)

606. Second day. My Jesus, I see everything wrong, bad, as if there were no grace in things. Australia. The itinerants, courageous, good, risking their lives. I'm distant, incapable, my Jesus, mute. And Kiko in good shape, founder. Of what? Lord, You, You are here and it's night and me in my doubts.

(Porto San Giorgio, June 10, 1981)

---

[565] Cardinal Giovanni Benelli (†), Archbishop of Florence, 1977-1982.
[566] Cf. Ex 3:14; Mt 14:27.

Written by Carmen on a picture sent to her mother, Clementa

CLEMENTICA! / THE SEA OF GALILEE / APRIL 1… / WE KEEP MARCHING TO THE BEAT OF THE DRUMS OF VICTORY… / A LIFE OF PILGRIMAGE… / "WE HAVE IN GOD A SOLID HOUSE NOT MADE BY HUMAN HANDS" AND IT IS ON THE HORIZON WITH ITS DOOR OPEN ND WE'RE GOING / ALLELUIA!!

607. My Jesus, to be present with this face of sorrow, of muteness. Kenya, Uganda. You give freshness to these poor people. Life? My Jesus, it's all madness where we disconnect in insecurity, in the "intangible." You, Lord. What sufferings. Sickness? Insanity? Faith? Lord, show yourself. Come.

(Porto San Giorgio, June 11, 1981)

608. Itinerants of nations. Bishop of Macerata.[567] Penitential. Brazil. And the boy in the well.[568] What a difficult kenosis, my Jesus. In the depths of your descent, death, human powerlessness. My Jesus, the mystery of the human psyche, a deep well of suffering and death. Salvation!

(Porto San Giorgio, June 12, 1981)

609. Itinerants of nations. Africa: Ivory Coast, Zaire. My Jesus, I look at you with admiration. I can't stand the heat here and they're in Africa. My Jesus, is it the years? When I was young in Javier, I, too, was up for anything. My Jesus, thank you for pulling me into the fight this morning with freedom. A day of suffering after all. Incredible peace. The heavens are open, my Jesus.

(Porto San Giorgio, June 13, 1981)

610. Eucharist. Bishops of Macerata. Sending itinerants throughout Italy two-by-two. Departure. My Jesus, shouldn't we be happy? I'm scared. I remain sad and the insanity comes to me again.

(Porto San Giorgio, June 14, 1981)

611. Porto San Giorgio – Rome – Madrid. Suffocating heat in Madrid. Incredible. It feels like we're in Africa. My Jesus, I'm floored. I love you. My Jesus, I'm in terror, terror about tomorrow: in the Seminary, pastors and Tarancón. My Jesus, have mercy. Kiko is also terrified.

(Madrid, June 15, 1981)

---

[567] Mons. Francesco Tarcisio Carboni (†), Bishop of Macerata, 1976-1995.

[568] An accident that shocked the world: in Italy, a six-year-old child fell down a well that was 260 feet deep and only two feet wide. He was stuck 115 feet from the surface, unable to move.

612. Seminary: pastors and Tarancón. My Jesus, between the suffocating heat, terror and poverty. Kiko and I, suffering. My Jesus, suffering and unbearable heat. Finally it ends. Serene, however: it went well after all, as You wanted. I'm left... My Jesus, nothing consoles me, absolutely nothing. My Jesus.

(Madrid, June 16, 1981)

613. My Jesus, what a day of suffering. I feel like I was bathed in it. Why, Lord? Something tightens around me. Is it You? Is it the devil? Lord, why? I must be sick, depressed. From my mother's bones[569] to the whole world, I see everything in fear, everything, every single thing demolished. I'm afraid of everything.

My Jesus, it's twelve o'clock already. Serenity. The sweltering air has lifted in this infernal heat of Madrid. I want to give you thanks. My Jesus, forgive me, because I don't see you.

(Madrid, June 17, 1981)

614. Madrid – Rome. My Jesus, lead us not into temptation.[570] Temptation, suffering... you teach me to fight. But the overwhelming suffering, not being free, my Jesus... this and that and this, and so what? And so what? Fight. And what will happen? Let it happen. Death, yes. God exists and I believe in You. Doing acts of faith. Stay awake?[571] Discovery: sleep, cigarettes, all escapes.

(Rome, June 18, 1981)

615. Rome – *Firenze* – Rome. My Jesus, back at four in the morning. Everything passes. My Jesus, what a surprise. Thank goodness, you have let me see many things. First, your continuous protection. Second, that I too, my Jesus, am a mystery because of your faithfulness. Third, understanding the others. It helps everyone. Lead us not into temptation, deliver us from evil.[572] Thank you, my Jesus.

(Rome, June 19, 1981)

---

[569] Afflicted with osteoarthritis.
[570] Cf. Mt 6:13.
[571] Cf. Mt 26:41.
[572] Cf. Mt 6:13.

616. Rite of the Our Father. Third *Martiri*, and the old ones of *Firenze*.

My Jesus, how is it possible? Temptation, sin… My Jesus, You are. One year arduously and anxiously carrying around books and more books on the Our Father, with the dread of a bullfighter or before an exam, all to never open my mouth and to suffer through every meeting. My Jesus, teach me to live. You are here. You lead this people. They are all so happy. My Jesus, I believe in You. And me? My Jesus, unbind me, teach me to live.

(Rome, June 20, 1981)

617. Jesus, my Jesus, thank you. The Pope at Gemelli: his voice sounded depressed.[573] My Jesus, do I have cervical osteoarthritis? I don't feel well.

Rome – Porto San Giorgio. My Jesus, travel, itinerants, I come back to what seems like nothing, with no interest, colorless. What's it all for? My Jesus, You. If You are, everything recovers eternity. Come.

(Porto San Giorgio, June 22, 1981)

618. My Jesus, so much complaining about the heat and now it rains and is as cold as winter. My Jesus, I feel absent, like an iceberg, passive. I listen tediously to team after team. And so? Lord, all is a mystery. Are you here? Where? Kiko is a continuous surprise. If You are not here, then what is?

(Porto San Giorgio, June 22, 1981)

619. India, Singapore. My Jesus, to the hospital. Two vertebrae: cervical osteoarthritis. My Jesus, You, truly a sign of contradiction; a sword in the soul, Sweet Virgin Mary.[574]

It's as if you weren't here, my Jesus, and yet were mysteriously in everything … Why, Lord? Command what is to be done. You can do anything.[575]

(Porto San Giorgio, June 23, 1981)

---

[573] He was admitted to the hospital Policlinico Universitario Agostino Gemelli, Rome, for a cytomegalovirus (CMV) infection.
[574] Cf. Lk 2:34-35.
[575] Cf. Mt 19:26.

620. Japan. My Jesus, what a mystery man is. My Jesus, what a mystery You are. Can it all be true? You. Suddenly you remind me of things: Barcelona, the Masses at Santa Maria del Mar, Abraham, the descendants. How blind I am. Without doing anything, You fulfill your Word and I'm blind to it. As if you didn't exist. My Jesus, my reservations, my fears... Come, You, my love.

(Porto San Giorgio, June 24, 1981)

621. Burundi. USA. United Kingdom. My Jesus, when You are, everything changes. Thank you, my Jesus, blessed are you. Peace, serenity, life, everything falls into place, with strength, normalcy. My Jesus, don't abandon me in the suffering, help me, even if I'm stupefied, blind and mute. Into your hands I entrust my life and death and tomorrow's waking. Free me from incredulity, apostasy, doubt, fear, misery. Jesus, Savior, wake me, free me, raise me.

(Porto San Giorgio, June 25, 1981)

622. America. My Jesus, day of worries, apprehension, fears; at night serenity, faith. Sweet Virgin Mary, everything is possible, everything is true, the mystery of the universe in your eyes. Sweet Virgin Mary, help me, wake me, alone, silent, with the sword in your heart[576] until the Cross. Woman![577] Blessed are you.

(Porto San Giorgio, June 26, 1981)

623. Loreto. Sweet Virgin Mary, Javier, Ain-Karem... You have believed.[578] Defend me. Quiet? Escape? My Jesus, a day of serenity and I become restless again. You are here and everything is divine, transcendent. You disappear and doubt returns and all falls to the ground, nothing remains. Jesus... Sweet Virgin Mary, help me.

(Porto San Giorgio, June 27, 1981)

624. Jesus, my Jesus, in the serenity of the night. You show me I must fight harder against the day's sorrows, the fear. But Lord, have mercy on me. Sadness grips me like an illness that doesn't come from

---

[576] Cf. Lk 2:35.
[577] Cf. Jn 19:26.
[578] Cf. Lk 1:45.

my radical powerlessness. Let me be a sacrifice, help me. No smoking? Help me. My Jesus, come. Do not hide your face from me when I awake. My Jesus, even if the whole world fought against me, with you, it's nothing. But You disappear and everything sinks into the nothingness of death, and the suffering terrifies me, it chokes me. Lord, lead me not into temptation; deliver me from evil.[579]

(Porto San Giorgio, June 28, 1981)

625. My Jesus, a night of revolution: the *merkaba* is moving: Spain, America… Oh, boy! My Jesus, the girls! Wow! In the end, I'm hurting because I don't know why I feel detached. I feel frustrated, alone. My Jesus, all this is incredible, insane. It is You, Lord. Don't leave me. I feel everything is distant, as if nothing depended on…

(Porto San Giorgio, June 29, 1981)

626. Four-thirty in the morning. An earthquake? Strong wind? At ten, impossible to wake up, pain, my head… heaviness. My Jesus, everything seems either like a dream or brainwashing. How can all this be? Is it You? Is it a mirage? Sweet Virgin Mary, if You are here, blessed are you. If these are all mental responses… my Jesus, where are we going? Jesus, have mercy on me. I have no energy.

(Porto San Giorgio, June 30, 1981)

627. Rest. Dentist. Hospital. I'm overwhelmed from every side, my Jesus. Fear, sadness, distress, and no consolation. Where? How? My Jesus, answer me, have mercy.

(Porto San Giorgio, July 1, 1981)

628. Rest. Hospital. More things. Alone! My Jesus, definitive cures… I'm always looking for what is definite, and it doesn't exist… Where are you? Only You are Eternal. Free me, Lord, for I cry to You. Day and night, I seek you, my Jesus.

(Porto San Giorgio, July 2, 1981)

629. Hospital. Dentist. All day in the mystery of suffering and death. And God? God, my God, where are you? Answer me. I'm

---

[579] Cf. Mt 6:13.

ashamed that I'm always saying the same things. Sadness and stubbornness. Jesus!

(Porto San Giorgio, July 3, 1981)

630. Free. Hospital. Not free, bound by the snares of death.[580] My Jesus, everything is terrifying, have mercy on me, I struggle in the anguish of death. You are here, Lord. *"Véante mis ojos."*[581] The darkness envelops me, the terror, the fear. My Jesus, you are possible. Where is your victory?[582] Jesus, Savior, show yourself.

(Porto San Giorgio, July 4, 1981)

631. Mountains. It's difficult to wake up. Accusing ghosts, calumnies. My Jesus, you have helped me. So what? What is the truth? Well, my Jesus, I'm a little better. The telephone call from Madrid has done me good. Or is it You? My Jesus, these sorrows, troubles, shadows seem to fit into their proper frames after reading St. John of the Cross. But then it all seems like spiritual illusions of these saints and I don't trust them. You exist, oh my God! How scary. I'm terrified that you may exist and yet I fear that only the nothingness and death exist. How is this possible? My Jesus, I love you, even if you didn't exist. Have mercy on me.

(Pieve di Cadore, July 9, 1981)

632. Terrible mountains, enormous. My Jesus, move the mountains...[583] Everything is possible for You.[584] I feel a bit better, freer. Not physically, my back, my arm… arthritis worsens. But I feel I am with you, my Jesus.

---

[580] Cf. 2 Sm 22:5-6.

[581] Verse from a popular song that made St. Teresa go into ecstasy: *"Véante mis ojos, / dulce Jesús bueno; / véante mis ojos, / muérame yo luego."* May my eyes see you, / good, sweet Jesus; / may my eyes see you, / and then may I die.

[582] Cf. 1 Cor 15:55.

[583] Cf. Mt 17:20.

[584] Cf. Mt 19:26.

Javier. Letter from Javier.[585] Everything is possible. The origins of Society. Everything seems to proceed on its own... and You, from behind, moving history. Life is in your hands. Blessed are you.

(Pieve di Cadore, July 10, 1981)

633. A day indoors. I burn the carpet, break a platter... My Jesus, I do everything badly, things don't interest me. I'm better, though... my Jesus, I don't know what to write. Everyone seems to be like me, indifferent, perplexed, lacking enthusiasm. My Jesus, not suffering much, but... my Jesus, may my eyes see you. To be able to say to you, kiss me with the kisses of your mouth.[586] Ah!

(Pieve di Cadore, July 11, 1981)

634. Mountains. Trout. My Jesus, I wake up feeling ill, troubled, amid the mountains. I pray, I read, I wait for you and I love you. Kiss me with the kisses of your mouth.[587] Your name is like a fragrant oil, poured out.[588] My Sweet Jesus, night falls, rain, and with it, serenity, but I'm distant from everything. My Jesus, St. Teresa makes me think of so many things and also to always see you in the actions of history themselves: the contradiction, the mystery. My Jesus, have mercy on us.

(Pieve di Cadore, July 12, 1981)

635. At the house, active. Jesus, my Jesus, the letters of St. Francis Xavier, India, the Creed... all mysterious. My Jesus, You are here. I see the saints as neurotic people with fixed ideas. St. Teresa, so many visions, my Jesus. Sickness, the mystery of men. You, mysterious, holy. You exist. May my blind eyes see you. Come, my love, come.

(Pieve di Cadore, July 13, 1981)

636. Mountains. It rains. It rains. Sadness permeates my soul. The sun comes out. The mountains, the sound of the river. My Jesus, if God were in my life, how gorgeous this view would be, the clouds,

---

[585] St. Francis Xavier from India.
[586] Cf. Sg 1:2.
[587] Cf. ibid.
[588] Cf. Sg 1:3.

the light, the trout, these companions that you give me. But doubt eats away at my life, and the dark darkness makes me wander aimlessly and mute. My Jesus, have mercy on me, tell me, yes, that all is foreseen by You, that You are and You know me. Blessed be your name.

(Pieve di Cadore, July 14, 1981)

637. Mario and Spandri[589] leave. House. Boredom. I go to Mass in town. My Jesus, these fantastic mountains rise up everywhere. Where are you? What am I doing here? What a mystery life is. My Jesus, I feel like I'm just waiting for the days, the hours to pass. Why? Reading about St. Francis Xavier in India, I'm almost scandalized. My Jesus, baptizing, baptizing, prayers, indulgences. My Jesus!

(Pieve di Cadore, July 15, 1981)

638. Virgin of Mount Carmel. Sweet Virgin Mary. We go out to new areas. More mountains. All immense and nothing revives me. I shut myself in the car to avoid meetings. New lake. My Jesus, sickness and fatigue in all things. "The annihilation." Contemplative purging? I wish! When I cannot find pleasure in anything, nor encouragement or consolation, or a place to sit, then yes, my Jesus, speak to me and cheer me up. Come, visit me, come, my love, come, turn a deaf ear to my terrible disbelief.

On the way back, the dire turmoil, "horror." My Jesus, I would like to escape and be by myself. Must I be my brother's keeper,[590] or is that my neurosis? "Freedom." My Jesus, your will. Show it to me, come.

(Pieve di Cadore, July 16, 1981)

639. Mountains. – Our battle is not against the creatures of flesh and blood, but against the powers and the spirits of evil. Stand firm, then, armed with the truth.[591] Resist courageously and you will see the salvation that the Lord will win for you.[592] Stand firm, then, armed with the truth. "Cling to Him, do not leave Him" *(Ecclesiasticus 2:3).*

---

[589] Antonio (Toni) Spandri (†), from the first community of the parish of *Santa Maria Formosa*, Venice.
[590] Cf. Gn 4:9.
[591] Cf. Eph 6:12-14.
[592] Cf. Ex 14:13; 2 Chr 20:17.

My Jesus, I spent the day better, with clearer perspectives. It did me good to discuss things with Kiko. My Jesus, it's possible to see things positively. Blessed are you. Defend me, unite me to You, do not separate me from You, let me believe in You. I love you, come, come, defend me when I awake.

(Pieve di Cadore, July 17, 1981)

640. Mountains. Rain, rain, rain. Alone in the house. From the depths, a little light wants to come out. "I believe in God, the Father Almighty, Creator of heaven and earth. I believe in Jesus Christ our Lord…" In your name, Lord. "Many followed him and he cured them all."[593] "Behold my Servant."[594] Most sweet Jesus, come, come, strengthen me in Rome, teach me to live in the present, to be yours, to love. Jesus!

It keeps raining buckets, twenty-four hours a day. My Jesus, even the newspapers terrify me: Sindona,[595] terrorism… You, my Jesus, crucified, have mercy. It rains, rains. The sound of the rain consoles me. Jesus!

(Pieve di Cadore, July 18, 1981)

641. Mountains. My Jesus, in bed the mountains rise, dragging me down like in a grave. My Jesus! If I could say like St. Paul, "Your grace has sustained me. When I was oppressed by anguish, your sweetness consoled me"[596]… My Jesus, I'm even afraid of God, Himself. Jesus, don't abandon me in the abyss of the human psyche. I'm tormented by mystery and fear. Jesus, my imaginings are like mountains. Teach me. Help me to see things less drastically, to live. My Jesus, come, come, I love you. I'm alone. Come, come with me, console me. I take refuge in You.[597]

---

[593] Cf. Mt 12:15.

[594] Mt 12:18.

[595] Michele Sindona (†), Italian banker, member of P2, the secret Italian freemason lodge linked to the Mafia, was poisoned while serving a life sentence for the murder of the attorney Giorgio Ambrosoli.

[596] Cf. Ps 94:18-19.

[597] Cf. Ps 143:9.

Talking to Kiko about my fears helps me see things less dramatically. Thank you, Jesus, that I see life naturally, with normality. Help me when I awake. Prayer!!!

(Pieve di Cadore, July 19, 1981)

642. My Jesus, defend me. Don't let me fall again into the swamp of intrigues, imaginings. Help me cut with it, not give it a chance, to forgive, to trust in You, my Jesus. Also to be on vacation and with Kiko, and the visits, the people. Lord, I believe in You. Jesus!

(Pieve di Cadore, July 20, 1981)

643. House. Cleaning up, leaving, my Jesus. The Pope, Lourdes,[598] the Church, I see everything emaciated my Jesus. Your word, your promises, "your mystery." God, my God, hidden, mysterious, savior, don't hide from my eyes, open them. Faith, Lord. I believe in You. Save me from this fierce and terrifying accuser,[599] who makes me see everything bleak so that my feet almost stumbled! My Rock, bind me to Yourself. Do not abandon me. I love you. You have given me all things. My life is in your hands. Help me to fight. Come, come. When You are here, the horizon changes, the present, the past, everything. Sweet Jesus, come, come, come. I love you. Don't remain distant.

(Pieve di Cadore, July 21, 1981)

644. It's late, almost three a.m. My Jesus, how sweet it is to see you, what a relief to see things with faith, with life. Jesus, living is sweet when everything changes. My Jesus, incredible: at night, during the day. How will I wake up? With you. Help me, my Jesus to simplify, to view things less drastically, to trust in You. Come, my Jesus, my mercy, my love, mysterious, holy. I love you.

After this night vigil, it's impossible to wake up. Pack up the house, always departing. Travel to Rome. Peaceful. My Jesus, help us.

(Rome, July 22, 1981)

---

[598] 42nd International Eucharistic Congress, July 15-23, 1981. The Pope, convalescing after the assassination attempt, did not attend.
[599] Cf. Rv 12:10.

645. My Jesus, everything gets old. Clothes that I don't need. I fill closets needlessly. I'm stingy. My Jesus, everything passes. You, the Eternal One. Where am I? The books, this house, everything feels like the nothingness. Lord, liberator, holy, unbind me from this miserable, stingy greed, that consumes me. Kiko is always like an earthquake of instability. My Jesus, everything fits me badly, I don't have anything to wear. I, I'm a horrible monster. Jesus, gracious, holy, my Lord, love me. I love you. Simplify me. The old order has passed away.[600] Teach me.

(Rome, July 23, 1981)

646. Dentist. Why, Lord, am I not happy with anything? You shower me with blessings. Your gifts are everywhere. And my conscience bothers me about everything: vacation, television, money, Kiko. Everything, everything weighs on me like a curse. My Jesus, what is it that I want? You know, Lord: to see you, to preach your name. Detach me from everything. Free. And with You. That You are, and that you love me. I love you, my Jesus. Make me trust in You. Gladden me.

(Rome, July 24, 1981)

647. In agony. Eucharist, yes or no? Santa Marinella, yes or no? My Jesus, the psalm resounds from the bottom of my anguished heart: I beg you, Lord, save me; the snares of death, anguish and sadness, surrounded me …[601] Lord, the tedium of the nothingness! When my existence holds no interest and time is dead, my Jesus… I'm a poor girl attacked by accusations, without memory, will, or understanding. I'm afraid of people, my Jesus, terrified of the human psyche, of myself. Have mercy on me. My Jesus, shelter me. I isolate myself in solitary confinement, in misery, my Jesus. Mercy, Lord.

Santa Marinella, finally. Lord, come!

(Santa Marinella, July 25, 1981)

648. Waking up in Sta. Marinella, buried by life. The destructive mentality of family, of myself, of life. This mystery of death

---

[600] Cf. 2 Cor 5:17.
[601] Cf. Ps 18:3-6.

destroying our existence. Jesus, my Jesus, savior, save me. Only your resurrection can enlighten this dark night, destructive, overwhelming, blind. My Jesus, where is your God?[602] I'm afraid. You, peacemaker, generous savior, save me, save me, save me. My Jesus, you give me a little encouragement in the middle of the night, so that I don't see life as such a tragedy. Thank you, my Jesus. Salvation?

(Santa Marinella, July 26, 1981)

649. Swimming. What for? Bicycle. Why? My Jesus, I have no desire for anything, everything is tragic. So what shall I do? My Jesus, I see everything is wrong, wrong, wrong, finished, destitute, a failure. My Jesus, television, television, television, all worries, everything seems wrong to me here, loneliness. I don't see life, life? My life. Where are you, my Jesus? Where are You, consoler, my life? Come, come, come.

(Santa Marinella, July 27, 1981)

650. Waking up as usual: pointless and in the nothingness. Swimming, why? I'm not going swimming. And then, stupidly, I slip! A tragic disruption, but I feel better: the boat, the sea, life is more normal. A sinner, a mess, miserable. My Jesus, You are the savior, Lord. My God, I love you, have mercy on me. I see things normally. Thank you, Lord.

(Santa Marinella, July 28, 1981)

651. To Rome. Dentist. Freedom, better, freer. My Jesus, I return freer, seeing things better. Will this last until tomorrow? I smoke stupidly. My Jesus, infuse me with energy. I sleep in peace. I had terrible dreams. Jesus!

(Santa Marinella, July 29, 1981)

652. A cleaning frenzy. Rome. Dentist. Mistrust eats away at my heart. I fall back into sadness.

I can hide better in this corner. It is almost better that it be obvious. My Jesus, the dead air; in the end, a hell of loneliness. My sweet Jesus.

---

[602] Cf. Ps 42:3.10.

You, Lord. The Church, holy assembly. Blessed are you. I love you, come.

(Santa Marinella, July 30, 1981)

653. My Jesus, how terrified I am of myself, of Kiko. Once more, my Jesus, take pity. Have mercy. Are you here? Are you here? My Jesus, don't abandon us, merciful, holy, for your name's sake,[603] for your holiness, your promises. Lift us up. Strengthen my will, my yearning, my faithfulness. My Jesus, wake me up from this dark, terrible hibernation stupor. My Jesus, I wait for you. Raise us up, Jesus.

(Santa Marinella, July 31, 1981)

654. All day, at the service of the Gennarinis, and I feel better. Today, ashamed again, my Jesus. Mario comes. Eucharist. I'm a little better. The trip will be cancelled. With just a little and the former glory returns, my Jesus. Everything is always precarious, everything passes, You remain, Eternal, only one, holy. Blessed are you.

(Santa Marinella, August 1, 1981)

655. The weariness begins. My Jesus, what are we doing here in the heart of this family? Jesus! My Jesus! The mystery of existence. Where are you? My Jesus, I cannot find rest in anything or anyone. Who are we? Who am I? My Jesus, merciful, holy, only one, come, come, come, give me the desire to be, to live, free me, heal me from this devastating, overwhelming pessimism. My Jesus, Madrid is cancelled. I don't know where to go and I don't know what I'm doing here. Come, Lord.

(Santa Marinella, August 2, 1981)

656. I can't see, Lord, not even the sea. Swimming, a sacrifice. Everything as if it didn't exist, and being here is like a syrupy mess, my Jesus… They have left. I close in on myself. Dangerous loneliness. You are and You are here, right? Thank you, my Jesus, You are Life for me Lord, the Only One. This crazy and mysterious existence… If You are, everything is wonderful. Yes, death and old age… everything seems horrible. My Jesus, resurrected, come, come, come.

(Santa Marinella, August 3, 1981)

---

[603] Cf. Jr 14:7.

657. Lauds. More spirit. I begin to enjoy the water. My Jesus, spending all day organizing the kitchen… I'm starting to become "*escorbútica*" and I smoke like an idiot. The lungs, the convivence, like menacing, overwhelming ghosts. Kiko, unbearable. My Jesus, the demands… Come, Lord, only one, generous, holy, come.

(Santa Marinella, August 4, 1981)

658. Alone. They've gone fishing. Everything scares me, my Jesus. I cry out to You all day and you don't hear me. "I called out to him but he did not answer."[604] My Jesus, I go for a walk with a sad, sad heart, crying. My Jesus, not swimming, not in the sun, only groaning, groaning and smoking like an absolute idiot. Have mercy on me.

(Santa Marinella, August 5, 1981)

659. Again, my Jesus, the afternoon. I'm terrified. Falling on your mercy, however, is better than the fears of gloom. My Jesus, when I cannot raise my head, nor boast of innocence, I'm seemingly better, without so many terrors. My Jesus do not abandon us, have pity. My Jesus, pity. My Jesus, pity. Mercy of mine, I love you. Forgive me!

(Santa Marinella, August 7, 1981)

660. Truly, "the Lord is compassionate and merciful; forgives sins and saves in the time of distress."[605] Blessed are you, Lord. I walked, walked looking for your forgiveness. Blessed age-old confession. Thank you, Lord. I rely on your mercy. Defend me. Raise me up from these crises of aging, of fear, of death. My Jesus, innocent, holy, blessed be your name. Open my lips to bless you, even if I don't deserve it. I love you. Save me!

(Santa Marinella, August 8, 1981)

661. Mimmo's birthday. Eucharist. Angela returns, thank goodness. I feel generous, my Jesus…

(Santa Marinella, August 9, 1981)

---

[604] Cf. Sg 5:6.
[605] Qo 2:11.

662. *S. Lorenzo*. I sleep for twenty-four hours. I'm groggy, sick. My Jesus, without a doctor in the villa, only You. My Jesus, how distant. I see everything as corruptible. If you are, it scares me, if not, it terrifies me. My Jesus, I invoke you day and night, where are you? Blessed be your mercy. Have mercy on me, have mercy.

(Santa Marinella, August 10, 1981)

663. My Jesus! The Pope's document: small communities, evangelizing dynamism; the Pope as an itinerant catechist.[606] A consolation? Must call Fr. Maximino. A more accessible Church. Books. My Jesus, a little bit better, but not really. Come, come, come sweet Lord, my Jesus, my mercy, come. Jesus!

(Santa Marinella, August 11, 1981)

664. My Jesus, all this past year spent in pain and nothingness, and now the terror of the future panorama… my Jesus, I'm happier. I read. What? What for? You know. I always wait for you. I'm a little better.

(Santa Marinella, August 12, 1981)

665. My Jesus! I don't know what to write anymore. Always the same sorrows. My Jesus! My Jesus! My Jesus! It's all held together by a string. You said something good to me: do not think of the immediate future, the present, the present. My Jesus, make yourself present and that is enough for me. Come.

(Santa Marinella, August 13, 1981)

666. Sweet Virgin Mary! *Assumpta in Coelis*. Blessed are You who have believed.[607] You have consoled me: two wings, the desert…[608] Sweet one, protect me, guide me, console me. Sweet Virgin Mary!

(Santa Marinella, August 14, 1981)

---

[606] Message of St. John Paul II on the occasion of the World Mission Day 1981 (6.7.1981), "It is a reason for great hope to see *small Christian communities* multiplying in the world, *dynamic* and open, which have understood their responsibility to *announce the Gospel*… I have traveled to many countries… I have wanted to announce the Gospel myself, in some way becoming an *itinerant catechist*."

[607] Cf. Lk 1:45.

[608] Cf. Rv 12:14.

667. Assumption. Sweet Virgin Mary. All this fishing makes me sad, afraid. My Jesus, why? This being here as one who doesn't exist, in the nothingness… idleness… without thanking you for being, for living, for being here, Lord, how can so much blindness be possible? What a mystery is man's unsatisfied heart. Only You, infinite, Lord, come.

(Santa Marinella, August 15, 1981)

668. My Jesus, willpower. What a word against laziness, boredom… my Jesus, defender, holy, savior…fight! My Jesus, the reason for this sadness, without grace… I see the tempter prowling around,[609] but then he moves on. The Pope, in good shape. My Jesus! You, You are eternal. Always, You are. Blessed are you, Come.

(Santa Marinella, August 16, 1981)

669. My Jesus, have mercy on me. What to do? My Jesus, I'm sad, I'm terrified of you, and my existence has no meaning. Have mercy, Lord.

(Santa Marinella, August 18, 1981)

670. Room change. The books open up to me. I sit in the sun. We set the longline. I can tolerate the visits. My Jesus, I'm better. Thank you, my Jesus, better!!! People, the sea, have done me some good. Jesus, revive me!

(Santa Marinella, August 19, 1981)

671. Parade of visits. Lord, the mystery of man. My Jesus, I have fears, turmoil, fright. I pace about in my sorrow, I sleep, I fear. I would kick everybody out. And then? Nothing. Jesus, have mercy.

(Santa Marinella, August 20, 1981)

672. Weather change. Stormy sea. My Jesus, restlessness, convivence, books… What, Lord? Only You. In conversion, calm, your salvation; in trusting abandonment, your strength.[610] My Jesus, abandoning myself to You. My Jesus, mysterious, holy, savior, I seek

---

[609] Cf. 1 Pt 5:8.
[610] Cf. Is 30:15.

You. Come. You have consoled me. Quiet prayer. I love you, My Jesus. Thank you. Serenity, peace, contentment, seem like wonderful gifts to me. My Jesus, how long since I lived. To live, Jesus, without so much fear.

(Santa Marinella, August 21, 1981)

673. Fell from the bicycle. Lord, how old I am, and what an "*estupidona.*"[611]

(Santa Marinella, August 22, 1981)

674. Eucharist, just the three of us. Thank you, my Jesus, that once in a while, you place some drops of balm on my heart that is always so full of tribulation, torment, and turmoil. My Jesus, the day is passing. Serenity. My Jesus, thank you. Fortify my faith, do not allow me to doubt You. Lead me not into temptation; deliver me from the evil one,[612] for I take refuge in You.

(Santa Marinella, August 23, 1981)

675. Peacefully watching the nightfall in front of the wonderful sea. The green, the first stars… your gifts, so great, parade before me. What are you complaining about? What could you desire that I haven't given you? Truly you are great, Lord. I'm a poor, petty wretch, who doesn't know how to live and let live. You, my Jesus, can cure me. Come, come, You, resurrected, alive. Lord, give me life, resurrect me, tear me out of the nothingness. My Jesus, Lord, I love you. I take refuge in You. Do not condemn me to myself. Save me.

(Santa Marinella, August 24, 1981)

676. The days trickle by. Like what? A burden? Lord, I'm struggling. In what? Lord, I take refuge in You. Give rest to my restlessness in every way: if I'm here, to be here; if not, to not be here. Paradise. Jesus, what a mystery is the human psyche! What fear of myself and of everyone and of the world and of history and of man. And You, Lord? What a mystery. My Jesus, have mercy on me. Gladden me. What am I defending myself from? From what? Jesus,

---

[611] Mix of Spanish and Italian, literally, 'big dummy' – *Trans.*
[612] Mt 6:13.

Jesus, savior, save me. May my blind eyes see you, Jesus; your voice, my deaf ears. Where are you? Who are you? Come, come, come, You, my Lord.

(Santa Marinella, August 25, 1981)

677. Time flies, flies. Stop it? Is it against me? My Jesus, devouring books, booklets, what am I looking for? You aren't there, my Jesus. I'm marching against time. This dark psyche, whiny, aggravating. I don't know how to live. Have mercy on me. I struggle in an existential tragedy. Where are you? Who am I? Where are we going? You, Jesus, You are here, You are, You have always been, you will be. I love you. Thank you, my Jesus. Forgiveness of sins. Come, holy one. Your answer is everything.

(Santa Marinella, August 26, 1981)

678. I finally find peace. Incredible. Dinner. Fish. My Jesus, you console us. Lord, I'm still terrified!!!

(Santa Marinella, August 27, 1981)

679. St. Augustine. My Jesus, memorable day for me. You pulled me out at great risk, with so much love. And now… Why do I fear the future? That embryo of promises is being mysteriously realized and I doubt. How is it possible? Have mercy on me. Arcinazzo terrifies me, convivence, family, Lord.

(Santa Marinella, August 28, 1981)

680. Counting time is like agony, agony, agony. Life is like an agony. I don't know how to live. Why, Lord, do I live in agony? With the sun, the sea, this house, that are all wonderful, and I'm in perpetual agony. Lord, will it pass? My Jesus, have mercy on me. With all my heart I cry out to you: help me!

(Santa Marinella, August 29, 1981)

681. I live like I'm in agony, dying, overwhelmed. Why? It seems like you are not here, that the convivence will be a ridiculous disaster, and terror invades me, terror. Jesus, come, come, come. Peace.

(Santa Marinella, August 30, 1981)

682. The month ends. Everything is ending. My Jesus, time! How scary. Everything terrifies me. I'm terrified, calm me down, Lord! And why? Document from the CEI,[613] the figure of Ballestrero... I have lived submerged in terror.

My Jesus, you visited me in the evening. Moses, history, the bush.[614] You know me, my Jesus, thank you. A little balm, of meaning. Thank you, Lord. Disregard my unbelief.

(Santa Marinella, August 31, 1981)

683. Dentist. So hoped for and so impossible. My Lord, neither money, nor friendship, nothing is of use to me if You don't want it. Sickness and death, my Jesus. Rome. I don't know how to be. I almost didn't return. Santa Marinella seems like a marvel for which I haven't thanked you... for anything.

(Santa Marinella, September 1, 1981)

684. Dentist again. Rome. My Jesus, what a small bill. The misery still pursues me, complaints. Suddenly the ghosts vanish. Reality. Reality. The events are not really enough to cause suffering. What a mystery, my Jesus: suddenly, freedom. Thank you, Lord!

(Santa Marinella, September 2, 1981)

685. Dentist: the piece of this well-known international tooth... My Jesus, an hour and a half lying here powerless before medicine and death, and without freedom. My Jesus, only You perform miracles. Jesus, Jesus, my Jesus!!!

(Santa Marinella, September 3, 1981)

686. Antoine,[615] France, the priests, the parishes... My Jesus, restless all day, with no time. What am I looking for in the books? What is it I want to do, since I have no time for anything? My Jesus, the *Sacramentinos*: the pastor is happy and so is Amadei. Thank goodness. My Jesus, at night, I laugh at the fears. Jesus!!!

(Santa Marinella, September 4, 1981)

---

[613] Italian Bishops' Conference, *Pastoral note: Ecclesiastical Criteria for groups, movements, associations* (5.22.1981).

[614] Cf. Ex 3:1-10.

[615] Antoine de Monicault (†), presbyter of the first community of the parish of *Notre Dame de la Bonne Nouvelle*, Paris.

687. Fr. Maximino's Day. The boat, the sea… symbolic. My Jesus, hope can only be placed in You, eternal, invincible. My Jesus, You have made all things wonderful. Day of suffering for Kiko. I'm doing better, more "battle ready", but the convinces have no other prospect than that of your presence. Thank you, my Jesus.

(Santa Marinella, September 5, 1981)

688. Eucharist. Finally, serenity, my Jesus. You listen to my cry. From the terror of the enemy, free us. My Jesus, I consume myself with waiting, the burdens, the convivences… Open my eyes to your presence. Revive me, My Jesus, savior. Deliver me, help me, my Jesus, my good, deliver me from the terror. Why? If You were not here… terrible. Jesus, open my mouth, help me.

(Santa Marinella, September 6, 1981)

689. My Jesus, you appear again, consoler. It was a trial, a preparation to announce your gospel. My Jesus, calm me down, because this helplessness troubles me. To speak. How? Inspiration! My Jesus, what will we say? You will be there. You have always been there, my Jesus, and regardless, I still cannot breathe. Restlessness, restlessness, ignorance, nothing. My Jesus, it's all a blank page to You, inspirer, wise, holy.

(Santa Marinella, September 7, 1981)

690. Anxiety, terror, agony. Lord, what suffering. Terrified by the convivences as if they were exams. Terror, life in the nothingness, helplessness. Finally, serenity: they've left. My Jesus, I feel free, blessed are you. Defend me when I awake.

(Santa Marinella, September 8, 1981)

691. Last day. Anxiety, anxiety, the convivence… everything ends. I want to have all the books present in my mind and nothing reassures me. Terror, terror, terror. Calm at nightfall.

(Santa Marinella, September 9, 1981)

692. Leave for Arcinazzo – Such fear that it makes me laugh. Arrival. Like sardines. Not one word. Jesus doesn't help me. Come.

(Arcinazzo, September 10, 1981)

693. I jump in. My Jesus, what labor pains, from jumping in. My Jesus, ahh! What a people.

(Arcinazzo, September 11, 1981)

694. My Jesus, a people. Weariness. Piemonte, my Jesus! Finally, Fr. Maximino. Eucharist. Peace, liberation, blessed are you. Help me!!!

(Arcinazzo, September 12, 1981)

695. Climate of inspiration. Your presence, my Jesus, what a consolation, what tranquility, what joy. My Jesus, strength, freedom, authority, grace. Thank you, my Jesus. I love you.

Rome. Trastevere. My Jesus, in peace, not suffering. It seems impossible. Blessed are you. Wake me up in peace. I love you. Jesus!

(Rome, September 13, 1981)

696. Sweet Glorious Cross, defend me. Salimei, consolation. My Jesus, I love.

(Rome, September 14, 1981)

697. Free. My Jesus, Kiko has nowhere to lay his head.[616] Television, Kiko, they both depress me. My Jesus, this house seems closed. And the street… there's no place to be. Movie? Restaurant? Why? You are the only refuge, life and strength. Fear already at the convivence… Jesus!

(Rome, September 15, 1981)

698. Rushing. Restless. Narváez. My mother arrives from Ólvega. My Jesus, thank you. Serenity, heat. Teach me to live in freedom. Help me!!!

(Madrid, September 16, 1981)

699. Jesus, again. A stable location. My Jesus, I'm angry: you don't inspire me, I make a fool of myself. My Jesus, why? What use am I to you? This coming and going, from here to there… I see everything gray, mediocre, without You, My crucified Jesus. Why? Do not leave me. Come, come, come.

(Valle – Madrid, September 17, 1981)

---

[616] Cf. Mt 8:20.

700. Catechists, Madrid and provinces. Itinerants. My Jesus, how much you make me suffer from helplessness, from darkness, from everything.

My Jesus, in the end, serenity. Psalm 22. To accept not speaking, not knowing or not being able. Either it is your will or it's my neuroses. My Jesus, I love you. Help me!!! I don't know what to say. Why?

(Valle, September 18, 1981)

701. My Jesus, this anxiety, like I get for an exam, for books I have to read, all over nothing. My Jesus, suffering, labor pains, is it from powerlessness or from evangelization? Eucharist. Frustration? No. You are always present in it. Thank you, Lord. My Jesus!

(Valle, September 19, 1981)

702. My Jesus, a bleak awakening. My Jesus, the power of your gospel. Loaded morning. I decide to open my mouth, as usual – disconnection. I love you. In any case, better toward the end. Peace. Thank you, my Jesus. When I awake, your face. Come!!! Freedom.

(Valle, September 20, 1981)

703. Narváez. I didn't fall asleep until six o'clock, from excitement. My Jesus, by day the fight. Alone. My Jesus what pain, what sorrow, my mother, her bones. My Jesus, what a mystery: everything oppresses me trying to bury me in the darkness. My Jesus, raise me up. Sweetest one, glorious, holy, victor, come, come, do not abandon me. Put the armor of light in my hands.[617] Battles. This world of darkness, of evil... My Jesus, love. St. Matthew today. Gospel, You mingling with sinners.[618] Come, come.

(Madrid, September 21, 1981)

704. Hospital *Primero de Octubre*. Treatment for cervical pain. My Jesus, good. Night in Elisa's house. Serenity at nightfall, thankfully. All day battling the darkness, death, pain. My mother. Physical and moral pains. My Jesus, bones completely dislocated without remedy. I love

---

[617] Cf. Rom 13:12.
[618] Cf. Mt 9:10-17.

you. Live for today. Blessed are you. Armor of light.[619] Fight. Help me.

(Madrid, September 22, 1981)

705. Hospital. My Jesus, you gave me a courageous, valiant ending. My Jesus, the darkness tries to bury me, but You appear glorious from the depths. Thank you, my Jesus. Help me. Jesus, my Jesus, my love, all of a sudden everything is nothingness and, when You want, everything has a meaning, even the smallest thing. Wake me up.

(Madrid, September 23, 1981)

706. My Jesus! Your language is unique, Lord. The newspapers, the television, my Jesus, all those voices, and at home… Man, man is poor: fear, the desire to be, to be loved… my Jesus, I feel pity for everything. My Jesus, free me from the fear. You are the only one, my Lord.

(Madrid, September 27, 1981)

707. Elisa's house. Painful awakening, as always. Hospital. Hurry. Racing. *La Paloma.* I'm happy. It's like a victory over the ghosts. My Jesus, free. Help me. My Jesus, the car window, broken. My notepad, stolen. Jesus.

(Madrid, September 28, 1981)

708. Insomnia yesterday. Joy. Jesus, to the hospital in the afternoon. You, Lord, blessed are you. Meeting at the Center. Vicariates. My Jesus, You always marvelously pull things out of nothing. Blessed are you.

(Madrid, September 29, 1981)

709. What dissatisfaction: groggy from smoking, fighting, yelling, my Jesus. So what's it to me? The day passes by like a breath. I smoke like an idiot. My Jesus, have mercy on me! The hospital, nothing. I don't see these treatments working.

(Madrid, September 30, 1981)

---

[619] Cf. Rom 13:12.

710. Hospital. Home. "*Escorbútica.*" Airport: Mimmo and Angela arrive. My Jesus, tired. My Jesus, I love you. This house, the marvels of the home. My Jesus, I love you.

(Madrid, October 1, 1981)

711. My Jesus, feeling neither sorrow nor glory, but deep down, I'm doing well. I'm comforted by this deep respite. Everything seems worthless to me. It seemed better before. Even disillusioned by Loewe… my Jesus, I love you so. Help me. Courage. To not give importance to things.

(Madrid, October 2, 1981)

712. Vigil of St. Francis. My Jesus. Let nothing trouble you. Thank you, my Jesus. The vineyard, no wild grapes.[620] Sweet one, your love is sweeter than wine.[621] Restlessness. My Jesus, calm me down. Eucharist. Peace.

(Madrid, October 3, 1981)

713. St. Francis. The Pope reappears. Beatification of Claudina Thevenet.[622] My Jesus, I love you. My Jesus, my neck is doing badly. Help me, encourage me.

(Alocén, October 4, 1981)

714. My Jesus, you train me in this intimate evil, my Jesus. Thinking bad, terrible thoughts, whatever my reason tells me. You convince me of sin.[623] When confronted with the absurd, it is better to accept the gospel. My Jesus, another nature! Jesus.

(Madrid, October 6, 1981)

715. Madrid – Rome – Arcinazzo. Itinerants of Italy plus Europe. My Jesus, thank you, happiness, encouragement, strength. When I'm

---

[620] Cf. Is 5:2.
[621] Cf. Sg 1:2.
[622] Founder of the Congregation of Jesus-Mary. Carmen spent her last years of high school in the *Colegio Jesus – Maria*, on calle Juan Bravo, Madrid. The religious suggested she enter their novitiate. Carmen stipulated she be allowed to go in mission. Her condition was not accepted.
[623] Rom 3:20.

well, I don't know what to write. My Jesus, I can even stay quiet, whatever You want. Inspire me, grant me the ability to speak about You, about your immense love, about your power. Open my mouth. Give me the chance, if You want. I love you. Help me.

(Arcinazzo, October 7, 1981)

716. Itinerants of Italy – Europe. My Jesus, my Jesus, you comfort me. You are. I feel courage, strength. But Kiko is always demanding. My Jesus, I can see everything with freedom and then, suddenly, the day becomes overcast by any small thing... What a mystery man is. I love you. Jesus, Jesus, I love you.

(Arcinazzo, October 8, 1981)

717. My Jesus, when you come, I no longer need to write down my sorrows, complaints. Ah, my Jesus, how unforgettable and fruitful are all the sadnesses, the suffering, the terror, the trial! My Jesus, open my lips.

(Arcinazzo, October 9, 1981)

718. Eucharist. When You are here, even if veiled, I don't know what to write.

(Arcinazzo, October 10, 1981)

719. My Jesus, listening, listening to the priests, to the boys... My Jesus, my strength, thank you. You comfort me deeply. I feel free. Thank you, my Jesus. When you are here, I don't know what to write. Open my lips, Lord, with mercy.

(Arcinazzo, October 11, 1981)

720. Arcinazzo – Rome. Incredible. We finished. Nigeria, Pakistan, Sudan and Italy. My Jesus, your chariot, You bring life, the nations, the Church, Rome. Good night.

(Rome, October 12, 1981)

721. St. Polycarp.[624] My Jesus, you train our hands for battle.[625] Blessed is your name, your power. Blessed are you, Lord. My Jesus, this world…

(Rome, October 13, 1981)

722. Chancery. Offices. My Jesus, from here one sees the poor administrators differently. My Jesus, You compellingly lead everything.

(Rome, October 14, 1981)

723. Cé, eighteen pages, my Jesus.[626] St. Teresa. Ballestrero in Avila.
Madrid – Valle. Two in the morning. My Jesus, teach me how to not worry, to rest in You. If you want me to open my mouth, inspire me. I abandon myself to You.

(Valle – Madrid, October 15, 1981)

724. Spain Itinerants. They are all more mature, without ringleaders. My Jesus, I love you. I don't listen. You keep me mute. For one word I said at Lauds… catastrophe. I love you.

(Valle, October 16, 1981)

725. Itinerants. Listening, listening, boys, girls. My Jesus, You love each one. I love you. Come, my Jesus, I love you. Eucharist. Lottery. Departure.

(Valle, October 17, 1981)

726. Valle – Madrid – Domund. Return. Landing in Madrid. Joy. My Jesus, you console me deeply. Your promises… they surpass the

---

[624] Parish of *San Policarpo*, Rome.

[625] Ps 144:1.

[626] Cardinal Marco Cé (†), Patriarch of Venice, 1978-2002. He was the successor in Venice to Albino Luciani after the latter was elected Pope, taking the name John Paul I. He published an 18-page pastoral letter, in which he presented his pastoral plan. In it, he forbade the celebration of the Eucharist in the Neocatechumenal communities, forbade new catechesis, even though there were then 45 requests, and reduced the Way to the two parishes in which it already existed, *Santa Maria Formosa* and *Santi Apostoli*. He sent this letter to various bishops in Italy and abroad.

promise of youth. You are great, Lord, the only one. I love you. With you… Come, Lord, You. To rest in You. "Let nothing trouble You."[627] The teams, the girls… my Jesus. New teams… labor pains. You are, Lord, holy, magnificent. I love you. I almost went into crisis: the people, each one, a world. You know each one by name. Blessed are you.

(Madrid, October 18-19, 1981)

727. Day off. Kiko and Mario at Alocén. I'm at the hospital. Order in Samaria.[628] My Jesus, I'm deeply happy. Thank you, my Jesus. I love you. And when You are here, it's useless to write. Blessed are you.

(Madrid, October 20, 1981)

728. My Jesus, You give us peace. The victory is in your hands. Everything is yours. You appear and are present. Catechists of Madrid in the Center. Kiko inspired. I'm even envious. My Jesus, it is You, and I'm happy.

(Madrid, October 22, 1981)

729. My Jesus, you awaken and visit me. And then I'm unbearable with Elisa, I don't understand her. I make Kiko's life impossible. Forgive me, Lord. You convince me of my sin, my Jesus, my love. How can you stand me? Inside I'm bad to the point of meanness. My Jesus, I love you. Help me.

(Madrid, October 23, 1981)

730. Intense day. *Canillas*: church, construction. Lunch at Josemari Soler's house. Like the old times! Lord, you have acted unceasingly. You understand everything. Night: *S. Sebastián*: everyone fighting to love. Mysterious discovery. You are holy.

(Madrid, October 24, 1981)

731. My Jesus, about to leave for Zamora and we give up: Mario's in bed. Moaning, complaining… my Jesus, deep down you comfort

---

[627] ST. TERESA OF JESUS, "Let nothing trouble you," in *Poems*.
[628] Street in Madrid where Carmen's older sister, Elisa, lived.

me, even against the terrible "kika" and "kikos" idea that used to destroy me; now I feel free. Blessed are you!

(Madrid, October 25, 1981)

732. Memorable day. Center meeting: program for the Vicariates. "The 35." Lottery:

North: Fr. Juan Manuel, pb;[629] Manolo – Paloma;[630] José María Soler – Carmenchu;[631] Antonio Camarero, pb;[632] Jacinto – Carmen.[633]

East: Pedro S.S., pb;[634] Carlos Sicilia – Mercedes;[635] José Agudo – Rosario;[636] Antonio (veterinarian), absent.[637]

South: Mondejar, pb;[638] Rafa – Marisol;[639] Antonio Varela, pb;[640] Ramón – Lidia;[641] Luis – Mari Carmen (catalinos).[642]

---

[629] Fr. Juan Manuel Ávalos Cuervos (†), pastor of the parish of *San José*, Madrid.

[630] Manuel and Paloma Atienza, from the first community of the parish of *San José*, Madrid.

[631] José María (†) and Carmen (†) Soler, from the community of the Neocatechumenal Center, Madrid.

[632] Fr. Antonio Sanz Camarero (†), then pastor of the parish of *San Antonio de la Florida*, Madrid.

[633] Jacinto (†) and Carmen (†) Cuesta, from the first community of the parish of *Santa Catalina Labouré*, Madrid.

[634] Fr. Pedro García Martín (†), pastor of the parish of *San Sebastián*, Madrid.

[635] Carlos and Mercedes Sicilia, from the first community of the parish of *San Sebastián*, Madrid.

[636] José and Rosario Agudo, from the community of the Neocatechumenal Center, Madrid.

[637] Antonio and Mariluz Molina, from the first community of the parish of *Nuestra Señora del Tránsito*, Madrid.

[638] José María Mondéjar Izquierdo, CM, then pastor of the parish of *Santa Catalina Labouré*, Madrid.

[639] Rafael and Sol Tomás, from the community of the Neocatechumenal Center, Madrid.

[640] Mons. Antonio Varela Verástegui (†), pastor of the parish of *San Roque*, Madrid.

[641] Ramón (†) and Lidia Domingo, from the first community of the parish of *San Roque*, Madrid.

[642] Luis and María del Carmen de Pablo, from the first community of the parish of *Santa Catalina Labouré*, Madrid.

West: Fr. Jesús pb;[643] Juan;[644] Luis Rivas – Ana;[645] Luis, pb.[646]

(Madrid, October 26, 1981)

733. Active day. My Jesus! Hyper, happy. My Jesus! Joy surprises me. My Jesus, with more heart, grateful to You, holy, liberator, my Lord. Visit to *S. Roque*. Announce the Our Father. Satisfaction, joy. Kiko inspired. Blessed are you. I am in grace. Fr. Antonio,[647] serene. Israel? Blessed are you.

(Madrid, October 27, 1981)

734. Running and grumbling all day. Why, Lord? Worries. To love You, to be with You, to abandon myself to You, my Jesus! The sorrows, my Jesus… I love you. Help me.

(Madrid, October 28, 1981)

735. My Jesus, on the go all day. Why? My Jesus, I love you. Help me slow down. I love you. Joy, meeting, inspiration. Center: catecheses of the steps, "the children", the new generation. I love you.

(Madrid, October 29, 1981)

736. Hyper. Fidgety. Hospital. Weekend. Lunch with Kiko's mother:[648] quail…

My Jesus, the Bible, having it bound. *Sta. Catalina*. I can't take any more. Dinner. I want to escape. I escape. My Jesus, my love!

(Madrid, October 30, 1981)

---

[643] Mons. Jesús Higuera Fernández (†), pastor of the parish of *Virgen de la Paloma y San Pedro el Real*, Madrid.

[644] Juan Fernández Ruiz, from the first community of the parish of *Virgen de la Paloma y San Pedro el Real*, Madrid. Ordained presbyter in 1983.

[645] Luis and Ana Rivas, from the first community of the parish of *Nuestra Señora del Tránsito*, Madrid.

[646] Fr. Luis Blanco Cerezo (†), pastor of the parish of *San Saturnino*, Alcorcón.

[647] Mons. Antonio Varela Verástegui (†), pastor of the parish of *San Roque*, Madrid.

[648] María del Pilar Wirtz Suárez (†).

737. Madrid – Zamora. Peace. Journey. Joy! Miracle of communities: incredible. The children – Eucharist. Lord, I love you. Thank you, Lord, help me.

(Zamora, October 31, 1981)

738. Communion of Saints. The lost sheep, forgiveness. Memorial of your sanctity: "Forgiveness." My Jesus, it seems like an eternity: Zamora… Travel to Madrid. My Jesus, help them.

(Madrid, November 1, 1981)

739. Day off, rest, free for my heart as well, my Jesus. How wonderful! To breathe, to live, in good spirits, with courage… My Jesus, grace! Blessed are you. The memory of the suffering, the helplessness, they all seem even funny now, gratuitous, good. Your sweetest love. Blessed are you!

(Madrid, November 2, 1981)

740. Madrid – Barcelona. Second community. My crucified Jesus, You pursue man. My Jesus, awesome, holy.

You wake me up happy, my Jesus. Thank you. Day of memories of Barcelona, of your faithfulness. Lost sheep catechesis.

Four a.m. Blessed are you! Bishop's residence. Alemany.[649] Farnés. Fr. Esteban.[650] Hurry. Airport. To Rome. Once again to the second of *Sta. Francesca.*

(Barcelona, November 3-5, 1981)

741. Barcelona – Rome – Sta. Marinella. Venice. Cé, my Jesus! I'm free, tired, happy. Smoking, my neck, my back… My Sweet Jesus, I see yes and no, that in the end only You, the only one, Lord of all things. My Jesus, I love you. The Russian ship in Sweden[651]… War? My Jesus!

(Santa Marinella, November 6, 1981)

---

[649] Mosén Joan Alemany Esteve (†), then Episcopal Vicar of Pastoral Zone 2, Barcelona.

[650] Fr. Esteban Casals Humet, SDB (†), from the second community of the parish of *Santas Juliana and Semproniana*, San Adrián de Besós.

[651] On October 30, 1981, the Russian nuclear submarine U-137 ran aground on the Swedish coast with a uranium load as big as that which destroyed Hiroshima.

742. Farnés. Letter to Cé. My Jesus, happy. Sweet one, you give me courage. I'm so tired. Your sweet love puts the brakes on my acceleration. I love you. Help us, my Jesus.

(Santa Marinella, November 7, 1981)

743. Eucharist. Paella. My Jesus, happy. Sustain me. I see things within your existence. You are immense, great, wonderful, and this makes me happy. Thank you, my Jesus. You come. Virgins awake; the oil.[652] You, Lord, the Bridegroom, my Love. I love you.

(Santa Marinella, November 8, 1981)

744. Active, agile. My Jesus, consoled by your sweet love. Blessed are you. I greatly love you. I love you.

Rome. In the car with Stefano and Claudiano.[653] Poletti, a consolation. Movie of the Pope. I fall asleep. Tired. But I won't say anything. Good night, my Jesus. I love you.

(Rome, November 9, 1981)

745. What can I say, Lord, of your greatness? You are indescribable, holy.

Visit with Poletti. Consoling. Thank you, my Jesus. Afternoon: second *Natività*. My Jesus, everything passes, develops, dies, mysteriously. History. Sweet Jesus, to be with you. Come.

(Rome, November 10, 1981)

746. Fr. Maximino. Sunny day in the Vatican. The light, peace. There's never any time, my Jesus. *S. Salvatore*. Martini. The history that is not playing out well, my Jesus. Lord, I trust in You. You, my Jesus.

(Rome, November 11, 1981)

---

[652] Cf. Mt 25:1-13.

[653] Mons. Claudiano Strazzari (pb), from the first community of the parish of San Leonardo Murialdo, Rome. Then itinerant catechist with Stefano Gennarini in Poland, Germany and Czechoslovakia. Later, Rector of the Diocesan College "Redemptoris Mater Seminary" of Rome since 1998.

747. My Jesus, you give me energy, encouragement, consolation, life. Blessed are you. I love you. Day in the house, active, ordered, holy. Prayer. Phone.

My Jesus! Second of *S. Luigi*. I love you. Your miracles, your presence your power, "the inspiration," my Jesus, the catechesis... I love you. Help me.

(Rome, November 12, 1981)

748. My Jesus, meek.[654] The phone gives me no rest. Giampiero's house. *S. Tito*. Mystery of mysteries. My Jesus, You are great, the only one. I fell asleep in the catechesis. Jesus!

(Rome, November 13, 1981)

749. First *Martiri*. Eucharist. Superior General of the Sacramentine Order. My Jesus, you are a genius in your plans, inscrutable, holy. Blessed be your name! My Jesus, I love you. Lord, "the strong woman"[655]... St. Augustine... you console me. Blessed your name and power!

(Rome, November 14, 1981)

750. Vatican. Went up to the Third Loggia in the Vatican:[656] Silvestrini. You, my Jesus, go before us, our history is yours. My Jesus, holy, blessed are you.

(Rome, November 15, 1981)

751. Rome – *Firenze*. My Jesus, You, Shepherd of Israel,[657] help me. The suffering! The old wounds! Give me a heart of mercy. Help me understand Kiko. Help him. I love you, my Jesus. The confusion!

(Florence, November 16, 1981)

---

[654] Cf. Mt 11:29.

[655] Cf. Pr 31:10-31.

[656] In architecture a loggia is an exterior balcony composed of arches on top of columns with a roof and is open on one or more sides. It functions as a balcony or porch and is entirely open on at least one of its sides and is supported by columns, pillars or arches. The Holy Father's residence and the offices of the Secretary of State are located on the third loggia (floor) of the Apostolic Palace in the Vatican.

[657] Cf. Ps 80:1.

752. Third community. My Jesus, it's late, late, intense day, fights, clarifications… my Jesus, work. You revive me after last night. It looks to me like the people aren't reacting, my Jesus.

(Florence, November 17, 1981)

753. *Firenze*. Beautiful. I stroll around with you alone. Lord, you are great, wonderful. I'm always in a hurry. My Jesus, I love you. Constantly like sheep. My Jesus, savior, holy, You love each one. Blessed are you, liberator. Catechesis second community of *Romito*.[658] And it's already 2 o'clock. We leave in the morning. And to return? Blessed are you.

(Florence, November 18, 1981)

754. *Firenze* – Bologna. Francesco.[659] Joy, fortitude, my Jesus.

In Ivrea. Communion. The enemies, all in the shackles.[660] My Jesus, You are the victor. Blessed are you.

(Ivrea, November 19, 1981)

755. Bettazzi. Meeting-nonmeeting. To forbid the Eucharist today can come only from the devil. Crushing attack. I'm free and happy, my Jesus.

Turin. Good environment. The ark; *"berit."*[661] Your presence moves me. I love you. Tomorrow Ballestrero.

(Ivrea, November 20, 1981)

756. My Jesus, I wake up in Turin, valiant, happy, eager to meet Bellestrero. Like an angry bull… He says no. Visit the Duomo. Pastors. Jesus, You direct us and know all things. After thousands of doubts. And Cé? And Martini?

---

[658] Parish of the *Sacro Cuore* in Romito, Florence.

[659] Francesco Cuppini (pb) (†), from the first community of the parish of *Santa Maria* in Calderara di Reno (Bologna). He collaborated as the itinerant presbyter with Kiko and Carmen in Rome from October 23, 1968 until July 1, 1971. T. Zani (ed.), Interview with Francesco Cuppini. *Fragments of the History of the Neocatechumenal Way and of the Church of Bologna* (Naples: Chirico, 2016) 36.56.

[660] Cf. Ps 57:6.

[661] Cf. Ex 25:10.

Finally, Venice. True brothers everywhere. My Jesus, I love you.

(Venice, November 21, 1981)

757. At St. Mark's.⁶⁶² The history, the paintings… magnificent. And the Masses… the singing… And the "parish community," which one? The one at ten? The one at twelve? The one at one-fifteen?

(Venice, November 22, 1981)

758. Leaving Venice in a fog. I call my mother beforehand. She's in a good mood, affectionate. My Jesus, I love you.

Bologna. Francesco. Doctor. My Jesus, the trip continues. I'm always hyper. Catechesis, my Jesus. Tension, tension, as the one who has to burst the "Kiko bubble"…

Firenze. Catechesis. Dinner. My Jesus, it's midnight: travel to Rome. It's already my birthday… Wish me a happy birthday!

(Florence, November 23, 1981)

759. Home. 51.⁶⁶³ Thank you, Lord, for having created me. Since no one else remembers — Kiko thinks only of himself, whether or not he did well — anger explodes in me, I remember the treachery of that date and I feel like escaping to anywhere else, of not being here tomorrow. It's four in the morning. My Jesus, let your love awaken me. I love you. Only You are faithful, holy, most sweet. Come with me. You, Lord, holy, consoling balm of conversion. The catechesis. What dare I complain of before You, crucified? Lord, forgive me. I love you.

*(Rome, November 24, 1981)*⁶⁶⁴

760. Day off. Wonderful, you are holy, my Jesus. Time flies. Service. I don't read. I don't do what I would have liked, but I'm happy and I love you. Simplify me. Free me from cigarettes. My Jesus, I love you.

(Rome, November 25, 1981)

---

⁶⁶² St. Mark's Basilica, Venice.

⁶⁶³ Carmen turned 51 years old.

⁶⁶⁴ The entries marked with an asterisk were written by Carmen in the second diary she kept in 1981.

761. A morning at home. Afternoon: Matías[665] furniture for Kiko. My Jesus, the joy of being with you remains with me and I love you. We we're starting a work that will never end. I feel free, good, and I love you.

(Rome, November 26, 1981)*

762. I wake up with strength, with joy. At eight, Landazuri:[666] battle plan; central point, catechumenate. I work with Kiko and Franco. You enlighten history, you fulfill it. In the light of our history together, you have powerfully extended your arm over us.[667] I love you, Lord. Singing of psalms. Dinner with Pino and Beatrice.[668] My Jesus, mysterious, holy, You lead your people.

(Rome, November 27, 1981)*

763. Restlessness. Smoking. Book. "Switchboard operator." You, merciful, holy, You come. Come, Lord Jesus, give me serenity because I'm troubled over a thousand worries. Eucharist. Crypt. Thank you, my Jesus, you have helped me. You, improvisor, inspirer, consoler. Your name be blessed eternally. Holy, holy, holy, You set me free. Blessed are you.

(Rome, November 28, 1981)*

764. My Jesus, joy, things accelerate, bags and bags, restless all day. Why, Lord? Sweet one, I love you. In return, I repay you with ingratitude… My Jesus, I love you. I'm moved by "the Ark, your Covenant, the Mystery", your sweet love. I love you, my Jesus, because of You. You move me. Call me.

(Rome, November 29, 1981)*

765. First week of advent. Lauds in *Martiri*. Poletti, the government is secure, tranquil. Airport. Travel to Madrid. I feel free, my Jesus.

(Madrid, November 30, 1981)

---

[665] Mattia del Prete.

[666] Cardinal Juan Landazuri Ricketts, OFM (†), Archbishop of Lima, Peru, 1955-1989.

[667] Cf. Acts 13:17.

[668] Pino and Beatrice Manzari, from the first community of *Nostra Signora del Santissimo Sacramento e Santi Martiri Canadesi*, Rome.

766. My Jesus, rushing around all day, rushing. My Jesus, this Kiko in action all day. I would like to sit with you in peace, with my books, with you. My Jesus, non-stop with so many things. My Jesus, everything hurried. Free me!

(Madrid, December 1, 1981)

767. Lauds at the Center. My Jesus, rushing all day. How is this possible? My Jesus, I didn't sleep. I can't take it anymore. What can I do? My life is in your hands. Help me.

(Madrid, December 2, 1981)

768. St. Francis Xavier. Jesus, sweet memories of your love. My Sweet love, running around all day. The hours go by quickly. I haven't slept, my Jesus. How it rains. My God, You love me. Meeting at the Center. Southern group, *Vallecas*. My Jesus, I love you. Kiko doesn't let me speak at all. He is impossible, my Jesus. I feel like crying.

(Madrid, December 3, 1981)

769. Lauds at the Center. On the way home, looking for furniture. No interest. Have mercy, my Jesus. Free. And so what? So tired. I can't sleep. I fuss all day like Martha.[669] Why? Iniesta.[670]

The fourth team: the East. My Jesus.

(Madrid, December 4, 1981)

770. My Jesus, delightful morning in your company. And then rush. Was it in vain? My Jesus, I love you. Eucharist. Lord, I love you. I'm dead tired. Kiko is impossible. Help me, Jesus.

(Madrid, December 5, 1981)

771. Madrid – Rome. Just the two of us, my Jesus. Restless all day over things, with no time to stop. My Jesus! Always preventing things, things. Always doing something, unable to stop and do what I'd like: to be with you, read. My Jesus, I worry about so many things. Why?

---

[669] Cf. Lk 10:41.

[670] Mons. Alberto Iniesta Jiménez (†), Auxiliary bishop of Madrid, 1972-1998 and Episcopal vicar of the IV Vicariate, Southeast Madrid.

To sleep. My Jesus, generous, immense, I love you. Come, come, come.

(Rome, December 6, 1981)

772. Rome – *Firenze*. Benelli at twelve. My Jesus, miraculous, great, the only one, holy, I love you. Joy of your presence, powerful, wonderful, invincible.

We continue the trip: Bologna – Porto S. Giorgio. Eucharist. Vigil of the Immaculate Conception. Sweet one, joy. Sweet Virgin Mary!

(Porto San Giorgio, December 7, 1981)

773. Lauds in the Center.

Loreto[671] – Capovilla.[672] My Jesus, what a mystery, these Bishops. I love you. Sweet Virgin Mary, so full of full grace. Return. I can't take it anymore.

(Porto San Giorgio, December 8, 1981)

774. Free. Rest. I wake up at midnight and in the morning at dawn. So beautiful. My Jesus, what joy, what enjoyment. I love you. It seems like a dream. You console me for the days of affliction. It seems impossible, my Jesus. Blessed are you. I trust in You.

(Porto San Giorgio, December 9, 1981)

775. Rest. Free. Gorgeous sunrise. Clouds, sun, joy, consolation. You wake me on time for the Office at night and for Lauds like a surprising miracle. You are holy, faithful, wonderful. Only You are God. Blessed are you, so generous. Finally, I sit and read. Catechetical Book of Madrid.[673] Market. My Jesus, I stroll alone with you. I love you.

(Porto San Giorgio, December 10, 1981)

---

[671] A step of the Neocatechumenal Way: before the "Our Father" is given to them, the Neocatechumens make a pilgrimage to a Marian sanctuary (the communities in Europe visit the shrine of Loreto), to receive the Virgin Mary as Mother, and profess the faith before the tomb of St. Peter and make an act of adherence to the Holy Father.

[672] Cardinal Loris Francesco Capovilla (†), Secretary to Saint John XXIII, territorial prelate of Loreto, 1971-1988.

[673] Perhaps the *General Directory of Pastoral Catechesis*. Bilingual edition in the *Directorium Cetechisticum Generale*.

Kiko and Carmen in the Philippines in 1992

776. Rest. Your wonderful presence consoles me when I awake. The Leviathan... Lord, You the victor, most holy. I finally read the book on the catechumenate. You are the only one, Lord, you have been present in all the work we have done. Sweet one, holy, I love you.

(Porto San Giorgio, December 11, 1981)

777. Rest. You always call me with your consolation at the right time, my Jesus. I don't know what to write anymore because You are ineffable. How can I sing and bless your name? I call Sevilla, with Felix,[674] and my mother. My Jesus, protect us. Eucharist.

(Porto San Giorgio, December 12, 1981)

778. Rest. My Jesus, I love you. I stupidly smoke nonstop. Coup in Poland![675] My Jesus, avert war. Stefano in Poland. My Jesus, I'm free and do little. I sleep. I'm tired. I love you. My neck hurts.

(Porto San Giorgio, December 13, 1981)

779. Restless all day. Phone. My Jesus, Bishops, Silvestrini... You are immense. Poland. Worldwide upheaval. I'm serene. The universe is in your hands and you are the only one. Blessed are you. To Fermo: x-ray. My bones... Only You are Life. I love you. Thank you, Lord. Make me serene.

(Porto San Giorgio, December 14, 1981)

780. My Jesus, I want to be with you in freedom. Sweet one, holy, magnificent, I love you. I await liberation. Magnificent in your deeds, invincible. Burial of Juan Avia.[676] Life passes quickly. My Jesus, You, eternal, resurrected, I want to be with you. Come, tame me!!!

(Porto San Giorgio, December 14, 1981)

---

[674] Her older brother.

[675] Leaders from the Armed Forces seized power and decreed martial law. The new military regime was announced over television and radio by general Wojciech Jaruzelski, prime minister and supreme leader of the Police Communist Party (POUP).

[676] Juan Avia Aranda (†), from the first community of the Neocatechumenal Center, Madrid.

781. Porto San Giorgio – Rome. Always departing, on the way. Joy. The night is falling, wonderful are your works. My Jesus. Second *Canadesi*. My Jesus!

(Rome, December 16, 1981)

782. First *Natività*. After Loreto. My Jesus, you give me strength, energy, grace, you allow me to speak. Blessed are you.

(Rome, December 17, 1981)

783. First *S. Luigi*. We listen to the experiences after Loreto. Stefano comes from Poland. My Jesus, intense day, nonstop. My Jesus!

(Rome, December 18, 1981)

784. My Jesus, wise, eternal only one. First *Sta. Francesca*. Round of experiences after Loreto. Free, my Jesus. I love you.

(Rome, December 19, 1981)

785. Fourth Sunday of Advent. My Jesus, happy when I wake up, happy at night. It's two a.m. Thank you, Jesus. Toured Rome with you: Via Giulia, Campo Fiori… My Jesus, most holy, I love you. Poland!

(Rome, December 20, 1981)

786. Toured Rome. My Jesus, I love you. Zevini.[677] First *Martiri*. My Jesus, I can't go on.

(Rome, December 21, 1981)

787. Hectic day. Vatican. Pouring rain. All day on the phone, gifts. My Jesus! Fr. Maximino: in the end, *turrones*[678]. Travel to Porto San Giorgio. We start the itinerants convivence of the nations. My Jesus, I feel free. Thank you, my Jesus.

(Rome, December 22, 1981)

---

[677] Cf. G. ZEVINI, "Il cammino neocatecumenale. Itinerario di maturazione nella fede", in A. Favale (ed.) *Movimenti ecclesiali contemporanei. Dimensioni storiche, teologico-spirituali ed apostoliche* (Biblioteca di Scienze Religiose 92; Studi di Teologia Pastorale 12; Rome: LAS, 1991) 239-278.

[678] Traditional Spanish Christmas treats.

788. International itinerants convivence. You move and console me. My Jesus, I love you. Lauds. The children. Lunch. Presentation. Dinner. And, I don't know how, it's already one in the morning. My Jesus, simplify me.

(Porto San Giorgio, December 23, 1981)

789. International itinerants convivence. Lauds and Penitential. Sweet Virgin Mary, holy, my most beloved Mother. You console me. You have comforted me in the midst of danger and tribulation. I love you. Christmas. An animated Nativity scene behind glass in the room. It moves me. My Sweet Jesus, blessed night!

(Porto San Giorgio, December 24, 1981)

790. International itinerants convivence. The hot chocolate at the end kept me up last night. My Jesus, most holy day, most blessed night, magnificent in everything, faithful. *Angelus*, Pope. Poland. The Pope: courageous. The liturgy: everything alive. The holiday meal at the Bellavista.[679] Vigil at night. My Jesus, I remember Fuentes:[680] the people in Exodus. You always make your holy history alive. Sweet one. I love you.

(Porto San Giorgio, December 25, 1981)

791. St. Stephen. My Sweet Jesus, you give me the wild ox's strength, you renew my youth.[681] Poor Kiko complains like a diva… My Jesus, you give me a little wisdom, lightheartedness, love. Thank you, my Jesus, I love you. After so many years being mute, you open my mouth, you give me courage. Thank you, my Jesus, I love you. Africa. Congo. Good night.

(Porto San Giorgio, December 26, 1981)

792. Solemn Eucharist, long, parish, wonderful. Free afternoon. Beautiful. My Jesus, I love you.

(Porto San Giorgio, December 27, 1981)

---

[679] Hotel Bellavista, Porto San Giorgio.

[680] An abandoned town in the foothills of Carbonero Mayor, in the province of Segovia, where the community of the shanty town of Palomeras had a convivence in 1966.

[681] Cf. Ps 92:10.

793. Holy Innocents. International itinerants convivence. Africa. The Bishop of Fermo.[682] We continue in the afternoon with Africa.

(Porto San Giorgio, December 28, 1981)

794. Lauds. St. Thomas Becket. The children at Lauds. Wonderful. We continue with Africa. Egypt. Consolation. I see a star over Palestine, my Jesus. Madagascar, mercy, Lord, only You can heal people. Consolation. Catechesis addressing the problems. Inspiration. All is well. Your most holy presence!

(Porto San Giorgio, December 29, 1981)

795. Lauds with children: excellent lectors. My Jesus, I feel free in You, Lord. The devil pursues me to take away my peace, again posing doubts: suddenly the future darkens. India. Boring exposition. My Jesus, St. Francis Xavier...

(Porto San Giorgio, December 30, 1981)

796. Admonition to the New Year's penitential celebration.[683] – I want to remind you of something I've said before. Conversion cannot be a last-ditch effort, "clenching your fists," but in entering into grace, into the gratuitous action of God. It's to let go, to stop relying on your own strength and to limp (Jacob)[684] = to confess your sins. Let it be seen that you are lame and so you pass, like Jacob, to meet the enemy,[685] to love, to grace.

You don't feel like you're a sinner today? Is there someone here who sees himself as so holy that he doesn't see the need to confess or doesn't know what to confess? The Church allows you to confess past sins, the sins of this year. Go to the root of your sin, that is greed, pride... Conversion, *teshuvá*: to remake the soul, the fabric of the Spirit, a new creation.[686]

(December 31, 1981)

---

[682] Mons. Cleto Bellucci (†), Archbishop of Fermo, 1976-1997.

[683] Written by Carmen in a different diary from 1981 on the pages of August 20-21.

[684] Cf. Gn 32:25-32.

[685] Cf. Gn 33:1-4.

[686] Cf. 2 Cor 5:17.

797. My Jesus,[687] sweet wisdom, your wonderful, incredible holy action, so powerful, your immense glory and your full work. You are the Living One always and forever. How loving you are in everything. Always prompt, nothing incomplete. You are the God of the universe and my Father. I love you, my Lord, so good, holy. I love you. How can I give you thanks? How do I eternally sing of your blessed love? My Jesus, I weep with tenderness seeing you like this, mocked, silent. Always victorious. Prayer, my Jesus!

(Rome, January 14, 1982

---

[687] This is a fragment that Carmen wrote two weeks later, on January 14, 1982. We have included it here as a preview and to conclude these writings.

TABLE OF CONTENTS

NOTE from Kiko Argüello 5
FOREWORD by Card. Ricardo Blázquez Pérez 7
PREFACE by Card. Ricardo Blázquez Pérez 11

DIARIES 1979-1981

1979 19
1980 63
1981 153

www.ingramcontent.com/pod-product-compliance
Lightning Source LLC
Chambersburg PA
CBHW031140160426
43193CB00008B/199